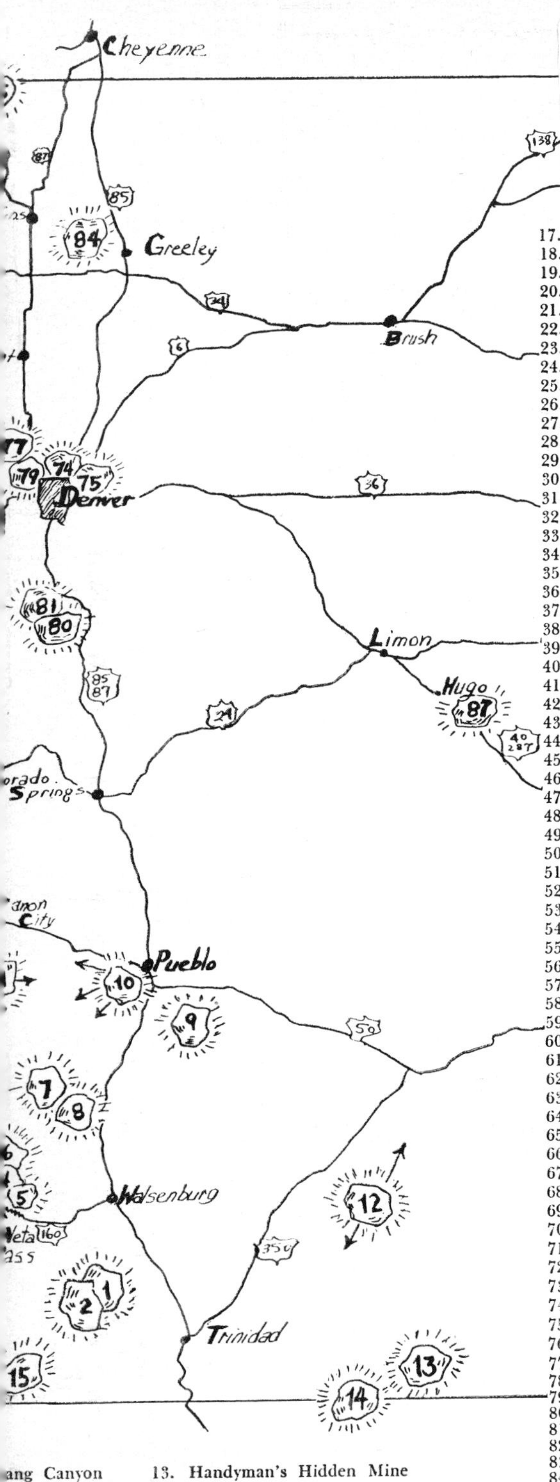

17. Secret Mine of Hidden Valley
18. La Caverna Del Oro
19. The Lost Brother Mine
20. The Golden Ledge
21. Treasure of Deadman Caves
22. Juan Carlos Gold
23. Moccasin Bill's Lost Mine
24. Treasure of Treasure Mountain
25. The Lost Philip's Mine
26. Kit Carson's Shining Stream
27. Jim Stewart's Lost Mine
28. Mark Biedel's Lost Lode
29. Spirits and the Highland Mary
30. The Lost Ute Mine
31. The Bear Creek Treasure
32. Newton's Lost Gold Mine
33. Treasure of Timber Hill
34. The Crazy Swede's Lost Lode
35. Lost Mine on Oak Creek
36. The Lost Trail Mine
37. Buried Treasure of Bull Canyon
38. The Lost Josephine Mine
39. The Montezuma Treasure
40. The Pish-La-Ki
41. Landlady's Lost Silver Mine
42. Bad Men of Brown's Hole
43. The Great Diamond Fields
44. Treasure of Pat's Hole
45. Snake River Gold
46. Jim Baker's Lost Mine
47. Elk Creek Treasure
48. Old Frying Pan Gold
49. Lost Ledge of Gore Range
50. The Rabbit Ears Lost Mine
51. Lost Treasure of Slate Mountain
52. The Disappearing Cliff
53. Lost Copper Mine on Meadow Mountain
54. Abandoned Mine on Cunundrum Gulch
55. Treasure of Cement Creek Caves
56. Legend of Snowblind Gulch
57. Buried Treasure on Round Hill
58. The Spanish Princess Treasure
59. The Search for Lost Gulch
60. Leadville's Haunted Mines
61. Lost Canyon Gold
62. Lost Gold Mine on Lost Gulch
63. Jesse James Loot on Halfmoon Gulch
64. Wonderland World of Orth Stein
65. The Reynolds Gang Gold
66. Lost Mine on Deadman's Gulch
67. The Whittier's Lost Mine
68. Lost Tenderfoot Mine
69. The Lost Missouri Mine
70. The Lost Mine Owner
71. Grand Lake Gold
72. Lost Bonanza on Soda Creek
73. Estes Park Gold
74. Spirits Join the Search
75. The Lost Spanish Bullion Case
76. Georgetown's Hidden Vault
77. Box Elder Lead
78. Lost Mine on Hicks Mountain
79. Underwater Gold on Standley Lake
80. The Devil's Head Treasure
81. The Rabbit Hole Tunnel
82. The Lost Dutchman Mine
83. Gunshot Lead
84. French Treasure on Cache La Poudre
85. Buried Treasure at Robber's Roost
86. Treasure of Italian Caves
87. The Clifford Buried Treasure

ang Canyon
shel
Fremont City
atory Canyon

13. Handyman's Hidden Mine
14. "Black Jack" Ketchum's Loot
15. Spanish Mine on Culebra Peak
16. The White Cement

TREASURE TALES
OF THE ROCKIES

An early trail in Colorado. Little wonder so many of the prospectors, their faithful burros and the treasures were lost. This could be any one of a hundred similar trails. No doubt it is similar to the perilous trail in the story of the Lost Brother Mine. Actually this is an early photograph of a San Juan trail by William H. Jackson.

Also by Perry Eberhart

GUIDE TO THE COLORADO

GHOST TOWNS AND MINING CAMPS

TREASURE TALES of the Rockies

by

PERRY EBERHART

Maps by Sandy Eberhart

Second, revised edition

SAGE BOOKS
Denver

Library of Congress Catalog No. 61-14373

Second, revised edition

Sage Books are published by

Alan Swallow, 2629 South York Street, Denver 10

TO MOTHER

Whose love is legend.

CONTENTS

MAPS

ILLUSTRATIONS

THE SEARCH . . . .

What is the gold you seek?
Here in the muck and the mud,
Is it a crystal palace, clean and cared for?
What is the gold you seek?
Here in the naked cold of nowhere,
It is warmth you seek?
This leather-hard skin,
This lean body, bent against the weather and the world,
Does it seek a softness, a velvet life?
In this narrow dirt gulch,
Do you seek refinement?
Beauty?
From a handful of dust
Do you seek power?
Fame?
What is the gold you seek?
In the stark, shrill aloneness of the night,
Do you pursue an ancient love?
A misty remembrance?
The warmth and tenderness of being wanted?
This time-tortured body,
Bent with age and age-old hurt,
Does it seek the lost wealth of youth?
In this rocky corridor
Do you seek eternal rest?
Do you see Heaven in the mud?
If this be the gold you seek,
Keep seeking, keep searching.
The glitter is along the trail,
The search is the thing.
When the search is over . . . .
The glitter is gone.

P.E.

INTRODUCTION

Every man has a lost mine or buried treasure—the road not taken, the close brush with fame and fortune, the gold still waiting, or just out of reach. Call it Hope, call it dreams, it is all the same thing.

In the old days in the early west, men were more honest about it. They called it by its right name—a lost mine or a buried treasure.

They told about these in the dancing campfire light, in the saloons. The treasure grew with each telling. One didn't belong to the group without a story. Each attempted to outdo the other. Many of the stories lived on, the listener took them for his own, added to them, gave them life. From these stories came legends.

Legends? Most of them had a smattering of fact, many of them had a lot. Of course, many of them were completely true. Why shouldn't they be?

I have been fascinated by stories of lost mines and buried treasure. The stories of the Lost Padre in California and the Lost Dutchman in Arizona—which I heard several years ago—captured my imagination. Later, as I traveled more and more through the rugged mountains of Colorado, I wondered if such tales graced this wonderland. Later still, in delving deeply into the history of the state, I discovered that Colorado is a gold mine—if you'll pardon the expression—of lost mine and buried treasure stories, many as interesting as any in the west.

Colorado affords an ideal setting for such tales.

In the first place, Colorado is more mountainous than any other state (with the exception of the new state of Alaska), and she has more high and more rugged mountains than any other state (again, with the exception of Alaska). Colorado's summers are short in the high mountains. It can, and has, snowed in the middle of summer. (An illustration is the old story of a Denverite asking a miner, just in from the San Juans, how he liked the summers in the high mountains. "I don't know," replied the miner, "I was only up there 18 months.")

People become lost in the Colorado Rockies every year, despite modern roads and facilities and plenty of population. Is it difficult to believe that many more people became lost in the old days when Colorado contained large areas of unpopulated, often uncharted, wilderness?

Not long ago, while exploring a ghost mining area, I gathered some interesting rocks and made a little pile of them in the center of a sloping field, to pick up on my return trip. Returning a short time later I searched the entire area, or what I thought was the area, and couldn't find a trace of the rocks. This happened in fairly open country. I wondered how easy it would be to lose something in heavily-wooded or rugged mountain country. Try it yourself sometime. Leave a marker somewhere in the mountains in the late summer or in the fall, then return the following spring and try to find it.

Many sections of Colorado contain mile upon mile of similar terrain, similar landmarks. To make matters worse, the face of the land changes continuously, a river changes its course, runoff waters wash out a prominent tree, or the tree burns down; rock slides and snow slides carve out a new face on the mountain and cover the markers at the foot of the hill.

The land changes with the season, too. Many of Colorado's great mining discoveries were made on the way back from the mountains in the fall, when the land had already begun its change. In many drainage areas, the land looks different in the early summer from the way it does in the late summer. And the winter appearance just doesn't look like the same place at all.

The old prospectors often aided nature by obscuring the openings of their propect holes, and hiding the trails. Another prospector trick was to claim a location was a gulch or so away from where it really was, to throw others off the track. Life was rugged, people died freely, some of them died with all their secrets still in them.

And, of course, the Indians played a major role in our little drama. They not only changed the look of the land but they also changed many a prospectors' outlook on gold, and things in general.

So, believe them or not, these tales of lost mines and buried treasure. Youngsters believe them, Heaven help us if they didn't.

The old man one often sees wandering beside the mountain road, believes them. His existence is based on them. He has spent his life following the rainbow. He mumbles the story over and over to himself. His eyes no longer see the road ahead but the gold behind. He may never find the gold ahead . . . but, what the hell . . . the search is the thing.

I. *IN THE BEGINNING*

QUIVIRA

An Indian slave first told New Spain's President Nuno de Guzman of the fabulous cities to the north. The slave said his father had been a dealer in ornamental Aztec artwork. The slave, as a boy, accompanied his father on sales trips to the villages to the north.

They visited seven great cities. The villagers lived in multi-storied buildings. The streets were exclusively occupied by workers in gold and silver. The glittering metals were everywhere in abundance here.

De Guzman firmly believed the slave's story. It verified the rumors of the "land of gold and silver" to the north. He dreamed of returning to Spain in glory . . . . and gold.

His plans for an expedition were spurred by the arrival of Cabeza de Vaca in 1536.

De Vaca had been a member of a Spanish sea-faring expedition that set out from Florida to explore the Gulf Coast. Off Texas, the ship was cast ashore in a storm. Only de Vaca and a Negro slave, Estevan, survived. They became the slaves of the Indian tribes. But de Vaca slowly won the favor of the natives through his magical healing powers. His medical kit contained nothing more than a prayer, the sign of the cross, and a few basic first aid principles . . . but they worked.

After six long years, de Vaca and Estevan, naked and scarred,

Coronado, the first fortune hunter. As many of the Quests that followed his search was unsuccessful. Above drawing shows the search for Quivira. Below. Coronado at Cibolla. Drawings by Frederic Remington, *Denver Public Library Western Collection.*

were granted their freedom and promised safe passage. They wandered from tribe to tribe healing the sick. Their fame spread. Indians came from distant points with their sick and ailing. The two men were regarded as miracle workers, they were feted, and presented with gifts.

They finally arrived at the Rio Grande, followed it northward. The tribes became more civilized. They lived in homes of clay and adobe, they tilled the soil, and raised animals for food and work. Among the gifts presented de Vaca by the Pueblos were arrowheads made of emeralds and other precious stones. The Indians said they found the precious stones in the lofty mountains to the north.

Traveling west (some believe he traveled northwest, even as far as Colorado) he came upon evidence of the Spanish, belt buckles and other relics left behind by wandering troops, picked up and worn by the Indians. Estevan elected to stay in this exalted position, raped a few squaws, and was murdered by the Pueblos. De Vaca was guided back to New Spain where he became an overnight sensation.

Before he set sail for Spain, De Vaca was asked, again and again, about the tribes and treasures of the north.

Shortly thereafter, de Guzman began to organize his expedition. But just before departure time he was relieved of his office and ordered back to Spain.

His place was taken by an up-and-coming young fellow named Coronado.

With Coronado now in command, the magnificent caravan began its northward trek in 1540. There were 400 conquistadores in plumes and shining armor, atop snorting, black horses, 1,000 Indian "allies" and slaves, 1,000 pack animals, herds of goats and sheep, and everywhere in and about the gigantic exodus were the priests, trademark of every Spanish expedition.

The moving city wintered along the Rio Grande and resumed its journey in the early spring of 1541. Scouting expeditions traveled in all directions and reported their findings to Coronado. One party led by Friar Marcos climbed to the top of a small hill.

There far below was Cibolla, one of the sought-for seven cities. The village, and other nearby villages, had buildings of many stories. The natives worked in the fields, at other more advanced trades. There was, here and there, evidence of precious stones and the Indians hinted of rich mountains of gold and silver to the north, but the Seven Cities of Cibolla themselves had been over-publicized and under-endowed.

Coronado made Cibolla his headquarters for expeditions in all directions. One party journeyed far enough into Colorado to view the Royal Gorge.

Another expedition came across a wandering Indian who had the appearance of a Turk. They called him "El Turko" and they listened to him. And the more they listened the more he talked.

He first told Coronado of the fabulous city of Quivira. The streets were paved with gold and the marble palace reflected in the pure blue lake nearby. The royal canoes carried golden oarlocks. The palace was hung with beautiful cotton cloth, and golden bells that tinkled in the breeze.

The vision, compared to the present neighborhood, blinded Coronado, and the caravan headed north.

The expedition followed along a trail near to, or possibly the same as, a much-traveled trail of later years that ran from Bents Fort to Taos, cutting across the southeastern corner of Colorado. Beyond the mountains, the parade headed east, over the plains, mountains of dust curling upward. All the while the Turk hopped along beside Coronado spinning the tales of Quivira. The wandering Indian tribes along the way—cued by El Turko—joined in the fabulous tale . . . and pointed to the north.

History books say the giant parade eventually arrived at a desolate point in Kansas, almost due east of Denver. This was the point that Quivira was supposed to be. Coronado halted the caravan and gazed over the burning prairie in all directions. They had seen only buffaloes and shabby Indian tribes. This was not gold and silver country.

The doubt had grown in Coronado's mind, now it boiled over on the Turk. The terrified Indian finally admitted that he lied. History books vary as to his reasons. On one side, legend says the Turk planned to lead the caravan out onto the endless prairie and then make off during the night with all the loot he could carry. Another story says the Turk planned to lead the caravan into ambush. And still another, and popular, story says the Turk's mission was no more than to keep the expedition going . . . and out from underfoot of the Pueblo tribes.

It could be that the Turk was merely a liar . . . and he had found a good audience.

But, alas, Coronado couldn't see the humor in the situation. He strangled the Indian on the spot.

Coronado, however, still believed in the gold, and adventure. He still dispatched expeditions in all directions. One, they say, journeyed into Colorado, possibly to the area at the foot of the Rockies where Denver grew some 300 years later.

Coronado planned to continue the trip the following spring, heading either north or west, to explore the lofty mountains he had heard so much about. But during a horse race, he fell from his mount and under the hoofs of the other horse. He was seriously injured and would be laid up for months. Rather than spend the time on the plains recuperating, he ordered his troops to pack up their tunics and their plumes and head home for New Spain.

Thus, the first, and perhaps the most colorful, gold-hunting expedition came to an ignoble end on the dusty plains of Kansas, only a few hundred miles east of Eldorado.

Coronado was just the beginning. He rode in the forefront of a long and colorful caravan . . . that's still underway.

GOLD, GLORY AND GOD

Historians know that many Spaniards clambered over the Colorado Rockies, all over them. Few historians doubt that they, the Spanish, undertook mining enterprises here and even established settlements. But few of these mines and settlements are mentioned in the history books. For want of detailed information the historians are cautious.

Legend is much more generous with us, and it takes advantage of many facts left lying around unused by cautious historians.

There's reason to believe that Hernando de Soto's party was the first to enter Colorado after Coronado.

De Soto, rich with the spoils of Peru where he fought valiantly with Pizzarro, returned to Spain in glory. He was top dog in the Spanish court for quite awhile. Then, this young upstart named

Cabeza de Vaca came along with his fantastic story of hardships and treasure in the New World.

By this time, de Vaca's story had grown to such proportions that the Spanish believed the New World contained inexhaustible mines of gold and precious stones. (They were right.)

De Soto saw the opportunity to eclipse the glory of De Vaca. He organized a new giant expedition, at his own expense, but with the blessings of the king. De Soto and his army of 950 Spanish and Portuguese adventurers landed in the new world in 1538. His expedition of fire, blood and pillage followed up the Mississippi, then into Kansas. Here de Soto became deathly ill. On the return trip he died.

His party buried de Soto in the wilderness. Then his men decided to continue the trip westward and join the conquering armies of New Spain. The Army, under the command of Louis de Moscoso, came upon the Arkansas River and followed it westward. The group entered Colorado in the summer of 1542, the same year of Coronado's return trip.

De Moscoso viewed the majestic mountains and spent several weeks inspecting them, expecting all the while that the gold would pour out of them. When the winds and the snow came the mountains lost their promise. De Moscoso led what remained of his army back over the route it had come.

The next Spanish visitor, according to the history books, was Juan de Oñate. About fifty years after Coronado, Oñate led 200 Spanish families, and a much larger number of horses, goats, pigs and such, into New Mexico. He claimed this strange new land for Spain and established the first colony here. History books usually say that Oñate sent out many an expedition into Colorado but the books hesitate to elaborate.

Local legend, taking advantage of official New Mexico records, gives Oñate much more credit. Old Spanish records in New Mexico say that Oñate first told of the gold in the San Luis Valley, and a mining settlement being established here, no doubt the first mining settlement in Colorado.

Legend also says that Oñate himself made extensive exploratory trips into Colorado, founding many settlements here and mining much gold. Evidence of ancient mining activity has been found near Poncha Springs, and local residents believe one of Oñate's settlements was near here.

After Oñate, the history books skip a hundred years, then they bring up such names as de Anza, Villasur, Rivera, Escalante and the like.

If it wasn't for legend, Colorado would have been a very dull place for the 200 years after Oñate. But legend says there was no end of Spanish prospecting trips and many a mining settlement made.

The legend isn't based on hearsay alone. First French explorers in the west learned from the Indians that the Spanish had done "extensive gold and silver mining" in the mountains in the early 1700's and earlier. In 1706, the Plains Indians declared that the Spanish had discovered "copper" far to the north of their settlements on the Rio Grande. The Plains Indians usually called all sorts of metals copper, including gold and silver.

Several arrastra ruins, or what could be arrastra ruins, have been found in several areas of Colorado. Armor, weapons and ancient mining equipment have been found in and around the San Luis Valley. The first Yankee and French travelers found prospect holes and worn trails in the mountains, and nearly invisible house foundations have been found near the foot of the mountains near Pueblo.

William N. Byers, first and longtime editor of the Denver *Rocky Mountain News,* told the story brought to Denver by a prospector named Samuel Stone.

Stone said his 1859 prospecting party found evidence of an ancient mining camp as far north as the headwaters of Big Thompson Creek near Longs Peak. Stone, who was positive his party was the first Yankee party in the area, found many prospect holes here and the relics of an old distillery.

To verify the story, Stone showed Byers a small copper distilling outfit which had been used in making brandy from wild berries that grow in profusion here.

No doubt these "shining mountains" swarmed with Spaniards during those dark years in the history book. The conquistadores discovered them as early as 1541. They believed the mountains held vast riches. The conquistadores were after "gold, glory and God," usually in that order, and it would be very difficult to believe they ignored the imminent possibilities of their "shining mountains" for 200 years.

THE FRENCH

The French had a vague influence in early Colorado and the west. They were among the best hunters and trappers in the wilderness. They came earlier and got around more than the early Yanquis. Surely they were numbered among the first white men to scamper over the Colorado Rockies—but we know so little about it.

Few mountain men, French or American, could read or write. Even if they could, they spent little time at it; there was nothing to write on and a decided lack of mailboxes in the mountains.

There was another reason, too. Most of the successful trappers and prospectors didn't want the news of their success to carry back home. They were afraid they would have to shell out some of the profits for the fatherland. It was expected of them, but the French weren't nearly so interested in glory and La Patrie as were the Spaniards.

But there is some information about the French in Colorado. They knew about the gold in the mountains.

As early as 1697 a French writer in Paris predicted that the north and central regions west of the Mississippi would be found "opulent in mines."

Three years later Le Sueur explored the upper Missouri River and reported that the Indians told him of rich Spanish tin and silver mines.

In October, 1717, a French official in Louisiana, Sieur Hubert (sometimes written as Hebert), said the richest mines were to be found only in the highest mountains. He said by ascending the Missouri River to its sources, mines as rich as the Spanish mines would be found.

The first official and detailed exploration of the "upper Missouri" by the French was made by Etienne Veniard de Bourgmont, a former commandant of Fort Detroit.

At the siege by the Fox Indians in 1712, de Bourgmont became acquainted with the Missouri Indians when they came to aid the French. Soon, de Bourgmont became the "White Father" of the Missouri tribes. He visited them in 1714. A short time later he deserted his official position, married an Indian squaw, and settled down in his own little tepee.

Fortunately, however, he wrote about his years with the Missouris.

He told of other French visitors, some of whom knew of, and sought for, the gold and silver in the mountains. One Frenchman told him that the mines should be as rich as the Spanish mines because the mountains were northern extensions of the same mountains in which the Spanish mines were located.

The French traded with the Padoucas, who had a village on the Platte River on the latter-day Smoky Hill Trail, near the source of the Republican River in Colorado. The Spanish also traded with the Padoucas for horses and cattle. The Padoucas said the Spanish mined great quantities of silver and gold in the mountains to the west. The Padoucas told tales of the Spanish enslaving Indians to work in the mines.

Some of the more patriotic Frenchmen urged France to chase the Spanish out and take over the mountains and the mines. The French may have considered the proposition as more and more Frenchmen headed west, some on official expeditions sponsored by the French government.

Brothers Peter and Paul Mallet led a prospecting party into Colorado in 1739. They followed up the Platte to the mountains, south along the Front Range, viewing the Spanish Peaks on July 10.

Perhaps, the largest—and most legendary—French expedition into Colorado ventured deep into the Rockies around 1800, leaving behind a tale of death and fabulous treasure.

In June of 1802, Louis Vilemont, captain of the French regiment of Louisiana, wrote home that the French found gold at the head of the Arkansas River. Vilemont didn't go into any detail, but he could well be verifying one of Colorado's greatest treasure tales, the Treasure of Treasure Mountain.

Some fifty years later—still before the Colorado gold rush—a French mountain man named Du Chet found what he thought was a beautiful stone along one of the creeks that run into the Arkansas. He put it in his hunting pouch and thought no more about it—mountain men were that way. The stone got in his way when he needed gunpowder and eventually he threw it away.

A few weeks later, in Santa Fe, he emptied the pouch and discovered particles of pure gold.

He searched for the spot where he had found the stone but he never found any more "beautiful stones." But then he didn't look very hard—mountain men were that way.

YANQUI GOLD

James Purcell left his home in Bairdstown, Kentucky, in 1799 to seek his fortune in the wilderness. A couple of years later he teamed up with two other adventurers in the frontier town of St. Louis and the three of them headed west to do some hunting. They had a successful season . . . until they headed home.

Some Kansas Indians made off with their horses one day as they returned to their camp at the foot of the hills. The three of them followed the Indians on foot, right to the edge of the Indian village. Purcell stalked into the village and demanded the return of his horses, as the tribesmen looked on in disbelief.

Despite the bravado of the paleface, the Indians refused to return the horses. At that moment, Purcell saw an Indian riding his horse at the edge of the village. Pulling out his knife, Purcell sprinted after the animal and ripped open its bowels—if Purcell couldn't have the horse no one else could either.

The frenzied Indian collected his senses and aimed his rifle at Purcell and pulled the trigger. Nothing happened. Purcell didn't wait for the second shot. He lit out after the redskin and chased him right into a tepee full of women. The Indian's life was spared with the promise that he would return the rest of the horses.

The horses were stolen again a few days later while the trappers went after their furs. They made a canoe out of pelts and began the trip back down the Osage River. Near the junction of that river with the Missouri, the canoe capsized, sending an entire season's furs to the bottom. Fortunately, they were able to save their guns and some ammunition.

The other two had had enough, but Purcell headed west again with two more adventurers going west along the Missouri.

In 1805, Purcell wandered into Santa Fe. He did a little carpenter work to finance another go at the mountains. A short time

Mountain man by Frederic Remington. The famous drawing was of no mountain man in particular, but the Nez Perce ponies, the scraggly beard—were it red—and harsh eyes make an image of "Parson" Bill Williams. *Denver Public Library Western Collection.*

later, however, he was arrested for making gunpowder, a criminal offense in Santa Fe. While in jail, Purcell told of his journeys into the mountains. Imprudently, or perhaps fortunately for him, he told of finding gold.

He was kept a prisoner-at-large by the Spanish for several years. The Spanish continually pressured him to lead them to the gold, but Purcell hedged. It may have been the only reason he was kept alive.

When Capt. Zebulon Montgomery Pike was captured by the Spanish the following year, he met Purcell in Santa Fe. The mountain man told the famous explorer of his find. Purcell said he found the gold near the headwaters of the Platte, either in 1802 or 1803. He put some samples in his gun pouch and carried them around for months. Eventually, however, he doubted if he would ever be able to use the gold, and also he was afraid that the gold would change his attitude toward the great outdoors, so he threw the nuggets away.

If it hadn't been for Pike's capture we probably would have never known of James Purcell. As it is, we know so little about him and the magnificent adventures he must have had. There may have been other Yankees before him, but if there were, they didn't run into Pike in Santa Fe.

As far as we know, James Purcell was the first Yankee in Colorado, the first Yankee to find gold in Colorado . . . and the first man to leave a lost gold mine behind him.

There was many another mountain man, and they all had their stories of lost gold.

William Sherley Williams had been a circuit-riding Baptist minister before heading west in the 1820's. That's why they called him "Parson" Bill. He wore a red beard and a thick mop of red hair . . . and had the most colorful vocabulary of any man or beast in the west. He rode a crop-eared, scrawny Nez-Perce pony, and Parson Bill cussed the poor animal all through the hinterland.

With this nag, Bill couldn't outrun the Indians so he had to outwit them. This he did, time after time. Sometimes he just held them spellbound by his appearance and his profanity. He lived among the Indians whenever he lived among anybody. Usually he was a lone wolf. He knew every inch of the west, and he was apt to show up any place.

In 1846, he met Colonel William Gilpin in South Park and he told the colonel of the gold he had found there. But Parson Bill wasn't much interested in gold.

Two years later he was a guide for Frémont's ill-fated fourth expedition into the Rockies. He almost lost his life, but his luck didn't run out completely until the next year when he was found propped up against a tree with an arrow through his chest.

Rufus Sage wasn't exactly a mountain man. Fortunately, he was a hobo historian, Colorado's first. Sage traveled up and down, in and around the Colorado Rockies during the 1830's and 1840's, and told us all about it. He gave us one of the popular legends about the Indians using golden pellets in their guns instead of bullets.

One time Sage was camping near the present site of Golden. He struck out into the mountains toward the head of Vasquez Fork when he found mineral which he believed rich in gold. It probably was, for they found a lot of gold around there twenty-five or thirty years later.

Another time Sage camped a half mile below the point at which the trail from Bent's old fort to Taos crossed the right hand fork of the Las Animas River, some twenty or thirty miles east of the Spanish Peaks. At this camp he met an American and an Englishman on their way back to the U. S. with pack mules laden with gold and silver.

Everybody found gold in Colorado.

George Simpson, a packer with Captain Randolph B. Marcy's troops sent out to settle the Mormon question, had a sudden impulse to pan in Cherry Creek, near the present site of Denver. Guide Jim Baker, standing nearby, laughed at the idea of gold being there. But Simpson induced him to try it himself. Sure enough, Baker panned about twenty-five cents worth.

William N. Byers, who later became the editor of the *Rocky Mountain News,* first traveled through the area in 1852. At a trading post at the mouth of Clear Creek, Byers learned that hunters and trappers brought small quantities of gold down from the mountains as early as the 1830's. Byers also heard rumors of gold found on Sweetwater and other places nearby.

Indians found their share of the gold, too. A bunch of Cherokees found some gold on the Cache La Poudre in 1849. Fall Leaf, the Delaware Indian guide, found some nuggets while leading Colonel Sumner's expedition against the Cheyennes.

Colonel Gilpin, surveying the area in 1849, said he found evidence of gold in five different areas of Colorado.

Some early Georgia hunters found gold on the Cache La Poudre. The Ralston brothers found gold on the South Platte in 1850. That same year and the year before, many a '49er bound for California located gold or evidence of gold in Colorado, but the call of the coast was stronger.

Another Indian chaser, General Thomas Taylor, said he found gold on Cherry Creek in 1852. Some Mexican prospectors from Sonora washed out some gold at the same place in 1857. The next year, John Cantrill, heading east from Salt Lake City, picked up some gold dust in Colorado. To prove his find he carried a bucketful of sand all the way to Kansas City, and washed out a few pennies worth of gold before a big crowd of people on the main street of the city.

All this gold was found before the big rush in 1859. Curiously enough, none of the finds was enough to bring on the rush. Many of the earlier discoverers weren't too interested in their finds. They left the gold in the mountains. Many of the locations were mined profitably later on. Perhaps some of their finds are still waiting to be re-discovered.

II. *THE ROMANCE OF SPANISH PEAKS*

1. SPANISH PEAKS

The Legend of Huajatolla

Perhaps the handsomest hunk of mountain in all Colorado sits midway between Walsenburg and Trinidad. The majestic Siamese-twin peaks tower above the area surrounding them. On a clear day they can be seen from Pikes Peak. They can be seen for miles out on the plains. The twin peaks have been sitting there smugly for ages, dominating the neighborhood and all the people that live, and have lived, below them.

The Twin Peaks, now known as the Spanish Peaks, have had many names: Dream Mountains, Double Mountain, and Twin Peaks, by the Americans; Las Cubres Espanolas (The Spanish Peaks) and Los Dos Hermanos (The Two Brothers) by the Spanish.

But the mountains are best remembered in legend by the name Huajatolla or Wah-To-Yah, given it, or them, by the Indians. The name means "Breasts of the Earth," and the Redman believed all living and growing things received their sustenance from the mountain and the many gods who made their home there. Looking at the peaks from certain angles they do resemble slightly lopsided breasts. And whether or not all living and growing things were weaned on the peaks, a mighty lot of legend suckled here.

The Rain God lived in the mountain. In his workshop he molded the clouds and sent them all over the world to bring on the summer rains, giving moisture to plants and all vegetation, which grew and gave life to all living things. The Indians called the Rain God, Tlaloc. He was in the shape of a man-headed pyramid, colored blue as the sky and green as the valley below.

When Tlaloc did not send down the rain, it was a sign he was angry. The most beautiful Indian maidens were sacrificed in the Sacred Well to appease Tlaloc.

Here in Huajatolla the Sun God lived also. He too was a source of life. He ruled the lives of the people with the brightness of day, and the long shadows of evening. He warmed the crops and made them grow.

Other gods lived here, too. The Thunder Gods battled with giant boulders. The whole world reverberated from the sounds of their battle. The huge rocks at the foot of the mountain were their weapons and the giant stone walls running from the mountain—called the Walls of Cuchara—were the breastworks of their battleground.

The early Indian tribes would gather at the first rays of the sun and follow them as they returned into Huajatolla. When a brave died, the body would lie in the sun from the first rays in the morning, and until the last rays of night would lead the departed soul into the land of eternal bliss.

The beautiful roses and ferns of Huajatolla were planted there by the gods and sheltered from the winds by the trees and the rocks. They bloomed on warm days and closed their petals in the soft dews of night. The flowers were held sacred by the Indians and the maidens danced among them by moonlight to banish evil spirits and bring happiness in their future domestic life.

On the mountain is the Indians' Lake of Singing Spirits. The ancient tribes performed rituals here to bring back the spirits of former chiefs from the spirit world. The dances and chants were carried on until the ghostlike figures of the dead appeared on the

The magnificent peaks of Huajatolla, the "Breasts of the World," where much legend suckled. The view from the northwest shows the "Walls of Cuchara," used as breastworks by legendary giants in battle, *U.S. Geological Survey photo.*

mesa and then disappeared in the direction of the small lake in the valley.

The gorge around the base of the peaks is a primitive area, once filled with wild turkeys and other wild animals. Here the Indians could hear the weird, sacred song of the mountain, sometimes resembling the deep chimes of bells, sometimes the deep tones of an organ, which began with a soft, smooth tone and ended in a piercing shriek. The canyon was haunted by spirits and was home of the gods, sacred land to the Indians. It was known as the Gorge of Weird Sounds.

The park nestling in between the peaks was a favorite resting place for eagles, and was called by the Indians, the Place of Many Eagles. The Indians hunted wild game here and gathered feathers for their headdresses.

About a mile from Eagle Park is the upper valley of Santa Clara, a spot covered with delicate ferns forming a soft carpet. Here the tribes built their altars to worship the Sun God. The entire region of Santa Clara was called the Valley of the Rising Sun. Sun worshippers practiced their ritual here during the summer solstice. All hostilities ceased and only brotherly love between the tribes existed. The last ritual took place in 1845.

But one day, many, many moons ago, dark clouds gathered over Huajatolla and warlike invaders swarmed down from the north. The people of Huajatolla were unaccustomed to fighting and were easily subdued and slaughtered. A few escaped into the hills.

This made the gods of Huajatolla very angry. The Rain God refused to send rain. The Sun God glared down on the people below. The land became parched and dry. The trees wasted away.

Legend also says the mountain burst forth with fire and boiling mud. Geologists believe the mountain was once an ancient volcano. The cleavage between the peaks may have been formed in one dark, angry day eons ago when the mountain burst forth and turned the sky to darkness and ashes. Bubbling, boiling pockets were seen coming from the mountain fissures in the last century . . . tiny, lingering burps from the ancient upheaval.

The blue and majestic peaks look down on modern highways and cities now, on fertile farmland and ranches. Perhaps the gods are no longer angry.

It's a workaday world to Huajatolla. But many of the old-timers sit on their porches, gaze up at the beautiful mountain, and recall the many tales the peaks have to tell.

The Demons of Gold

Indian legend tells of advanced tribes of Mexico mining gold in the Spanish Peaks to decorate their idols.

Long before the white man came, even before the alliance of the three great Indian nations of Alcolhua, Aztec, and Tepance, gold was a precious article used to offer to the dieties. The metal was used to decorate the fabulous shrines of Huitsilopochtli. Much gold from the Spanish Peaks was taken to the Mexican communities of Tlacopan and Tezcuco, where Nezhuatcoyotl reigned in splendor.

And the gods of Huajatolla placed gods on the mountain which spit fire and smoke (could this be the makings of a volcanic eruption?) and forbade all men to approach.

No more gold came from Huajatolla to decorate the temples of the south, and thereafter all those seeking gold at Huajatolla became cursed.

The Evil Priest of Huajatolla

Coronado traveled through southeastern Colorado in 1541 and 1542 in his futile search for Quivira. On his return trip three of the fourteen priests who accompanied the expedition remained in New Mexico to teach Christianity to the heathen tribes. They were Fray Luis de Ureda, Fray Juan de Padilla, and Fray Juan de la Cruz. The first two became martyrs to the cause of Christianity. But Fray de la Cruz heard of the fabulous Indian mines to the north, and the call of the gold was stronger than the call of the cloth.

According to legend—and ancient Spanish documents—Fray de la Cruz ventured to Huajatolla and "reopened" the mines here. The mines had been closed by the mountain demons. But Fray de la Cruz told the Indians that he had conquered the demons

A very early drawing showing the Spanish enslaving the Indians to work in the mines. Source of the drawing is unknown. *Denver Public Library Western Collection.*

and had penetrated the evil mountain and found vast treasure there.

Through various means, the priest enticed the Indians to the mountain, promising them rich rewards. Then the good Friar would enslave the Indians, torture them, and make them work in the mine. And when he was through with them, he killed them.

After the friar was satisfied with the quantity of gold he had accumulated, he packed it all on mules and headed south. He traveled a devious and secret route, fearing reprisals by the Indians.

Fray de la Cruz with his ill-gotten treasure was never heard from again.

In 1811, a traveler named Baca found some gold nuggets along an old trail a short distance south of the Spanish Peaks. He also reported evidence of an earthquake. He found open fissures in the valleys southeast of the peaks where vapors still issued.

Fifty years later, another traveler found a golden cup with the name "Hermoine" impressed upon it. It was found in a natural grotto at the base of the east peak by the side of a tiny spring.

It would be easy to believe that this was evidence of Fray de la Cruz and his trip back to New Spain. Perhaps the ground opened up and ate him for all the evil he had done.

Evidence of his work on Huajatolla has also been obliterated. Many have sought for a trace of the vicious priest on the mountain, but the ages have covered up his dirty work.

Yanqui Gold of Huajatolla

The white man tells many stories of gold and lost mines on Huajatolla, or Wa-To-Yah, as he called it. The first travelers took up the legend where the Spanish left off, and added to it.

Rufus Sage, Colorado's hobo historian, told of his experiences near Spanish Peaks in the 1830's and 1840's. He wrote that he and his companions chased what they thought were enemy Mexicans. Instead, they found the two men to be an Englishman and an American who were driving two mules loaded with gold and silver back east. Sage reported seeing the rich specimens of ore which verified the reports he had heard of gold in this region.

Local history tells of trappers coming down out of the mountains with burros loaded with rich ore which they took to Bent's Fort to be processed. Two trappers made several trips down from the mountains to the fort. Each time they carried much gold and silver. Legend grew around the two men and the legend named Spanish Peaks as the source of their treasure. Many tried to follow them or find their mine, but none succeeded. After a while the two trappers returned no more.

George S. Simpson, a Bent's Fort resident, grew to know the trappers. He verified the gold, but said the trappers never indicated where they found it.

Several years later, outdoorsman Joseph Davis camped one night on the peak while traveling the old trail from Bent's Fort to Taos which went by way of the peaks. By the light of his campfire, while looking toward the west peak, he saw indications of an old winding road leading up the peak. Investigating the next day, he found slight evidence of an old path and even a trace of where some repair work had been done on the trail. But a little farther along heavy timber obliterated the route.

Colonel Francisco came to this region in 1850, and in 1860 he built a fort along the Apishapa River. The rumors of gold here brought many a prospector. During the next few years, many prospectors scoured the mysterious peaks for gold. Several prospect holes still visible attest to their search. Some mining was done here. There is a Bullseye Mine on the West Peak. The Spanish Peaks Mining Company, located by John Hudson, mined some silver in the 1890's and early 1900's. There were others but none of them showed much profit.

No one has found the Spanish Mine. Many believe any evidence of such a mine has long since been obliterated by rockslides.

Andrew Merritt of Walsenburg, a well-known mining engineer and geologist who knows more about mining in this area than just about anybody else, believes the Spanish sluiced their gold from the streams on Spanish Peaks. He said ruins of ancient sluices have been found here. He said La Veta shoemaker William Krier reported seeing one below Lover's Leap, at the foot of the cliff at the mouth of the canyon.

There are still some active prospects on the peaks. But mountain cabins and ranches are just about the biggest businesses on the mystic mountain today.

The gold of Huajatolla is another of the many delightful legends of the magnificent peaks.

2. THE ARAPAHO PRINCESS TREASURE

Ancient Indian tribes lived at the foot of Huajatolla. Here can be found signs of their life, including paintings depicting their fabulous times.

The paintings say the land was fruitful beyond imagination. The paintings show the tribes carved out jewelry from gold and other precious metals to adorn their gods. No doubt the gold came from Huajatolla.

Then, legend says, an invasion came from the north. This, coupled with the long drouth, left the land barren for hundreds of years.

Finally, the Indians returned. This land was inhabited by a latter-day tribe—the Arapahoes. Their life was not as prosperous . . . but, legend says, they too had their gold.

Rufus Sage, Colorado's first census taker, told tales of the Arapahoes using golden pellets in their last big war against the

Indian pictograph found in Apishapa Canyon below the Spanish peaks. The drawings found here told of the great prosperity enjoyed by the ancient Indian tribes that lived here before the Gods of Huajatolla became angry . . . and the Spanish came. *U.S. Geological Survey photo.*

Pawnees. Golden pellets were so much better than ordinary pellets because each one hit the mark. The Arapahoes attributed their victory to the little yellow balls, and some of these balls were buried with their great Chief Whirlwind, who led the battle against the Pawnees.

Latter-day historians denied the use of gold for shot by the Indians, but it was a very popular story way back when. Several Indian tribes used precious metals for this and that, so who are we to deny the Arapahoes the use of gold to protect their tepees and squaws? There are several legends concerning Arapaho gold. The best known and, perhaps, the most authentic (if we may use that word) is the Lost Arapaho Princess Treasure.

Such legends of gold as the one mentioned above brought many Spanish prospectors into Colorado. Some parties set up what could well have been the first settlements in the state.

One such party of eight or ten Spaniards settled in the foothills of the Spanish Peaks in the early 1800's.

The Arapahoes were here but the Spaniards found them friendly and the two peoples lived side by side.

After several days of prospecting the Spaniards located a rich vein of gold, in which the pay stream was one half inch of solid sheet gold in places.

The Spaniards began mining the gold, melting it down into 50-pound bars, storing the bars, planning to ship them back to Spain. They hired the Indians to work for them and the work progressed wonderfully well.

It just so happened—as in all good stories—that the chief had a beautiful daughter. It followed that the leader of the Spanish settlement fell in love with her. The chief approved the marriage, and there was a grand ceremony. Before long the couple had a daughter.

It was just about this time that the Utes began to fuss with the Arapahoes again. Some believe it was over reports of gold that had filtered back to the Utes. There were some minor skirmishes along the border but nothing serious until one day Arapaho scouts heard that the Utes planned a grand attack to chase the Arapahoes out and kill the Spanish.

The Arapahoes advised the Spanish to leave until things cooled down. The Spanish followed the advice. The bars of gold were packed on eight burros, the Spanish leader kissed his wife and daughter, and the little caravan began to leave.

But apparently the Utes got wind of the immigration because before the Spanish were out of the village, the Ute braves bore down on them. The Spanish realized that they had no chance of escape with the heavy gold shipment, so they hurriedly buried the gold and left on swift horses.

The treasure was buried along a line from some houses, about 300 feet away from a strange arrangement of rocks. One rock was bigger than the rest—about thirty feet high—and formed much like a doll. It was so doll-like the Indians had named it Muñeca—the doll. The Spaniards buried the treasure under a smaller rock near the Muñeca.

They had no sooner finished than the battle started. Six Spaniards were killed. The leader and two others escaped to Santa Fe, where they recuperated and eventually returned to Spain.

But during his months in Spain, the leader's loneliness grew for his wife and daughter. After ten years he returned to Huajatolla.

He was welcomed back into the tribe by the chief. But he learned that his wife, the Princess, had died. However, his daughter, now thirteen years old, was very much alive, and was blossoming into the beautiful image of her mother.

The Spaniard was tired of fighting and mining gold. He sought only peace and contentment. He refused to open the mine. He wanted no more than to settle down and farm, with his daughter by his side.

He lived happily ever after and didn't mention the gold until he lay dying. His daughter was at his side, and he told her of the fabulous treasure, which was estimated at between one and two million dollars.

The daughter cared naught for the gold either. She merely mentioned it in passing when she was married. Years passed. One day, her oldest son, Carlos, overheard his parents speak of the gold hoard. From then on he and the other children often begged to see the gold, but their mother didn't tell them where it was, fearing it would corrupt them.

More years passed. The Princess' husband died and Carlos became chief. When his mother, the Spaniard's daughter, grew old, she told Carlos the secret of the treasure, but she cautioned him not to touch it until she died.

She said he could find the gold buried near the Muñeca, the place marked with a shovel.

After his mother died, Carlos and his brothers and sisters searched for the treasure. They found the Muñeca, but, look as they might, they never found the shovel.

Only after they looked for it did one of them remember finding the shovel many moons before while out hunting. He said he used the shovel to clear a spot in which to eat and then he had cast it aside.

3. THE GOLDEN MUMMY

Taylor Markley and Jim Coleville worked overtime at the Coyote Mine on Silver Mountain, near La Veta, one day in 1892.

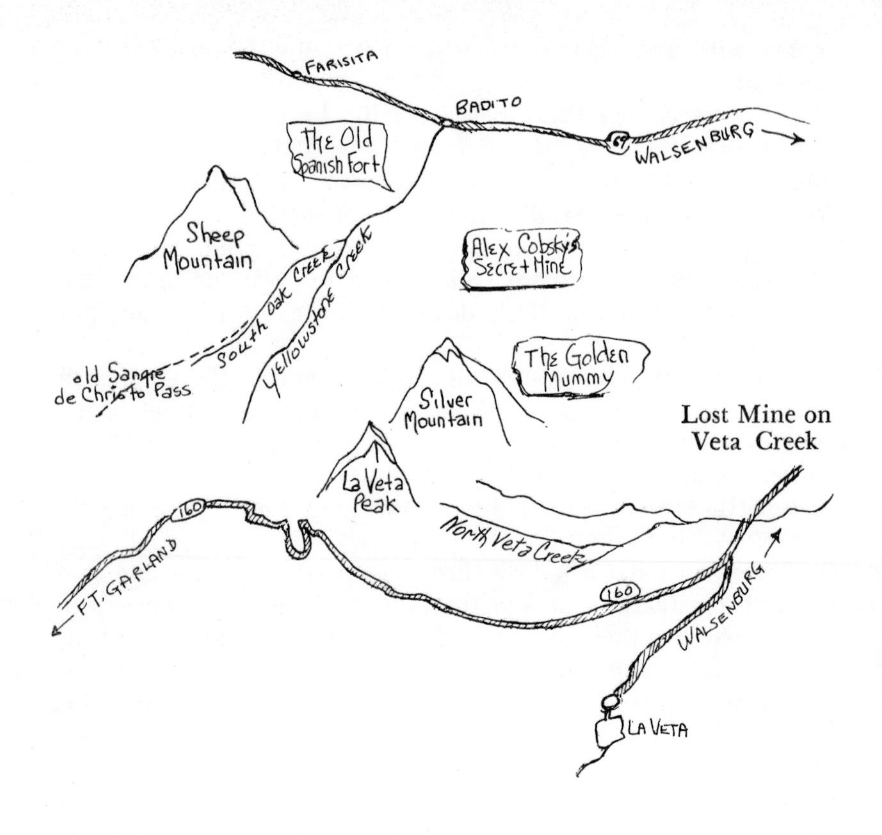

Lost Mine on Veta Creek

They finished work just as the snow started falling. To avoid being trapped by a possible blizzard, they took a shortcut over the mountain.

While crossing a large body of snow on the mountain, the ground gave way under them. They fell through the snow, through the surface of the ground, and into a cave.

After recovering their footing, they examined the cave. It was about eight feet wide and about thirty or forty feet deep. Exploring farther, they found what seemed to be a mine tunnel. They had only penetrated the tunnel a short distance when they decided they'd better hurry back and save the exploring until later. Feeling their way along the sides of the tunnel, they ran into a niche or shelf at one point. They saw a peculiar-looking form in the niche. It appeared to be that of a child about two or three years old.

They attempted to lift the form and found it hard and extremely heavy, weighing about 140 pounds. Closer examination showed the form was wearing a string of beads around its neck and a bracelet on its arm. In the feeble light of their mining candles the jewelry glittered like the finest gold filigree. As they were working with the figure, a piece of it was chipped off and its inside surface glittered with gold. The small piece was later assayed and found to be almost solid gold. Local experts speculated the figure was either of Indian or Spanish origin and had been carved out fifty or more years before.

The above story appeared in the 1892 *Denver Times.* That would date the object in the early or middle 1800's. There was no record of Indian or Spanish mining activity in this area at this time. The story may have been a fake, as many such stories were at that time. Such finds, however, were not unknown. It could well have been a true golden moment in Colorado's past.

4. ALEX COBSKY'S SECRET MINE

Alex Cobsky died at the state hospital in Pueblo in March of 1937, one year after he had been hit by an auto while guiding his burro along the highway in southern Colorado. He was about eighty when he died, penniless and incoherent. His death would have passed unnoticed had not a couple of alert reporters recalled the legend that clung to Alex Cobsky . . . and his "secret" mine.

Alex received national attention in early 1901 when he appeared at a Pueblo smelter with two burros packed with ore. The ore assayed at $40,000 a ton, some of the richest ore ever found in Colorado. Alex Cobsky got $12,500 for the load. It was the most sensational mining news of the year in Colorado, and the find received attention in newspapers throughout the country.

The story had little time to spread, however, before Alex Cobsky disappeared back into the mysterious mountains.

He created another stir a few months later when he brought another big ore load into Pueblo. Altogether, Cobsky got $30,000 for his ore, a pretty fair price for two small shipments.

One of the rare pictures of Alex Cobsky. He lived in his cabin with his animals during the winter. *Colorado Historical Society photo.*

The good people of Pueblo didn't discover much more about the man and his find than they had on his first trip into town. Putting together what little they learned, it seems Cobsky had found an old shaft while herding goats . . . somewhere in the southern Colorado mountains.

Putting two legends together, it became an accepted fact that Cobsky had found the long-lost Simpson Mine. It seems that Jack Simpson had found a streak of almost free gold somewhere on Silver Mountain near La Veta Pass in 1869. Simpson took one rich shipment of the ore into town and was killed by Indians before he could make another trip. Scores of men searched for the Simpson shaft, but it was never found . . . that is, until Alex Cobsky and his goats evidently stumbled upon it. The richness and similarity of Cobsky's and Simpson's ores made people believe they were one and the same.

One couldn't prove it by Alex Cobsky. One couldn't prove anything by Alex Cobsky.

The exciting young man of the mining world was actually two people in one. Gold has done strange things to many men. Alex Cobsky had little enjoyment from his; rather, for the rest of his life, he was fearful and animal-like in his protection of his hoard.

On his rare trips into town—two or three times a year into La Veta and a few trips into Pueblo and Denver—he had been pleasant, and even interesting to be around. The people of La Veta said Cobsky treated his infrequent trips into town as a holiday. He always ordered two ice cream sodas and devoured them with boyish delight.

The publicity his discovery received throughout the country brought Cobsky back together with what few relatives he had. He had been orphaned while a baby and had been separated from his brothers and sisters. The news of his discovery brought the family together again and they moved to Denver.

Over the years, Cobsky made very few trips into Denver, but he was always welcome. He made his visits something special. He stored up his talk all year long, to spend it on his family. He brought presents with him. And one trip he gave the youngsters in the family gold nuggets to play with. When Cobsky came to Denver it was Christmas and he played Santa Claus.

But, alas, the change that came over the man when he went back up into the mountains!

The people of La Veta all knew his ritual, they talked about it, laughed about it, but had no mind to change it.

Cobsky usually left La Veta in the late afternoon or early evening. Just outside town he would hide beside the trail, usually for hours, to make sure he wasn't being followed. Like an animal, his fear-filled eyes peered from behind the branches. He moved only at night, doubling back frequently to make sure that there was no one behind him. He was back in his den by daylight. Up in the mountains he was hostile, sometimes vicious. He always carried a gun and if anyone chanced to meet him in the mountains, the gun was loaded, cocked and aimed at the visitor all the time. One time, Undersheriff Carl Swift threatened to take the gun away from him if he saw it again. So Cobsky made a quick trip into Denver for a permit.

For years and years, Alex Cobsky kept the location of his mine a secret. Even up to the time of his death very, very few people knew of the mine. His family didn't even know its location. But as La Veta became more populated, it was natural that some people, albeit a very few, ran into the man in the mountains. A few people apparently knew of his cabin built into the side of the mountain, but few guessed that the cabin was built over the entrance of the mine. Alex Cobsky usually wasn't in sight whenever anyone wandered up his way, but they didn't go near the cabin anyway. They knew Cobsky was probably peering at them with a rifle in his hand.

Only once in the thirty-odd years the old man lived in the mountains did he let down his guard and invite someone into his cabin. Theodore C. Gibbons, then a Grand Valley farmer, told of the visit many years later, after Cobsky's death.

He said he made the visit when he was only fourteen years old. Gibbons said he and his brother and some friends were prospecting in the hills. Gibbons was the youngest of the group and wore down long before the others. The others wanted to go on, but Gibbons couldn't go another step. For want of anything better to do, the older boys left him with an old man they met in the mountains.

The old man was Alex Cobsky. And Cobsky, for want of anything better to do, invited the boy to his cabin.

Gibbons said the mine was in plain view inside the cabin, but the mine entrance was covered by a heavy vault-like door. Gibbons recalled what the old man said as the boy approached the vaulted door:

"You can't go any further, boy. I'm the only man in the world who can go past that door and I'll always be the only one."

Cobsky told him there was a lot of gold behind the door but that there were all sorts of death traps if anyone tried to get into the mine.

Gibbons recalled that a large collection of guns hung on one side of the cabin. On the other side of the cabin was an animal feed stall, lending credence to the rumor that Cobsky invited his burros and two cows inside the cabin to live during the winter.

Gibbons said he kept the visit a secret so long because he liked Cobsky and because "that old man was a good shot and he made me promise."

All the people around La Veta came to know the strange old man. They knew him as two people, a twinkling, happy man, so full of life and talk when he came to town. Then there was the frightened, hostile man of the mountains. The legend grew around the latter. The legend grew, aided by Cobsky himself, that the cabin and the mine contained all sorts of death traps, pitfalls, booby traps and the like.

So, as might be expected, even after Cobsky was struck by a car, and after his death, people stayed away from the cabin.

But eventually, Undersheriff Carl Swift and a deputy decided it was in their best interest to check into the death trap stories. They did find an old box of dynamite in one corner of the cabin, but it wasn't hooked up to any death trap. In fact, the two men searched the cabin and the mine thoroughly and discovered nothing of a sinister nature.

Cobsky willed his mine to Denver relatives: Mrs. Anna Reicht and Mrs. Elizabeth Wiebelt, his nieces; and a grand-nephew, Howard Roepnack, an Arvada attorney. But trouble brewed over the mine right after the old man's death. Apparently he had never patented his claim and some people in the La Veta area contested the property rights.

Roepnack took a mining engineer down to La Veta to inspect the mine and to see if it was worth fighting for. The engineer found little ore of value and recommended that the Denver relatives not contest the suits against it, even if they thought they had grounds. The relatives never realized anything from the mine.

There is little evidence that anyone ever got anything out of it after the old man's death. It's on the property of a local rancher and they say he keeps the mine open and once in a while fiddles around inside it, but he's never showed any good ore from it.

Maybe it's as some people around La Veta believe—Alex Cobsky didn't want anyone else to have his gold.

He took it with him.

5. LOST MINE ON VETA CREEK

During the years just prior to the Civil War many men came west, not only to seek their fortunes and find adventure, but also to avoid the strife back east. Among this number was one who took a devious route and eventually found himself at the foot of the majestic mountains. Here the man became acquainted with a friendly Indian tribe and soon became a part of it.

He hunted game with the tribe. But he was not converted completely because he hunted gold, too.

Finally, in his wanderings, he discovered free gold quartz at the head of a creek known as North Veta. The discovery was enough to make him forget his life as an Indian. At the site of his discovery he built a cabin and began work, digging and storing his gold.

Later, when Denver became a city, the man journeyed all the way from his cabin to sell some of his gold and buy a few knickknacks . . . like food and clothing. He attracted some attention, but since he was a fugitive from the Civil War and since he had already found his gold, he was wary and secretive.

During the next few years the man made a few more trips to Denver . . . as few as possible. But in the early 1880's, when he realized he was getting old and he would not be able to make many more journeys, he went to a lawyer's office and made out his last will and testament.

In his will he gave everything to his only sister, a Mrs. Clark, living in Kansas. He said he had a rich gold mine and four bags of the gold already stacked inside the entrance. He gave detailed directions for locating the mine, saying it was near an old fort close by an Indian trail (possibly the old Spanish Fort near Sangre de Cristo Pass). He said the mine was well hidden and not likely to be found without the directions contained in the will. Its location could be verified by a pick hidden in the roots of a nearby tree.

After making out his will the old man headed west, never to be seen again.

Mr. Clark, husband of the old man's sister, came to the town of La Veta in 1884 and searched for the mine, with no luck. He returned the following year, a little more desperate and a little more talkative about it. He even showed the will to a few people, and with some coaxing he imprudently displayed the directions on how to find the mine. Within days several persons heard of the mine and became extremely interested in it. Several parties searched for it during that summer.

If the mine was found, the fact was not recorded by the finder.

But late in the fall, two men, Morgan Peterson and George Dotson, were heading back to civilization in the face of the first snowstorm of the winter.

While scrambling along the canyon they paused to rest a moment and noticed the roots of the nearby tree had been dug up. Upon investigation they found an old rusted pick. Not knowing the story of the lost mine at the time, the two men thought little of their find. They carried the tool along with them a while and then finally cast it into some bushes along the way as the snow began to fall and they had to hurry on.

The lost mine was never found and its most important landmark has disappeared.

6. THE OLD SPANISH FORT

In 1819, when the west was overcrowded with gringos and Frenchmen—there must have been some twenty or thirty out here—the Spanish built a fort to keep all trespassers out of Spanish territory.

The Spanish selected a site at the eastern foot of an ancient

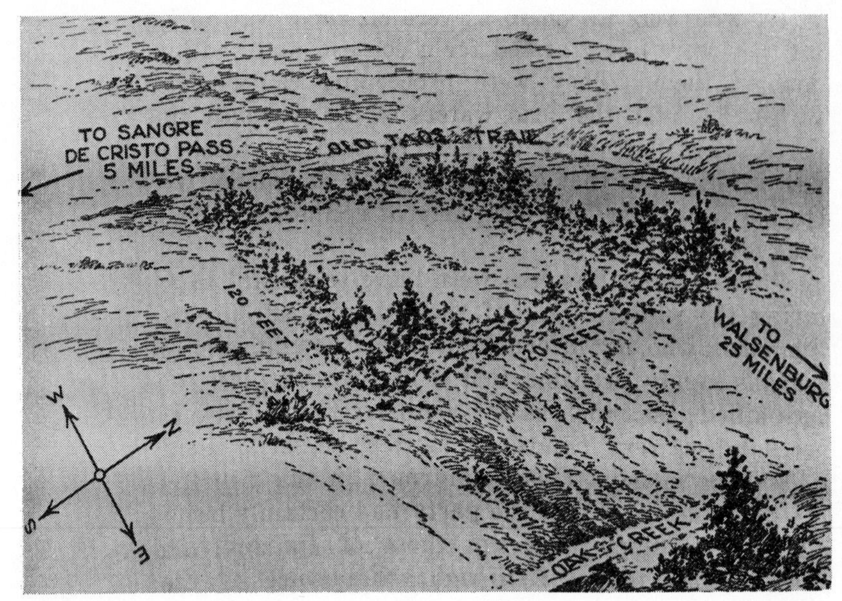

Sketch of the ruins of the old Spanish Fort as seen by Colorado Historian LeRoy Hafen in the '30's. *Colorado Historical Society photo.*

Spanish trail, which later became known as the Sangre de Cristo Pass trail. The pass lies between Veta Mountains to the south and Sheep Mountains to the north. The fort, a triangular one, was located about twenty-five miles from present-day Walsenburg.

The fort had a short but violent life. In the fall of 1819 it was attacked by about 100 Indians, and, as some think, a few Yankees and Frenchmen dressed up as Indians. Many of the Spanish defenders were killed.

Later the same year, the United States and Spain finally agreed upon the Arkansas River as the southern boundary of the Louisiana Purchase in Colorado. So the fort was no longer practical and the Spanish abandoned it.

The fort was forgotten for about 100 years. In fact, if anyone ever located it, they never made mention of the fact.

In the 1920's, however, an old man came into the nearby town of Gardner and bought supplies with authentic eight-sided Spanish gold pieces. He did this frequently during the next few years.

Finally, he let it slip that he had found a cache of the Cpanish coins inside the walls of the old fort.

The great Colorado historian, LeRoy Hafen, heard the story and verified the existence of the Spanish Fort. He located the remains of the crumbling adobe walls.

He said he dug around the fort site but didn't find any Spanish coins.

Perhaps the old man had recovered all there were.

Or, perhaps, more coins are scattered in the dust at the foot of the majestic mountains.

III. *THE LEGENDS OF PUEBLO*

7. THE GOLD OF GREENHORN RANGE

A short distance west of Pueblo are the serene, green hills known as the Greenhorn Range. The range and the nearby creek are named for the famous Comanche Chief, Cuerno Verde (Green Horn), who was killed at the foot of the mountains in 1819 by Spanish Captain De Anza.

The mountains have been fairly peaceful ever since with nothing more exciting than an occasional prospector searching for lost gold.

One of the most-told tales is the one of a Pueblo prospector who spent much of his time combing the range. After several years of futile search he thought he had finally hit it lucky.

He came riding into Pueblo hell-bent for leather, pulling a wagon full of ore, which he believed to be rich. He took the ore to the first assay office he came to in Pueblo.

To his great disappointment the assayer said the ore was worthless.

The news broke the prospector's heart—he had been positive that he had finally found the end of the rainbow.

Dejectedly he took the wagon load of nothing and dumped it in a vacant area on the outskirts of Pueblo. The next few days

he packed up his gear, said farewell to his friends, and headed over the range, never to be seen again.

A few months later another man found the ore dump. It looked promising to him, too. So he took the samples to another assayer.

The second expert said it was some of the richest ore he had ever seen.

But the first prospector, the only man who knew where it came from, had long since departed.

8. TREASURE OF APACHE GULCH

There are several prospect holes up Apache Gulch. Prospectors have searched the gulch fairly thoroughly but haven't found too much worth bothering about.

According to legend, however, the Spaniards fared better. They found some good gold here and are said to have mined quite a bit. Then, according to legend, the Indians came along and made with the slaughter, killing all the Spaniards except a 12-year-old boy.

The years passed and then came the gringos. They farmed nearby, ranched nearby, and always there were the prospectors. Prospectors didn't find much paydirt in the gulch but some of them claimed to have found some evidence of Spanish civilization around, some old prospect holes, ancient tools, and other knick-knacks. What must have been an old Spanish arrastra, a primitive tool for crushing the ore, was found up the gulch. A farmer, a few years ago, claimed to have found a gold brick while working in his field.

Some prospectors put the legend and the evidence together and began looking for the youth who survived the Indian ambush.

They finally found the Spaniard in Santa Fe. He was an old man now, but he agreed to come to Colorado and look for the gold mine.

After several days of looking he gave up in despair. He found some vague landmarks of long ago, but the other details were clouded with age.

The Spaniard died a few years ago. He was over 100 years old.

Few of the legends down Walsenburg way are more controversial than that of the lost Spanish mine on Apache Gulch. Residents are about evenly divided on the credibility of the legend. Most skeptics base their skepticism on the fact that very little good ore has been found up the gulch. One well-known mining man in the area, however, claims to have seen Apache Gulch ore worth about $58,000 to the ton, some of the richest in the state.

There are always two sides to a legend.

9. SUNKEN TREASURE OF MUSTANG CANYON

About twenty years ago Walsenburg rancher and amateur archeologist R. R. Holderman created a bit of a stir when he claimed to have found evidence of buried treasure in Bottomless Lake of Mustang Canyon.

Holderman said he found markings on the canyon wall that were apparently made by an ancient Indian tribe, possibly Aztecs, who migrated to this region from Mexico after the Spanish invasion.

Holderman read treasure into the markings.

He said it was part of the religious practices of some advanced tribes to make a sacrifice to rain gods by dumping valuables into lakes and pools. Holderman figured the Indians used the blind canyon as a corral for game roundups. It followed, according to Holderman, that Bottomless Lake would be a good place to bury the sacrifices.

Mustang Pool is a large natural reservoir pounded into solid rock by the constant hammering of a 60-foot waterfall. It has never been sounded. Years ago, during the construction of a railroad through the region, engineers pumped water from the pool for locomotives. But the hose never reached the bottom and the pool was never drained, despite the millions of gallons pumped from it.

Holderman planned on hiring a noted skin diver, able to dive 170 feet, to search for the treasure he was sure was there.

Holderman has long since left the area. Most people in the region never heard of his plans of hiring a skin diver. However, old timers doubt if a skin diver ever did search the murky bottom of the pool, and they are positive no treasure was ever pulled out.

It may have been as Holderman feared . . . that the mud and silt of the centuries have buried the treasure even deeper.

10. GOLD NUGGETS BY THE BUSHEL

There was gold excitement down Pueblo way about the time of the great diamond excitement in the west (see the Great Diamond Fields), and for a short while—in Pueblo—the gold outdid the diamonds.

While most fortune hunters were chasing the elusive diamonds all over Colorado and the west, a fellow named Mike Clay showed up at Pueblo to outfit himself for prospecting. At that time rumors put the diamond fields in southern Colorado so it was taken for granted that Gray was joining the diamond search.

Not so.

Gray told them in the tavern that he didn't give a hoot for the diamonds, but that he was here "to take possession of one of the most astounding gold mines ever seen by mortal eyes."

Gray said he was following the lead of a Frenchman who affirmed "in a solemn manner" that he had visited a valley where gold in nugget form could be gathered by the bushel.

The confident stranger said that, three years before, the Frenchman, with a party of Mexicans, had explored the region where the gold fields lay, when the party was attacked by a band of Apaches. All but the Frenchman and two Mexicans were killed. The three survivors barely escaped with their lives.

A while later, the Frenchman told Gray that a white woman who had been held captive by the Utes for years knew exactly where the gold was to be found, and she used to gather it herself.

"But the Indians," said the Frenchman, "apprehensive that she might disclose the valuable secret, murdered her, and thus destroyed the last dangerous possessor of it outside their own tribe."

Gray said the Frenchman pledged his life "to be sacrificed in any manner they might elect" if he didn't lead them to the gold fields.

Gray left Pueblo and was never seen again. As Colorado's early historian Frank Hall puts it: "What became of him has not been related, but certain it is that Gray never found the mine."

11. LOST TUNGSTEN MINE IN FREMONT COUNTY

Somewhere in Fremont County is a tungsten mine, believed richer than the world-famous mines in Boulder County. Of course, tungsten is not gold or silver, but it's nothing to be sneezed at, and at one time—during World War I—it was more valuable than any of the precious metals given up by Mother Earth.

It was during World War I that knowledge of this lost tungsten mine came to light. It all came about in a very unusual manner.

Colorado State Mines Commissioner Fred Carroll began the search. It seems Carroll was browsing through several ore samples sent in many years before for a mining exposition. The examples were well labeled when sent from Colorado to the international exhibit. But when the ore samples were returned many of the labels had been lost.

Carroll said the rich tungsten sample was found among the rocks from Fremont County, but the individual label telling of its location was missing. Carroll had the ore assayed and found it to be worth $7,500 a ton—at that time. He went to Fremont County in an attempt to find the location of the rich mine, but no mining expert there could identify the land the ore came from.

The problem came about by the fact that when the sample was submitted, tungsten had no appreciable value and no one became too excited about it. At least not excited enough to keep particulars about it. With the end of the war, the value of tungsten took a nosedive. It lost most of its allure.

But it could still be valuable property . . . wherever it is. Carroll believed, from its appearance, it was found near or at the surface, and was a part of a large ore body.

IV. *BORDERLAND TREASURE*

12. SPANISH TREASURE OF PURGATORY CANYON

The full name of the river is El Rio de Las Animas Perdidas en Purgatoir, The River of Lost Souls in Purgatory.

The name stems from an ancient Spanish tale told by Franciscan Friars in New Mexico.

It seems a large party of conquistadores set out for another search for Quivira a few years after Coronado made the search in 1540-42. The party was commanded, strangely enough, by a Portuguese gentleman, with a Spaniard second in command. Also along on the trip were several priests. This was not only a Spanish custom but a rule for all expeditions by the conquistadores.

After only a few days out, the Spanish lieutenant killed the Portuguese captain in a fit of jealous rage. The Spaniard claimed command of the expedition. But the priests charged the Spaniard with murder and refused to continue on the unholy journey. They, and several other members of the party, turned back.

The ill-fated expedition was never heard from again. It was believed they were all killed by Apaches somewhere in southeastern Colorado. Since there were no priests along to deliver the last sacraments, they are still floating around out there in Purgatory. Hence the name.

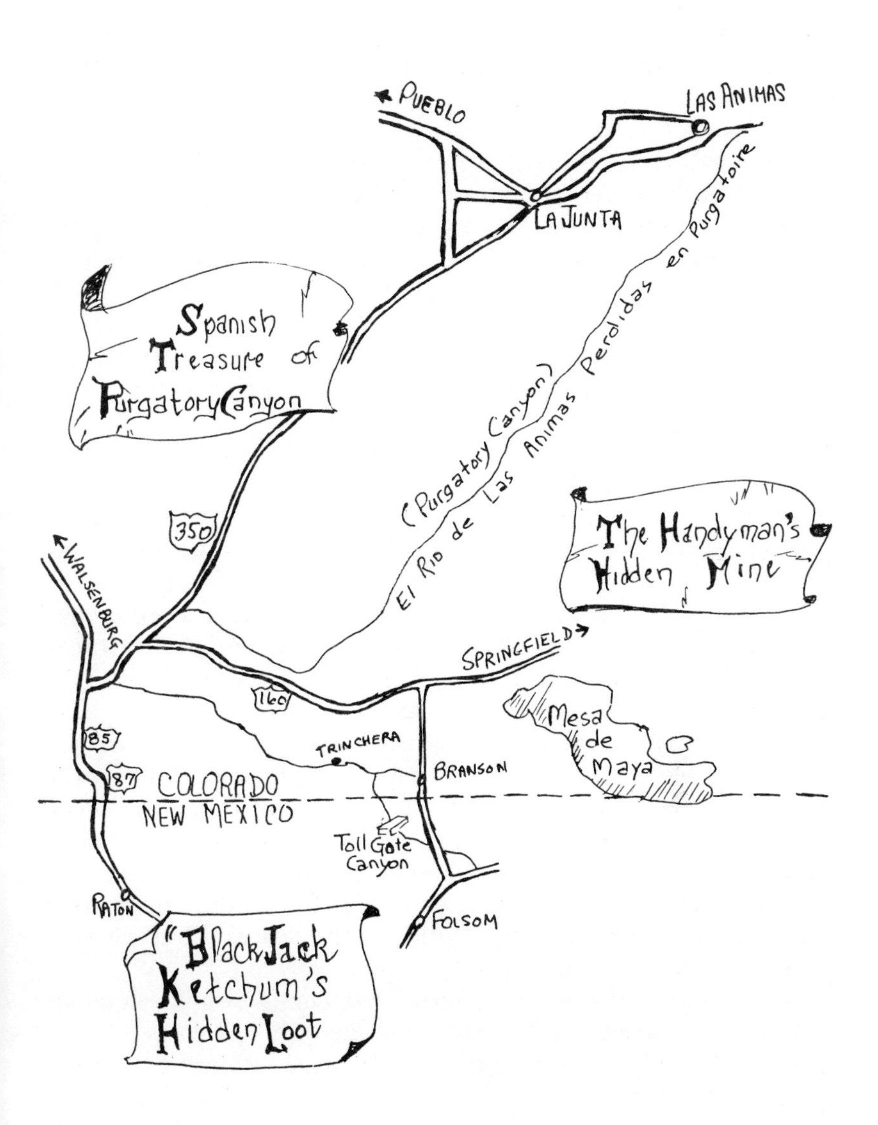
PUEBLO
LAS ANIMAS
LA JUNTA
Spanish Treasure of Purgatory Canyon
(Purgatory Canyon)
El Rio de Las Animas Perdidas en Purgatoire
350
WALSENBURG
The Handyman's Hidden Mine
SPRINGFIELD
160
Mesa de Maya
85
TRINCHERA
BRANSON
87
COLORADO
NEW MEXICO
Toll Gate Canyon
RATON
FOLSOM
"Black Jack Ketchum's Hidden Loot

Later rusted armor, skeletons, and arrows were found along the river. Parts of a skeleton and rusty metal belonging to a gun were found in a cave east of Willow-Vogel Canyon Junction in 1924.

The French later changed the name to Purgatoire. The Americans found this hard to pronounce so they Americanized this to Picketwire. One historian even went so far to say the name came from an early settler with an unusual name.

A river with such a historic beginning was bound to gather momentum as it went along. And it did. Full many a legend is gathered from the broiling waters of the Purgatory River and the Canyon it runs through.

The richest legend concerns twelve chests of Spanish gold doubloons either buried along its banks or rusting at the bottom of the river.

Around 1700, a large Spanish regiment left Santa Fe bound for the Spanish garrison at St. Augustine, Florida. The regiment convoyed twelve chests of gold with which to pay the soldiers at the garrison. The regiment was commanded by Carrasco Rodriguez.

Ignoring the guides, Rodriguez marched in a northeasterly direction. Winter found them near the present site of Trinidad, where they camped until spring. Spring came, and once again they took off . . . in the wrong direction.

The regiment was never heard from again. But five years later a dying Apache said the entire regiment had been killed in an Indian ambush. Pieces of Spanish armor and other equipment showed up from time to time among the Indians. Many years later a Spanish suit of armor was found alongside the Purgatoire.

It is believed the Indians were satisfied with the armor, guns, rum and other personal belongings of the Spanish, but were not interested in the gold.

Some believe the Spanish buried the chests of gold along the banks of the river. Others think the Spanish somehow managed boats and were racing downstream when they dumped the chests overboard at the last moment. In either case there's a pretty good chance that there are twelve chests of Spanish gold still to be found somewhere in the Purgatory River area.

Purgatory Canyon took on an even more mysterious air in later years with tales of a treasure wagon darting from shadow to shadow in the canyon. According to records nobody, officially, saw the mysterious wagon and its more mysterious rider. But legend grew until, eventually, anybody who presumed to know the canyon had seen the apparition at one time or another.

The wagon was black, and pulled by six jet black horses with manes a-streaming in the dash up and down the canyon. The driver wore luminous gloves. Somehow, the legend grew that he was a Spaniard carrying treasure to his own hiding place.

The reports of the discovery of gold ingots along the trail, and other evidence of Spanish visitors, were credited to the mystery rider, but legend was vague about where the gold came from and where it went. A logical solution to the puzzle were the many caves along the canyon. Searchers began to probe the many grottos and holes along the route.

The closest the legend came to reality was the story of one searcher finding Spanish equipment and a few golden pieces of eight in one cave. Sure the secret of the legend and the treasure was near, but unable to thoroughly search the area at the time, the discoverer marked the area by thrusting a knife into the closest tree.

A short time later, however, he fell while climbing in the canyon and broke his leg. Unable to move, he lay for two days and nights before found. Near death from exposure, he was able only to gasp out his story and die.

Of course, all this story did was add a tree with a dagger stuck in it to the search for a treasure cave and mysterious rider. No doubt the mysterious rider is dead now but the cave and the tree are still there. Legends don't die easy.

13. THE HANDYMAN'S HIDDEN MINE

One story of lost gold in the Mesa de Maya area was told several years ago by one of the leading ranchers in the region.

The rancher said he hired a Texan for a handyman. This fellow performed all sorts of miscellaneous tasks around the ranch.

Late in the fall the rancher sent the handyman off in a wagon to gather firewood for the winter. On the Texan's return he produced what he thought was an exceptionally pretty rock, and asked

Moody and mysterious Mesa de Maya, source of many a legend. It was here a handyman is said to have found a gold mine. This picture is taken from the south. *Picture courtesy of Willard Louden.*

the rancher if he knew what it was. The handyman said he had chipped it off a larger rock with an ax.

The boss inspected the rock and found it to be gold-bearing quartz. The handyman said there was plenty more where that came from. The rancher knew a good thing when he saw it and agreed to finance a mining venture for half interest. The handyman thought about it for a while and then agreed upon the plan on one condition—he would be given a wagon and team of oxen to visit his family in Texas. The rancher agreed.

But before the handyman was ready to travel, winter was upon them. It looked as if it would be a particularly severe winter, so the handyman decided to put off his trip until spring.

Early in the spring the handyman took off.

He never returned.

Usually, when one gets taken like that, he doesn't like to talk about it, but the rancher was a jolly good sport. He told the story on himself.

14. BLACK JACK KETCHUM'S HIDDEN LOOT

People down Mesa de Maya way claim "Black Jack" Ketchum hid some loot in the neighborhood and didn't get a chance to come back and get it before he was hanged. It may or may not be so. Jack wasn't famous for leaving loot around, but at least it gives the people a feeling of belonging . . . to the Black Jack Ketchum legend.

Black Jack was just about as bad a man as the southwest produced. Like "Butch" Cassidy, Black Jack was a "nice" outlaw in many ways. He didn't ever want to hurt anybody, he just wanted to get rich quick.

Jack rode out of Texas in the middle nineties and in a few short years rose to the top of his profession, which was robbing trains. He concentrated on trains in New Mexico and Arizona, but several other states around claim "business visits" by the man and his gang.

Running beside Mesa de Maya is Tollgate Canyon, a toll road offshoot of the Santa Fe Trail. The canyon was so narrow in parts that a wagon couldn't turn around and had to pay the toll. In one of these narrow sections, near the New Mexico border, Black Jack, or some other highwayman, set up shop.

It seems the highwayman used dummy confederates. Behind rocks the robber would prop up stuffed dummies, so when the highwaymen held up a wagon or stagecoach, it looked to the victim as if he were caught in an ambush.

The take from the robberies was said to have been buried nearby. When the bandit was chased off by a posse, they say he didn't have time to stop and pick up his treasure.

People in southeastern Colorado said the enterprising bandit was Black Jack Ketchum. It would seem that Black Jack wouldn't bother with a slow way to make money, and, according to the records, Jack was pretty busy down in Arizona and New Mexico.

Ruins of the old toll house in Tollgate Canyon near the New Mexico-Colorado border near where Black Jack Ketchum is said to have done some highway robbery with the help of phony confederates. *Picture courtesy of Fred Smith.*

Tollgate Canyon, so narrow a wagon couldn't turn about and had to pay fare. A rock, since pushed off the road, stood opposite the one above. A toll gate ran between the rocks. It was in this narrow passage that Black Jack Ketchum is said to have practiced his highwayman trade. *Photo courtesy Fred Smith.*

Black Jack Ketchum. His brief but hectic era in the southwest gave cause for many a buried treasure tale. Below, the hanging of Black Jack at Clayton, New Mexico, on July 24, 1899, where he allegedly said, "hurry it up, I'm due in Hell for dinner." *Denver Public Library Western Collection.*

Some of Black Jack's train robberies were south of Mesa de Maya. In November of 1896, Ketchum and his gang robbed a train of many thousands of dollars near Separ, New Mexico. Some of the gang members were killed, but Ketchum escaped to ride again.

In 1901, Ketchum held up a train single-handedly at Twin-Mountain Curve. Although wounded, Ketchum escaped the posse only to be found wandering around the desert in a dazed condition the next day.

The jig was up for Black Jack Ketchum.

He was taken to Clayton, New Mexico, where he was tried, convicted, and sentenced to be hanged. His last requests were that he be buried face down and that he have music at his hanging. A violin and guitar played Ketchum's favorite music, but the stage-struck hangman muffed his part as he fumbled with the ropes. Upon this, legend says, Black Jack scolded:

"Hurry it up, I'm due in hell for dinner."

15. SPANISH MINE ON CULEBRA PEAK

The first settlers in the Trinidad area heard rumors of a rich Spanish mine somewhere nearby. Five generations of settlers went about their business, every now and again finding themselves in the mountains, recalling the rumor and searching for the mine.

According to the legend the Spanish prospected in this area about the time of the Revolutionary War. Somewhere near the Colorado-New Mexico border they found their gold. They dug a shaft, timbered it, made cleaning sloughs and melting ovens, and then put the Indians to work.

Work had not progressed very far, however, when they were either called away or chased away, legend varies. Anyhow, the Spanish left, but before they did, they ordered their Indian slaves to cover the shaft, hide the evidence of their work, and destroy the trail to the mine.

The Spanish never came back.

Many have sought the mine since. One of the latter-day searchers was Manuel Torres, a former post office employee in Trinidad and

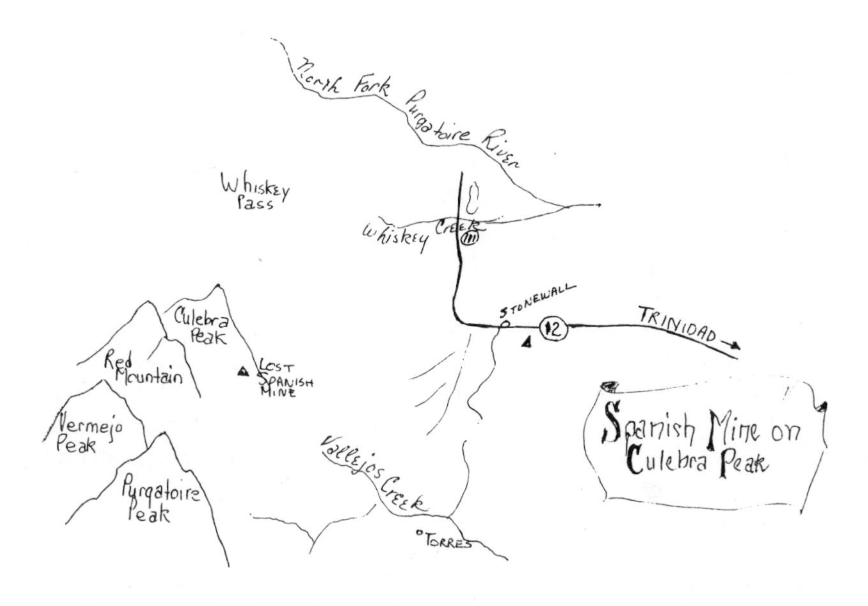

member of a large and well-known Trinidad family. Through the years Torres had spent much of his spare time seeking the old Spanish mine of legend. Through research and a process of elimination, he came to believe the mine was on or near Culebra Peak. During one vacation in 1939 he made another study of Culebra. He followed a circuitous route up the peak. It was a slow, but thorough, process. Finally, about a mile above timberline on the north side of the peak, he discovered a part of a rotting timber among a pile of rocks. He began digging into the rock pile and eventually struck water. He followed the water until he came to a mine shaft extending deep into the crown of the peak. Investigating the surface around the drift, he discovered a rock dump a distance away from the mouth of the mine. Three miles from the mouth of the mine he found evidence of an ancient mine slough and some mining masonry.

Torres found that the ancient mine was on property belonging to the Colorado Fuel and Iron Co. He secured papers from the corporation giving him permission to continue his explorations. With his son, Elias, and grandson, Simplicio Vallejos, he quietly but methodically went to work.

During what remained of the summer of 1939 he was able to uncover the entrance of the shaft. It had been well-timbered at one time, but now the timbers were rotting. Inside the mine but near the mine entrance, he found an ancient tool sharpener.

The summer of his discovery ended too soon and he could do no more.

Torres returned the following spring and continued his work. Penetrating deeper into the mine he found ore which showed some gold or silver, although of poor quality. He spent much of the summer retimbering the shaft.

Torres hadn't gone far into the shaft, however, when his work became hampered by seepage and gases. The farther into the shaft he went, the worse the water and gases became. About the farthest he could penetrate was 180 feet, although some reports said he went a distance of about 300 feet. From his deepest penetration, Torres saw evidence of a crosscut shaft a short distance beyond, but out of reach. Torres believed a rich body of gold ore was in this shaft.

Trying to go deeper into the shaft became the frustration of Torres' later years. He returned frequently but he never discovered anything more than what he had found before. He was positive this was the old Spanish mine of legend, but he was never able to find good gold. Torres was over eighty when he died in 1956. Although he never found his treasure, he, at least, died happy in the thought that he had discovered the old Spanish mine.

About forty-five miles west and a little south of Trinidad is the small community of Tercio. Some relatives and friends of Manuel Torres live here. They all know the story of Torres' Spanish mine. In fact, on a good day one can see the small opening high on the massive peak just to the west. They believe, as Manuel Torres did, that an ancient Spanish treasure still waits deep in the mountain.

16. THE WHITE CEMENT

The ragged, dead-tired old man shuffled into a prospecting camp in Horsehead Gulch, in northeast New Mexico, on a day in July of 1858. The prospecting party was headed by Henry Sharron, brother of New Mexico Senator Sharron.

The camp members took the old man in, fed him, let him rest his weary body, and tended the equally frazzled old mule the old man had dragged into camp. With all the tender care, the man was once more in fine shape that night as the men gathered around the fire. As at many western campfires, one hundred years ago, the talk eventually turned to tales of gold and treasure, lost gold and buried treasure. Each tale topped the other. It was always that way. The old man kept his tongue and listened, but with each story his eyes became brighter. Until, finally, his story burst forth.

His name was White and he said he came west from New England in 1849 to try his luck with all the rest of the fortune hunters in California. He searched for years but had no luck. Finally, he turned east again to make his disillusioned way home. In the high mountains, the Rockies, to the north, he stumbled on a lode of white rock which looked like cement. He had been around the hills long enough to discern that the stuff was rich in gold. And White topped off the story by pulling some white nuggets from his bag to show around.

The camp assayist processed the nuggets and said they assayed at 1,000 ounces of gold per ton. The old man made the mistake of saying there was plenty more where that came from.

The camp was excited that night but they didn't want to force the issue. None of the men slept, and by morning each had his plan for sharing or owning the White Cement Mine. Before the men became violent, Sharron stepped in. He told White that he must show them the treasure site. The old man would be given the choice claim and the surrounding claims would be shared among the rest. Sharron said there was no other way, that the old man's life wouldn't be worth a nickel if he didn't cooperate.

White, realizing his blunder, concocted all sorts of alibis in an effort to escape his predicament. He said he had made up the story. He said he had no idea where the site was. He hemmed and hawed. But the prospecting party was adamant, and eventually the old man realized that he had no other choice but to show them where the White Cement Mine was located.

The party lost no time in getting underway. The trail led northwestward and it became more and more difficult. At the end of the first day many of the party were sore and weary, not used to such tortuous traveling. Travel was equally rugged the second day, which found the party in the heart of mountains unknown to any but the old man. In fact, White, seeing the animosity growing in the party, told them he had lost the way for a while, but was now back on the trail. The party made camp in a blind canyon near the New Mexico-Colorado border.

"Boys, we'll be there tomorrow," the old man said.

He said he recognized all the landmarks, and the site was about thirty-five miles farther north.

The party, once ready for murder. was again hungry for gold. They were excited but too tired that night to do more than fall to the ground in sleep. The old man said he was too excited to sleep and volunteered to tend the horses.

The next morning White was gone.

The party immediately set out in pursuit, but it soon became evident that they could never catch up with the old man in the strange, rugged terrain. Nonetheless, the party searched for days. Some became lost in the mountains. Supplies were running low. Finally, they made their way back to civilization. Despite the fact that almost half of the first party was lost and despite the hardships of the trek, they organized another search party of almost 100 men. The large party combed the area for weeks but found no trace of the old man and his mine. The search was finally abandoned.

The White Cement Mine was all but forgotten during the next few years until a man named White showed up in Salt Lake City. He was incredibly rich and spent his money lavishly. According to reports he lent $60,000 to a rancher in Provo. Then he disappeared. He never collected on his loan. He was never heard from again.

But the story of the old man and his fabulous find became a well-known tale in the Colorado Rockies. Scores of search parties scoured southern Colorado for the mine. Legend says Nickolas C. Creede joined in the search, and the story goes on to say that it was during his futile search that he struck his pick into the ground in disgust and discovered the famous Holy Moses Mine and began the story of Creede. Many other rich mines in the San Juans and southern Colorado were discovered during the search for the White Cement.

Millions of dollars in gold and silver came from the mines, but the White Cement has never been found.

17. THE SECRET OF HIDDEN VALLEY

The legend was a popular one in the early gold and silver years of Colorado. It concerns the Spanish and the Indians. The story is not supported by the history books, but, then, how much history is?

It begins shortly after Coronado's trek in 1541 in search for Quivira. Along with the stories of Quivira, the Spanish saw Indians wearing rich gold ornaments. They say the gold trinkets gave rise to the stories of Quivira.

Anyhow, many Spaniards attempted to follow the Indians to the source of their gold. Most of them met disaster: they were killed or became hopelessly lost in the wilds to the north. But eventually one party successfully tracked the Indians to a fully developed mine, located, it is believed, on the Colorado-New Mexico border.

The Spanish party killed every last Navajo working the mine. They established a colony in the Hidden Valley and began working the mine themselves. Before long, more Indians came, but the Spanish got along with them, and even lured them to work for them. Things progressed very well.

Until in 1560, Cortez came north and he heard of Hidden Valley —quite by accident. He forced an old Indian to take him to the mine. When he came upon the valley he killed all the Spanish on the pretext of punishing them for their crimes against the Indians. Then he slaughtered the Indians, men and boys, and outraged the Indian maidens.

Then Cortez left a force of his own men to work the mine and went on about his business of being a conquistadore.

But his workers were not as successful at mining. They couldn't force the Indians to work for them. Soon there was open hostility. One night, a large band of Indians descended upon them and killed them all.

And Hidden Valley was forgotten for centuries . . . except in legend.

Some three hundred years later the story got to two young Leadville prospectors, Charles Ackerman and William Ramsey. Like many others before them, they decided to try their luck with

Hidden Valley. With two pack burros loaded down with equipment, and two ponies, the two men headed south from Leadville.

Leadville didn't hear from them for weeks, but finally friends in the silver town got a long letter.

Ackerman and Ramsey said they had searched through southern Colorado for weeks, avoiding the hostile Indians but following the Indian trails. One dark, stormy night they sought shelter in a cleft in the mountains and built a campfire. The fire cast eerie shadows on the walls of the cave and showed things that couldn't be seen in the daytime.

They decided to take torches and search the cleft of rocks further. They eventually found an opening in the wall of rocks, one that couldn't be seen except on close inspection. The opening emptied into a wide open area, the extent of which was far beyond the range of their torches.

They were convinced that they had found the Hidden Valley and were too excited to sleep. They talked and whiled away the endless night, and at the first light of dawn they began their examination.

There was a hidden valley!

What's more, there were many signs of ancient activity that were well preserved within the valley. Here were massive adobe walls, and a number of skeletons that turned to dust at their touch. They found mining equipment that was too modern for the Indians. Some of the equipment had Spanish inscriptions on it. But they did find many Indian relics, including numerous arrowheads.

They searched the whole valley carefully and found a gold-bearing quartz dump. They also found why the place had been so illusive—the mouth of the valley had been entirely choked up with rocks and boulders.

After their curiosity had been satisfied, Ackerman and Ramsey staked their claim, made careful notes of the location and its surroundings. When this was completed, they returned to Del Norte and filed application for the entire valley under the Homestead Act.

Along with their letters to Leadville, which appeared in the Leadville paper in 1880, they sent specimens of rich ore found in "their" valley.

Again, the two men dropped from sight. Their fabulous story

was all but forgotten. Some authorities had brushed off the story as a farce. Some believers said the two men had possibly stumbled upon one of the many Indian Pueblo ruins in southern Colorado or northern New Mexico. A friend of the discoverers in Leadville claimed, months later, that he had heard from Ackerman and Ramsey by letter, and they had said they were unable to find the well-hidden opening to their valley again. Hidden Valley was hidden once more, and Ackerman and Ramsey were never heard from again.

'Tis a pity, they wrote such interesting letters.

V. *TREASURES OF THE BLOOD OF CHRIST*

18. LA CAVERNA DEL ORO

The legend was here when the mountain men came west—the Spanish Cave of Gold. It was one of the earliest, and greatest, legends in the west. Many western states claim the treasure, or one similar to it, but Colorado had prior right . . . and the best location.

According to the old legend, the Spanish worked a fabulously rich underground mine somewhere in Colorado. They enslaved the Indians, who did all the heavy work. Things went quite well for a while. The Spanish were able to store much bullion. But, lo, after several moons, the Indians had had enough. They turned on their captors. Many Spaniards were killed. The others escaped—legend says through an underground passage—burying or spilling their bullion along the way.

Almost every section of Colorado with a spare cave or hole in the ground lays claim to La Caverna Del Oro. But discoveries during the past thirty years have led most experts to believe the famous cave is in the Sangre de Cristos.

In fact, most students of things like that are positive the legendary cave is in the Marble Cave or Spanish Cave area, near the mighty Crestones, only about twelve or thirteen miles from Westcliffe.

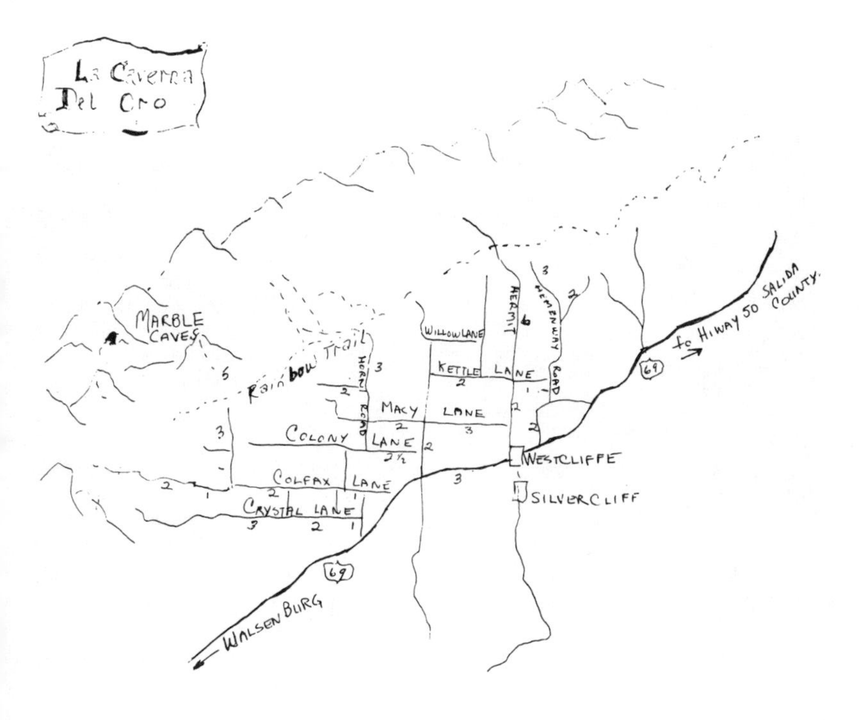

Men have been exploring the caves here, off and on, for several years. Many interesting discoveries were made, other discoveries were claimed but never supported.

But the most exciting finds were made as recently as 1960. These discoveries have led followers to believe that the study of the Spanish Caves has only begun.

The modern study of the cave, or caves, began nearly 100 years ago. In 1869, Captain Elisha P. Horn, one of the first settlers in the Wet Mountain Valley, discovered a faded Maltese cross over a cave entrance high in the Mountains. The cross was old when found by Horn. It measured two feet square and was colored with red pigment. Exploring further, Horn discovered evidence of rude fortifications and many arrowheads, testifying to a struggle. Nearby, Horn found a skeleton clothed in Spanish armor, an arrow piercing his heart.

The cave has been explored in part many times since, but nobody has made a serious study of it until this century.

Forest Ranger Paul Gilbert heard of the cave in 1919 from an

The beautiful Sangre de Cristo mountains where many a treasure has been lost over the years. *U.S. Forest Service photo.*

old Indian squaw, who at the time was 105. The woman said she had heard stories when she was young of the Spanish taking gold from the cave. She said if one descended to a sufficient depth, a set of oak doors would be found, disclosing the source of the gold. She called it the Three Steps Mine.

The old Indian said that when she was a child living near the caves, her people would throw a stone wrapped in a blanket down the shaft. In a short time the blanket would be blown back, minus the stone, by the strong winds in the cave.

Following the woman's instructions, Gilbert located the cave the following year. He reported the cavern was more of a volcanic fissure than a cave. It is entered by a vent, and at ninety feet was a circular shaft twenty feet in diameter. Near the cave, Gilbert found an old, rusted shovel and a piece of rope.

Gilbert was unable to interest anyone in further exploration until 1929, when a party of ten from the Colorado Mountain Club and a Ranger Truman of Westcliffe undertook a scientific exploration.

The party descended deep into the shaft without finding its bottom. At seventy feet, on a small ledge, they discovered the remains of a crude ladder that scientists in the party judged to be at least 200 years old. At approximately 300 feet was found a hand-forged hammer, believed to be of 17th-century manufacture. Two of the party made their way down the shaft to a depth of some 500 feet, at which level, according to Gilbert, "the hole was little more than a cold and muddy shaft-like cave with dangerous loose rock in the walls."

Exploring around the entrance of the cave, the party found evidence of the remains of an ancient log and stone fort.

A later exploration was headed by LeRoy Hafen, former historian of the State Historical Society. The party made a very detailed study of the cave, but went no farther than the Gilbert party and found little else of interest, although they did find evidence of ancient occupation. Mrs. Hafen, in writing up the expedition, said, "apparently the whole cavern had been eaten out from limestone by trickling water working its way for centuries in the heart of the mountain."

Peter Moser of Denver and two companions, Victor Donald and Jack Barth, entered the cave with ropes in 1932. All three went down to the 100-foot level. From here, Moser lowered himself another 250 feet and then followed the passage for another fifty feet to another level. At this level, he said, he made a grisly discovery—particularly for one alone in the black bowels of the earth—a human skeleton chained by the neck to one wall of the cave.

One vague report said a 1932 expedition, possibly the Moser one, went down 1,000 feet and found evidence of activity at that level.

Another scientist, a Carl Blaurock, lowered himself into the cave to make a geological study. He said it was a natural cave, water carved, and probably lifted from its original location—possibly the floor of an ancient sea—to its present location by nature's most recent upheaval. Evidence to support such speculation might be found in the deposits of marble spreading across the mountainside not far from the entrance of the cave, and over an area of several acres. The marble is almost solidly packed with fossilized forms of chrinoids—crazy, mixed-up sea lilies that

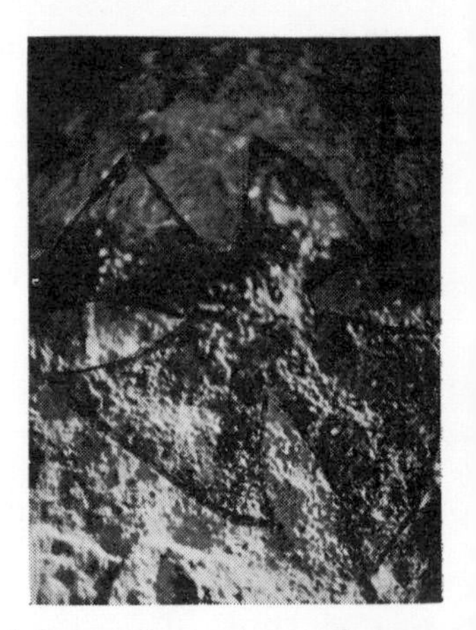

The Maltese Cross near the entrance of the Spanish Caves. The outline of the cross has been darkened by the author as the old Spanish symbol is barely visible due to time and vandals.

Spelunkers from the Colorado Grotto of the National Speological Society exploring the famous Spanish Caves, better known in legend as La Caverna Del Oro. Above photo left, shows location of cave entrance on Marble Mountain. The entrance is in a ravine that is filled with snow much of the year. Photos below show a seplunker descending the main shaft of the cave, and spelunkers at the entrance of the cave. *Photos courtesy of the Colorado Grotto of the National Speological Society.*

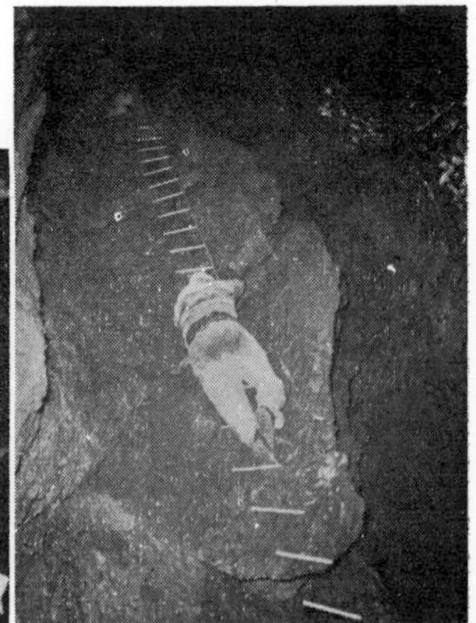

couldn't decide whether or not to be a flower or a predatory organism that preyed on other living things of the old oceans.

But you might say La Caverna Del Oro was left in the dark until the Colorado spelunkers became interested in it.

The Colorado Grotto of the National Speological Society, unquestionably the most expert of the cave scientists, has made several exploratory trips to the Marble Caves in recent years. Their early explorations seemed to debunk many of the early stories, and take away much of the romance of the caves.

The spelunkers made the most complete study of the cave ever made in their early trips. The cave was mapped and measured and every nook and cranny was explored . . . they thought. Samples were made of the rocks and the sediment in the cave. Pictures were taken, temperature and humidity were measured.

On the floor of the main chamber, the spelunkers found remnants of rope and hemp. Much of it, they believe, were remains of fairly recent explorations. They have no way of telling if any of the remains were Spanish. They did find, however, at the bottom-most level of the cave, an ancient shovel imbedded in the sand. Thus, the shovel, a couple of hand-carved logs in the entrance of the cave, the Maltese Cross over the entrance, and the rude fort down the hill, were singular items testifying to early activity by the Spanish.

The Colorado cavemen didn't find a chained skeleton, they didn't find precious metal. In fact, they were just about satisfied that they had investigated all the cave had to offer, when, in 1960, they made exciting new discoveries that showed them that their work had just begun.

In their earlier explorations they passed by what they thought was just a short pocket across the drop near the entrance of the cave. After cursory examination they were sure that the pocket was no more than just a short dead-end passage, and they thought no more about it.

During the summer of 1960, however, the passage was tested. It turned out to be the entrance to another section of the cave, easily as large as the known section.

Time was too short to explore the new section completely, but they have already found some curious items.

For example, the floor was covered with many animal bones. Samples of several of the bones were sent to the University of

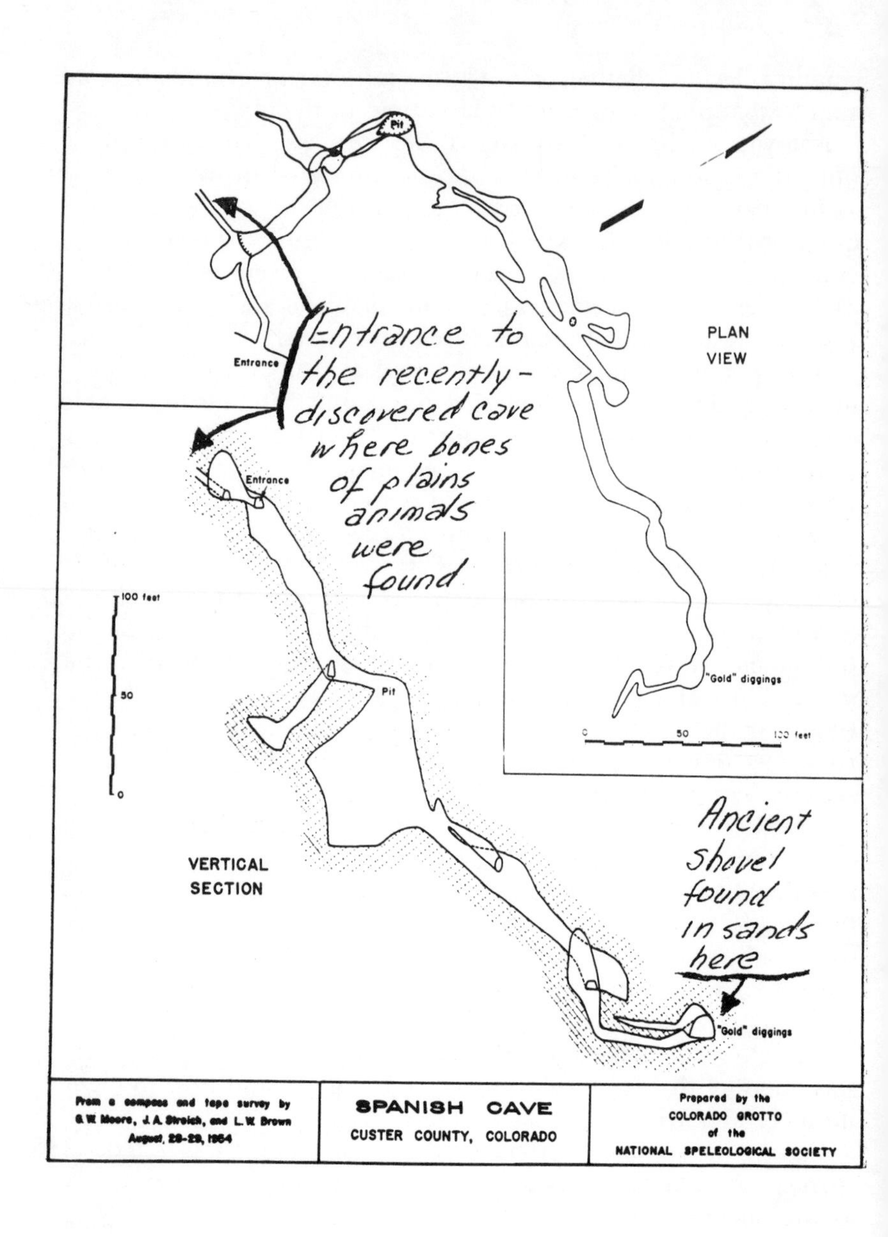
Pit
Entrance
Entrance to
the recently-
discovered cave
where bones
of plains
animals
were
found
PLAN
VIEW
Entrance
100 feet
50
0
Pit
"Gold" diggings
0
50
100 feet
Ancient
shovel
found
in sands
here
VERTICAL
SECTION
"Gold" diggings
From a compass and tape survey by
G. W. Moore, J. A. Streich, and L. W. Brown
August, 28-29, 1954
SPANISH CAVE
CUSTER COUNTY, COLORADO
Prepared by the
COLORADO GROTTO
of the
NATIONAL SPELEOLOGICAL SOCIETY

Colorado for analysis. Many of the bones came from deer, elk and mountain sheep—animals that had every right to be there.

But there were also some bones of the plains animals, bison and antelope, that had no right to be there at all, unless, of course, their carcasses were dragged up there by man or by some mighty strong animals. The spelunkers found no evidence of any earlier explorations in the new section. It may take several trips and several years to completely explore and chart the new area. No doubt many more interesting items will turn up.

Another discovery made in 1960 may well be even more illuminating.

There are about fifteen caves in the area of the Spanish Cave. Until 1960, they figured they had them all marked out. Then they found the new wing of the Spanish Cave . . . and another cave that could well be the largest and most interesting one of the bunch.

It was near the end of the short caving season on Marble Mountain when the spelunkers found a niche in the mountain, a few hundred feet above the entrance of the Spanish Cave, that was full of loose rocks. No doubt the spelunkers and others had passed the section many times and thought little about it. In 1960, however, one enterprising caveman decided to investigate further. He and some friends cleared the rocks away and—sure enough—there was another cave entrance.

Little exploratory work has been done on the new cave, but preliminary explorations indicate that no one has been in it before—at least, in recent times. The new cave appears to be the largest one yet, and experts believe it may connect with one of the others below it.

There's so much to be done still, maybe the greatest discovery is yet to come. That's the romance of caving.

But the cavemen are cautious in selling the mysterious songs of the caves. They are afraid of too much public participation in the explorations because the caves are dangerous, even for experts. Amateurs take their lives in their hands in attempting to seek the answers to the questions the caves ask.

Secondary to the danger involved is the fact that non-serious students of caving may well destroy the secrets of the caves. Vandals have already destroyed much of Colorado's historical landmarks. They do the same dirty work on caves. For example, the first thing many non-scientific people do when they come upon a cave is to throw stones or debris in it. Many Colorado caves and grottos are full of debris thrown in by unthinking tourists.

An example of the limits the vandals go to is the Maltese Cross above the entrance of the Spanish Cave. It is slowly being blasted from sight by sharpshooters that look upon the marker—hundreds of years old—as nothing more than a target.

Perhaps one day the caves will be made safe and open to public inspection with all the information available and the safety devices in working order, as is the case with many another cave. But solving such deep and ancient mysteries is not done overnight and by amateurs.

Perhaps one of the caves on Marble Mountain is the famous La Caverna Del Oro of legend. The caves may tell us many well hidden secrets from Colorado's dark and mysterious past, secrets hidden for centuries . . . and only now beginning to come to the surface.

See Addendum, p. 281, for further information.

19. THE LOST BROTHER MINE

One day in 1868 a stranger knocked on the door of a farmhouse in the Wet Mountain Valley.

He said he was looking for his brother. The stranger in the doorway said his brother, George, came west in 1860 from Illinois, and the family had not heard from him since.

The young stranger said that during his extensive search he had run across a grocer in Denver who had sold some groceries to George. George had left some money with the grocer for safekeeping, saying he would return for the money in the fall but that he didn't need it in the mountains. He had never returned.

The grocer said he wasn't sure where George was headed but somehow he had got the idea he was heading for the Sangre de Cristos.

The stranger, Bill Skinner, told the farmer that he had just arrived in the valley, and was anxious to get started on the search, but that he didn't know where to begin. The farmer said he had never heard of a George Skinner, but he invited the boy to stay the night and said he would help him search the next day.

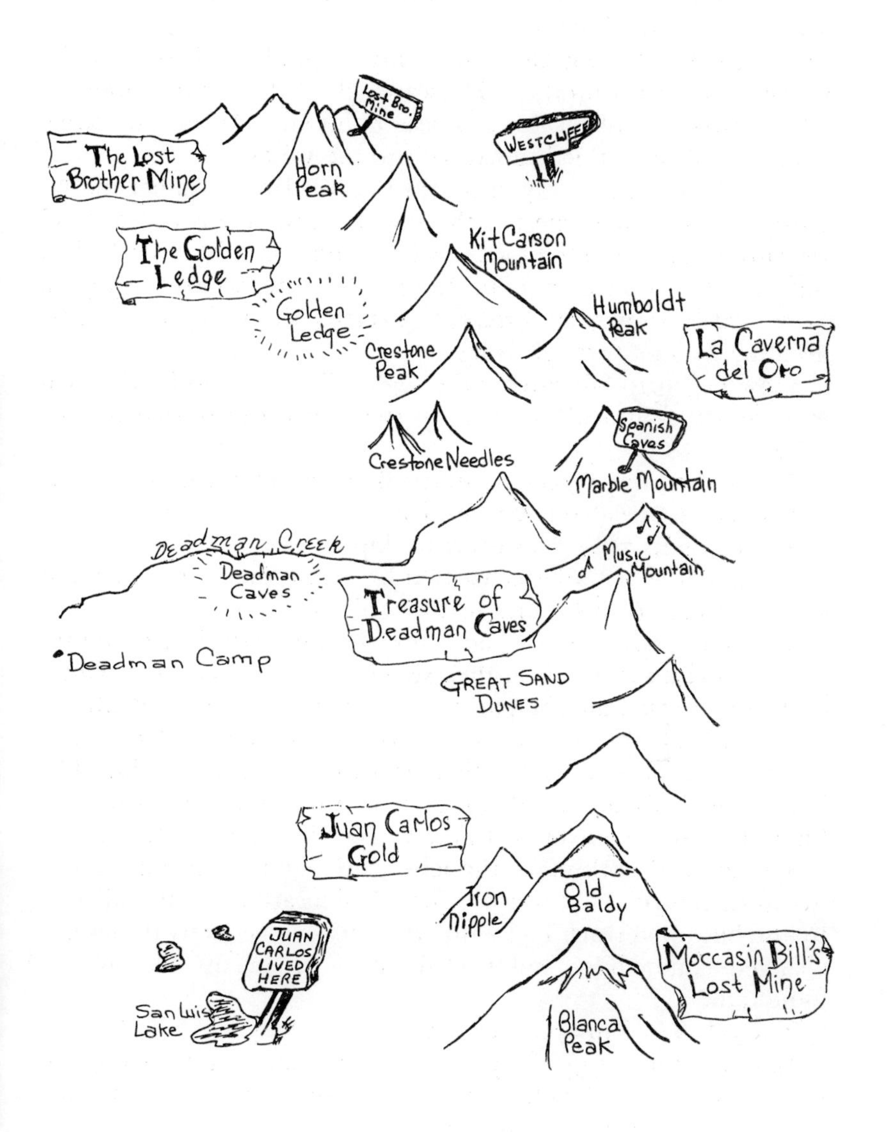

The Lost Brother Mine
Lost Bro. Mine
Horn Peak
Westcliffe
The Golden Ledge
Golden Ledge
Kit Carson Mountain
Humboldt Peak
La Caverna del Oro
Crestone Peak
Crestone Needles
Spanish Caves
Marble Mountain
Deadman Creek
Deadman Caves
Music Mountain
Treasure of Deadman Caves
Deadman Camp
Great Sand Dunes
Juan Carlos Gold
Iron Nipple
Old Baldy
Juan Carlos Lived Here
Moccasin Bill's Lost Mine
San Luis Lake
Blanca Peak

The next few days the farmer and the boy wandered through the valley asking questions of everyone they met. But nobody had heard of George Skinner.

Eventually, the boy decided to hire a guide and look in the mountains for his brother. He searched all during the summer, asking questions of all the prospectors he met. When fall came, Skinner and the guide headed back to the valley.

One night, on the way back, they camped near timberline on Horn's Peak. They selected the spot because it was a near-level clearing and because there was a small cabin here. Skinner looked through the cabin and found nothing of interest except an old black wallet wound in wire. He casually threw it in his pack, deciding to look through it later.

Snow began to fall during the night. The cold woke the men early and they quickly packed up their gear and started for the valley.

The wallet was forgotten until Skinner ran across it a short time later and decided to go through it.

The contents caused his heart to skip a beat.

In the wallet was a letter written by his brother, George, about six months after his brother had left Illinois.

The letter said George had found a "wonderfully rich mine" and was planning a trip to the "settlements" to spend the winter outfitting himself and preparing for a mining venture. Realizing the hazards of traveling in those days, George put the location of the mine in another letter that he had left in the cabin. The letter, which Skinner had not seen in the cabin, instructed the finder to mail the envelope to the writer's brother in Illinois.

Skinner said nothing of the letter, but the next spring he and his guide returned to the cabin site. The location was not difficult to find but upon reaching the site they discovered many things had changed. Snowslides had peeled off much of the face of the mountain.

The cabin had disappeared completely.

Skinner and the guide spent the entire summer searching for further clues of the brother, but they had no luck at all. Came fall, they began their weary way home.

They followed a different route back than they had the year before. The trail followed along the face of a deep precipice. Had they known what to expect they would never have taken the trail, for the footing was narrow and insecure, and the loose rocks and boulders threatened rockslides all along the way. Although they traveled very carefully, one of the burros tumbled over the ledge and down the cliff. Skinner and the guide scrambled down to where the animal had fallen to salvage what they could of their equipment.

As they approached the dead animal they saw two skeletons, one of a man and one of a pack animal, which had apparently been there for years. Among the equipment strewn all around was considerable gold . . . and a little black, weather-beaten book.

The book turned out to be George Skinner's diary. On one of the weathered pages of the book he referred to the letter left in the cabin. The final entry, apparently written just before his death, told of planning a trip to town.

George Skinner and the burro had apparently fallen from the same spot from which the other burro had fallen that day.

Skinner buried the remains of his brother at the site. He returned to Illinois and sadly told his story to the rest of the family.

The next spring he returned to Colorado. He found more rock and snow slides had further changed the face of the mountain. He found no gold mine, and he never found any more clues about his brother and the lonely life he had led.

20. THE GOLDEN LEDGE OF THE SANGRE DE CRISTOS

In the early days of Colorado just about everybody was a prospector. Few were experts but they all searched. Lawyers, doctors, merchants, chiefs, all performed their various tasks during the week and then headed for the hills on the weekends . . . or whenever they could get away.

Three spare-time prospectors were Dan de Foe, prominent Denver businessman; M. M. Warner, a practicing attorney in Aspen; and a friend of De Foe remembered only as Bert.

The three had heard of the legendary Gold Ledge of the Sangre de Cristos. The legend had gained followers over the years after more and more prospectors reported finding fairly rich gold float in the majestic mountains. But no one, it seems, was able to find the mother lode, although many, very many, spent a lot of time looking. Somehow, the golden ledge found its way into the legend, a mammoth golden ledge traversing the range on the western slope of the range.

The three spare-time prospectors decided to spend a vacation looking for the ledge.

The search extended far beyond their vacation-time. They looked for several weeks without any luck. Just like die-hard fishermen, they hated to call it quits. Eventually, however, they decided to make one last run and head for home.

On the way back from final search they were traveling through typical Sangre de Cristo country of endless small hills edging the mountains. Each hill had the same scrubby cedars and pinon trees.

On one of the hills they stumbled upon an old prospect hole. Apparently at one time the hole had been much deeper, but now loose dirt and rocks had fallen into it. Going through some of the rocks in the hole, they came across what seemed to their unexpert eyes a poor quality lead ore.

The ore seemed typical for this part of the country. But although it was quite lean-looking and not too promising, it was on the steep side of the hill and the structure of a vein they found in the hole told them it might be worth checking into further.

The three men worked until nightfall, putting a ten foot face around the hole and putting up location notices. They also surveyed the area with a pocket compass and set up regulation claims at the corners of their claim. De Foe took notes and made detailed charts of the location while the other two were sorting through the ore samples for the best ones to take back.

After they were satisfied that they had done the job properly, they headed back to their camp.

When they reached the edge of the San Luis Valley, they discovered their estimations had been off and that they were on Cottonwood Creek, some two or three miles beyond their camp.

When they finally reached their camp they were greatly encouraged by the luck they had that day, the best luck they had had all summer. Just like a fisherman who gets his first bite in hours, and decides to keep trying in the same hole while his luck is hot, they decided to stay on for a few more days.

But their luck was all bad after that. To make matters worse, De Foe lost his notes and charts and other essential items. They decided they had had enough prospecting to last a lifetime. So they folded up their tents like the Arabs and silently stole away . . . disgusted.

As you might suspect, however, Warner, a few weeks later, ran across the samples he had picked up at the prospect hole. For want of anything better to do he had them assayed, and they showed more than twenty ounces of gold to the ton. Warner wrote De Foe in Denver and told him to have his samples checked. They showed as much as forty-five ounces to the ton.

A few days later Warner showed up in Denver enroute to Wisconsin. The three men decided the ore was well worth mining. Warner told De Foe to get their claim recorded and the three of them could get an early start on their mining venture in the spring.

De Foe and Bert rode down to the Sangre De Cristos in the dead of winter to get details for their claim. The snow was three feet deep in places, which added to the hopelessness of their task.

They searched again in the spring but didn't have any better luck than they did in the winter. They searched for the site much of the rest of the summer.

In fact, De Foe recounted the story eleven years later—in 1891—and said he and his partners had just about given up on it.

21. THE TREASURE OF DEADMAN CAVES

The Marble Caves are not the only mysterious caverns in the Sangre de Cristos. There are many of them. And many of these have attracted stories of lost gold and buried treasure.

One of the more authentic often-told stories came from three well-known prospectors, S. J. Harkman, E. R. Oliver, and H. A. Melton.

The trio was prospecting in the Sangre de Cristos on the San Luis side, about two miles north of what is now known as the Dead Man's Camp. A heavy snowstorm hit them, making traveling difficult, so they decided to seek shelter under a ledge of rocks. From their shelter they saw the mouth of a cave on the nearby side of the canyon.

They decided to investigate and found a long tunnel, not very high. The three men gathered some dry pine branches for torches and started in the cave. They had to enter the opening on their hands and knees in single file. The passage extended about ten or twelve feet when they came to what seemed to be a large vault. The vault was about twenty feet wide and in the far wall there was another small passage.

The second passage was not more than ten feet long and it too emptied into a chamber. This one, however, was much larger than the first and it was necessary for the men to feel their way along the sides. While doing so, Oliver, who was in the lead, struck his foot against something.

He found it was a human skull.

At this point, the three men built a fire on the floor and, in doing so, they discovered four more skulls and skeletons scattered about nearby. Just skeletons, no tools, guns or knives.

They retraced their steps, went outside the cave, gathered as much firewood as they could, and returned to the second chamber to investigate it further.

They found another skeleton a short distance off. They also found another narrow passage, longer and not so narrow. It led to a smaller chamber, the walls of which were very irregular in some places, resembling shelves in a room.

On the western side of the chamber, near the far end, the shelf-like cuts extended a considerable distance from the wall and were about ten inches from the floor of the cave.

Melton lowered the light and looked under the ledge. He found some peculiar-shaped stones. Lifting them, he found them very heavy. On closer inspection he found them to be crude dusty gold bars.

Excitedly the men gathered them up and headed out of the cave. On returning to Silver Cliff, they found the gold bars were worth $900 each. In their hurried inspection of the cave they picked up only 5 bars, but they were sure many more could be found.

Of course, three prospectors selling crude gold bars aroused not just a little curiosity. And the three told their story willingly, saying they had noticed other passages in the cave that needed to be explored. But the trio refused to tell anyone the exact location. They said they planned to go back to the mysterious cave at the earliest opportunity in the spring and continue their investigation.

The men slipped off in the spring. But they never found the Deadmen Cave. They had thought it would be easy, but on their return they found so many places that looked like the area in which the caves were found. In fact, practically the entire area seemed strange to them. They went back frequently. Many others went back frequently. Nobody found anything.

22. JUAN CARLOS' GOLD

Juan Carlos came from New Mexico into the San Luis Valley leading a large pack train and many peons. They say the pack train carried many books and many manuscripts, and some say it carried much gold. It was known from the first that he had plenty of gold, but he was very secretive and miserly with it. Actually, nobody knew too much about him at all.

He erected a cabin at the foot of Mt. Blanca and turned the peons loose. He attempted to live like a hermit . . . just he and one servant. But a man so strange cannot live in peace.

The first day of May that first year, Juan Carlos headed off for the hills by himself. Everyone was interested in his actions but nobody knew where he was going. They say he headed for his secret gold mine. On the last day of October Juan Carlos returned, his pack train loaded down . . . with gold dust, they say.

The second year on May the first, Juan Carlos disappeared again. He returned on the last day of October. More gold dust, they say. Some Mexicans had tried to follow him but Juan eluded them.

The third year they were ready for him. They followed him very closely. Juan Carlos saw that he could not shake them, so he circled around and returned home.

He never went to the hills again.

For the next few years he did live as a hermit. His servant transacted all his business. No one heard or saw much of Juan Carlos until 1868. That year he hired a number of Mexicans to build him some fancy cabins alongside San Luis Lake. When the job was finished Juan Carlos paid the men and sent them on their way . . . all except two of them. The other workers believed Juan Carlos purposely selected these two to remain behind because they were the most stupid.

When three months had passed and the two ignorant workers had not returned, members of their families set out in search of them. Juan Carlos acted surprised that the two men had not returned to their families. He said the men had finished their work over a month before and he had sent them on their way. The families said they did not believe him and pressed him further. Juan Carlos thought and thought about it and finally decided it might be due to the Indians. He said the day after the men had left, a band of Indians had visited the area. He suggested that maybe the men were captured and killed by the Indians.

The families of the two men still did not believe Juan Carlos. To this day the people in the San Luis Valley believe Juan Carlos had the two men do some special work—like hiding a gold cache—and then had them killed.

Within a year after the cabins were built, Juan Carlos lay dying. Perhaps his last act before he died was to dispatch a letter to the priest in Calabra. His faithful servant was found murdered on the road. The letter—or part of it—was found near the body. Juan Carlos had said in the letter that he wanted to confess his serious wrongs and to leave his fortune to the church. But the letter was either not finished or part of it was missing. No mention was made of where the gold fortune was and the serious wrongs were not listed.

Juan Carlos' cabin was searched and a grand scale investigation was undertaken but no clue to the fortune—if there was a fortune—was found.

Less than a year later, however, two Mexicans in the village suddenly became very rich. They purchased large herds of sheep and cattle. They said they had earned the money doing government work in Santa Fe. Nobody believed them.

Despite the many legends that have evolved from the story of Juan Carlos, none of the essentials has ever come to light. There was a Juan Carlos. He was well known in the San Luis Valley. They say the only friend he ever had was Colonel Head, who became Colorado's first lieutenant governor. They say their friendship ended when Colonel Head married a beautiful Mexican lady. Some say Juan Carlos had worshipped this woman.

Relics of Juan Carlos are still with us. The cabins he built alongside San Luis Lake were remodeled long after his death, and have been used in recent years by fishermen.

In recalling the story of Juan Carlos, many say his well-hidden gold mine was the same as the one discovered by Kit Carson. But no one ever knew. Perhaps the only reason they attach the two stories is because they were popular legends of lost gold that ran concurrently in southern Colorado.

There are many things we would like to know about Juan Carlos, his hidden fortune, his secret gold mine, his serious crimes . . . secrets blown away by the gentle winds of the San Luis Valley, well covered by the sands of time.

23. MOCCASIN BILL'S LOST TREASURE

William Perkins was a well-known hunter and story teller in the Wet Mountain Valley in the 1870's and 1880's. He was known for the Indian moccasins he wore year in and year out. He said they were the best footwear for hunting. It was easier to sneak up on your game wearing moccasins. Few people knew the name of William Perkins, but everybody knew "Moccasin Bill."

He lived in Ula, now a ghost town about five miles northeast of Westcliffe. He claimed to be the best hunter in the valley and nobody at the time was able to dispute it. He was in constant demand on hunting trips not only for his prowess but also for the tales he told. No doubt Bill invented some of the stories and jazzed up some others just to keep things going. But many of the things that happened to Bill were true. There were people along to verify them.

Take the time in 1877 when he was attacked by a panther while on a hunting trip. Bill fought the animal until his hunting companion could draw a bead on it. It took twelve bullets, three in the head, to kill the beast.

He had a guest along on another hunting trip during the 70's when he came close to his fortune. Moccasin Bill and the companion searched for the treasure off and on for the rest of their lives but never found it.

It seems Moccasin Bill and his friend, whose name was never known, were hunting one day on Sierra Blanca Peak in the Sangre de Cristos, when a soldier came running into their camp. The soldier was breathless and excited. Bill discovered the lad was deserting from the army and had taken the unlikely trail over the mountain to throw any possible pursuers off the trail.

The cause of the soldier's excitement, however, were the gold nuggets he clutched in his hand. Bill had lived around this rich mining area long enough to be able to tell good ore when he saw it, and it took only a short examination to see that the nuggets were among the richest he had ever seen.

The soldier had gathered up as many nuggets as he could carry and he said that Bill and his friend were welcome to the rest. He told them he was leaving this part of the country for good. He told Bill he didn't dare take the time to lead them to the site of his find, but he would do the next best thing. He sketched out as detailed a map of the place as he could remember. The spot was located on the other side of the hill.

Bill and his companion hurried over the hill as soon as the soldier had departed. Game was forgotten for the rest of the trip as the two searched high and low for gold. Using the map, they attacked the area from every possible angle. No luck.

Bill herded several subsequent hunting safaris into the area so he could keep on looking. Some of his companions also took up the search. But no trace of the gold nuggets was ever found.

VI. *RIO GRANDE COUNTRY*

24. THE TREASURE OF TREASURE MOUNTAIN

A majestic mountain just south of the summit of Wolf Creek Pass in southern Colorado is called Treasure Mountain. It is well named, for somewhere in its bosom is said to be from five million to thirty-three million dollars in gold bullion, buried nearly 200 years ago by a huge French expedition.

The story of the treasure, for which the mountain is named, is one of Colorado's most fabulous tales of buried treasure. Its veracity is said to have been proved in ancient French documents. Its repercussions are deeply imbedded in the history of the southwest.

About 1790 (although one source puts the date at 1828, which seems improbable) a huge expedition set out from a small French outpost near present-day Leavenworth, Kansas, to determine the mineral resources of New France. The expedition numbered 300 men, including skilled miners, mechanics, geologists, soldiers and many laborers. The group had some 450 horses and the most modern equipment.

The giant brigade followed down the Platte River and down the Colorado mountains, everywhere prospecting for evidence of gold. They were believed to have mined the first gold at Cripple Creek, Summitville, and other areas in the mountains that later produced in large quantities. But nowhere did they find the metal

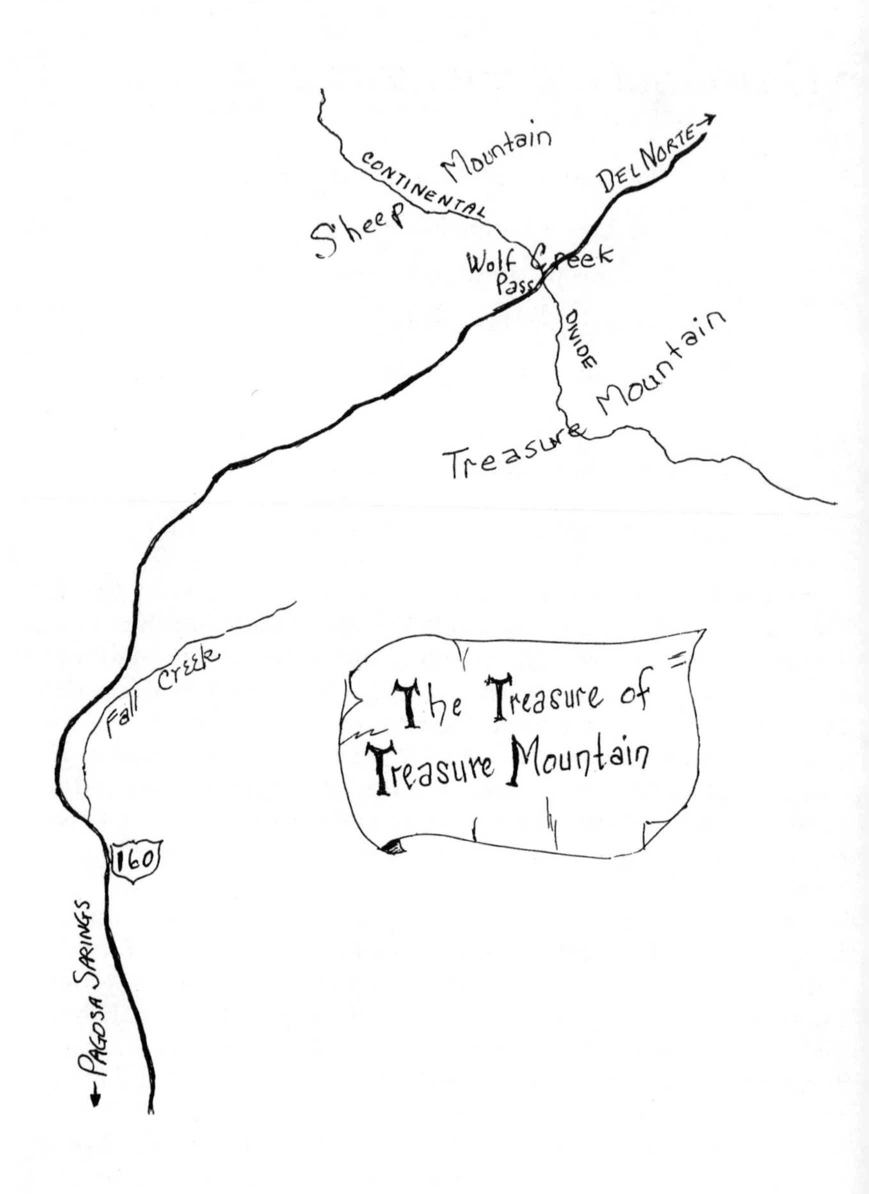
Sheep Mountain
CONTINENTAL
DIVIDE
DEL NORTE
Wolf Creek Pass
Treasure Mountain
Fall Creek
160
PAGOSA SPRINGS
The Treasure of Treasure Mountain

in sufficient quantity to merit their pausing—that is, until they reached Treasure Mountain.

Near here (and some believe their discovery was at Summitville) they found ore rich enough. They made permanent camp near the peak about three or four miles from the summit of Wolf Creek Pass and not far from Summitville.

Whether the group knew it or not—and it's quite possible that they did know it—they had made camp in Spanish territory. They mined their gold in Spanish territory, melted it down into gold bars, and stored it in Spanish territory. If this wasn't enough, in the winter when they could not work in the high mountains they wintered brazenly in Spanish Taos. The French outpost in Kansas was hundreds of miles away and the pilgrimage to Taos was out of necessity. Of course, they kept their spring and summer location and their discovery a secret, telling the Spanish only that they were making a survey of New France. They were believed and accepted by the Spanish, who needed allies at the moment. In fact, the French were treated quite royally.

This particular French expedition needed allies also. Other than the friendly Spanish in New Mexico, there were nothing but Indians in the vast uncharted west. The French found some of them friendly but found many other hostile or suspicious. While mining, it was necessary to keep guards posted at all times.

According to later reports the gold was cached in three places, only known to the top officers of the expedition. A key chart was made of the entire area and kept by the officer in command.

Despite the fact that the Spanish were friendly, as were most of the Indians, and the game was plentiful, the life on this wild frontier had taken its toll. Many of the original party died of disease and privation until, months later, when the expedition made plans to return to France, fewer than one hundred of the original group of three hundred remained. They were satisfied with their gold, anyway. Most sources estimated the value at some five million dollars, although one source estimated the cache as worth thirty-three million dollars. (Perhaps this estimate included the interest accumulated over 170 years.)

The Indians begrudged the French their departure. Perhaps they realized "Indian gold" was going with them. Whatever the reason or reasons were, the once-friendly Indians suddenly turned hostile just as the French started their expedition back to France.

Treasure Mountain, where legend says one of the West's greatest treasures was buried by the French. Picture was taken from near Pagosa Springs. *Picture courtesy Erika Schramm.*

The savages struck before the French had even left camp. During the thick of the battle, the gold was reburied and the French leaders made hasty, but detailed, maps of the new vaults.

One report claims seventeen men survived the battle, while another puts the number at thirty-five. No matter, because shortly after they had regrouped along the Arkansas and begun the long journey back, they were attacked once again. Only five survived.

The larger expedition had planned to return to New Orleans and then go on to France. But the five saw that this was impossible and set out for the French outpost near Fort Leavenworth. Even this, however, was an impossible trip for most of the small group. They ate bark and wild berries, but still could not fight off starvation. As a last resort, they drew straws and the loser was eaten by the others.

There had been three losers by the time they reached the outpost. Only two made the trip—a man by the name of Le Breu or Le Blanc, the historian of the expedition, and one other man, who was more dead than alive by the time he reached safety, and he died shortly afterward.

Le Breu, as we shall call him, recovered from the arduous experience after several weeks and returned to France. Enroute, he made two copies of the treasure map. One he gave to his government on his return and the other he kept with his family documents.

This was at the time of Napoleon, and France was having enough excitement as it was without being bothered by a treasure buried thousands of miles away. So the maps were forgotten for nearly forty years.

Reports differ on the next episode of our story. One source says a party gotten up by a member of Le Breu's family set out to regain the lost treasure, while another source claims France needed money desperately at the time and dusted off the old map and organized an official French expedition. Anyhow, these men were led by a man named Le Breu or Le Blanc, said to have been a relation of the only surviving member of the original group.

The second expedition numbered between fifty and sixty, and it was well equipped. It reported in at Taos, where Bernardo Sanchez was hired as guide. The party worked diligently for three years, combing the entire area, with no apparent luck.

Then, shortly after the caravan left Taos for another assault on Treasure Mountain, Sanchez returned alone. He said the entire expedition, except him, had been slaughtered by Indians.

It was a great scandal in the settlements in New Mexico. They accused Sanchez of desertion. Apparently it was believed at the time that a good scout should go down with his expedition. They accused him of making deals with the Indians. They accused him of everything until finally the government officially accused him of murder.

In what was recorded as the last Mexican murder trial ever to be held on U.S. territory, Sanchez proved his innocence and was acquitted.

Some believe the whole affair was a put-up job. They say Sanchez made a deal with the French, who may have found the gold and returned to France in another direction so as to throw any and all persons off their track. Believers of this yarn point out that the gold was still in Mexican territory and to get it out they would have to travel either through Mexican or U.S. territory. If the plan was not well executed all sorts of governments and lesser highwaymen could lay claim to the treasure. According to this theory Sanchez was promised a tidy fortune by the French if he would keep their secret.

There are several arguments with this theory. In the first place, it is doubtful if a man would be able to keep a secret in the face of his own execution for murder. Also, the French themselves estimated it would take a pack train of some 600 mules to move such a tremendous treasure. This they did not have. Even if they had managed some other way, a caravan so large and so wealthy would still receive some notoriety.

Anyhow, the Mexicans reported that some French equipment was later found in possession of the Indians.

It is thought the treasure is still there . . . on Treasure Mountain. The story is believed by the people of the southwest, enough so that they named a mountain after it. Many, many have searched, have dug up the mountain. They have found much evidence of ancient activity. They found graves, they found mounds, said to have been part of the landmarks on the treasure map; they have even found an ancient tunnel shaft . . . but no treasure.

Sanchez said years later, after the trial, that he knew but one clue to the location of the treasure. This landmark was a "mock grave with three spruce trees equidistant around it." According to Sanchez if one stands on the grave at six p.m. on September first, the head of his shadow will cover the treasure spot.

Sanchez is said to have searched many times himself. Don Archuleta, Archuleta County land and cattle owner, and his son, Jose Manuel Archuleta, are said to have spent more than $50,000 looking for the treasure. They got the facts first hand from Sanchez.

A Le Breu, or Le Blanc, supposed to have been a grandson of the survivor of the original expedition, was said to have spent much time in the vicinity with a copy of the original map but he had no luck.

The map was next heard of from a man named William Yule, who claimed to possess a tracing of it. He searched the area many times, as far away as Saguache, but he found nothing.

Asa Poor was a well-known prospector in southern Colorado.

Years before, while prospecting, he ran across a grave on Treasure Mountain. He remembered the grave years later when in a tavern he heard the story of the fabulous French treasure. Poor traced down Yule and found him in New Mexico and became the next owner of the so-called treasure map.

Poor went about his search very diligently. He took on Leon Montroy and A. T. Stolsteimer as partners. Montroy was superintendant of Senator Bowen's Little Annie Mine in Summitville. He was a mining expert who was perhaps more acquainted with the territory than anyone else. Stolsteimer was Indian agent for the Southern Utes at Ignacio. It was believed he could glean new clues from the Indians. His part in the scheme of things just didn't pan out, however, as the Indians either didn't know anything or wouldn't talk.

But the three claim to have discovered several landmarks from the treasure map.

Asa retraced his trail to a little park near the summit of Treasure Mountain where he had seen the grave many years before. He found the grave, dug it up, and found it empty. They also found blazes on a few trees around, also mentioned on the map. But apparently one of the trees on the map had been destroyed many years before. Nonetheless, they attacked the treasure spot from every possible angle, completely dug up the area, but found no treasure.

Systematically, they probed out in every direction. About two miles from the false grave they found some loose ground and dug into it. They uncovered a shaft about three and one-half feet in the clear and boarded up to about twenty feet. They went to the bottom of the shaft and found nothing. They dug four shafts from forty-two to sixty-three feet long in all directions of the original shaft, and still found nothing.

Poor claims the three had destroyed the landmarks they had found, including the blazed trees and the false grave, apparently with the idea that if they didn't find the treasure, no one else would either. Montroy was said to have retained the map for several years and then it disappeared. It apparently wasn't much good anyway, and many doubt that it was the original.

This, according to their own reports, was the most scientific search for the treasure. But many others have joined the hunt. The one-time mayor of Pagosa Springs once organized a search party. A man named Crouse, also from Pagosa Springs, used a mineral rod in looking for the treasure.

But apparently the treasure has withstood all the assaults on the mountain, and there are still large areas that haven't been excavated yet.

25. THE LOST PHILLIPS LODE

Old Man Phillips made his first appearance in Del Norte in the 1870's. With rich gold dust he purchased what supplies he needed and then slipped out of sight. For the next fifteen years he reappeared every few months, paid for all his supplies in gold dust, and then disappeared.

Every attempt to follow him into the mountains—and there were many—failed. All that was known about his gold source was that it lay southwest from Del Norte; at least that was the direction the old man took.

In the late 1880's, the old man came into Del Norte shaking and feverish. He was put to bed. Soon he was delirious. He died while still in a coma, taking the secret of his gold source with him.

Searching for the Phillips Lode was a favorite occupation of the good people of Del Norte and other southern Colorado towns. Every now and again someone would make the claim that he found it, but the report always turned out to be false.

In 1902, however, some men discovered a shaft that came the closest to sounding like the Phillips Lode.

The claim was made by H. C. Schroth, Dave Ray, Ed Gause, and O. G. Nesbitt of Alamosa. The men had made a study of the Phillips legend, learned that it was true, and had even spent some time looking for the long-lost lode. They had just about come to a dead end in their search when they heard that two strangers had spent some gold dust in Del Norte for mining supplies and had disappeared back into the mountains.

The four Alamosa men took up lodging in Del Norte and waited. While waiting, they learned that the two men had been in town before to spend their gold dust, and there had even been attempts to follow them back into the mountains, but the attempts failed.

The two gold-dust-spenders came into Alamosa a short time later. The four Alamosa men kept an around-the-clock watch on them, and when the two strangers left town the four men from Alamosa were ready. They were fortunate in that a light snow and rain had fallen the night before, and they could follow the tracks at a good distance behind and not be seen.

Although the tracks were easy to follow, the trail wasn't. It went up the south fork and over the range to the west. It went over some mighty rugged country, up and down steep slopes and around many a perilous ledge. The four men were ready to call it quits many times, but each time they decided to go on "just a little farther," until they felt they had gone too far to turn back.

Three days and thirty miles later they came upon the camp of the surprised miners. It was a rude cabin built a short distance from a shallow mine shaft.

Since the original two had not taken out a patent on the claim, they were forced to divide the property with the men from Alamosa. The shaft was sunk on a lead of gold-bearing ore about forty feet wide, according to the four. The original party was given the main shaft while the Alamosa party staked some of the best claims around it.

The four men patented the claims on returning to Del Norte when they told of their discovery. They said the find was located on the west slope of the range where Silver Creek flows toward the San Juans, about fifteen miles west of the town of Elwood.

The find was the climax to the story. It became just another Colorado mine, not one of the best and not one of the worst. Little is left to talk about.

Except, of course, the fact that we have no way of telling whether this was the famous Phillips Lode or not. It could have been, but more people think it isn't than think it is.

26. KIT CARSON'S SHINING STREAM

A lost mine story was standard equipment in the early west. Everyone had one or two in the repertoire.

Kit Carson was no exception. His well-documented story was known far and wide and has been recorded in the history books.

Just prior to the war with Mexico, Kit was commissioned to transport messages between Santa Fe and California. On August 29, 1847, he left Santa Fe bound for California. With him were sixty Americans and five Mexicans. Only two of the party were officially with Kit—a Lieutenant Stewart of the U.S. Army, and a Mexican named Archuleta. The rest went along for the ride.

They traveled over rough uncharted country and they never knew what to expect from the Indians. When the party reached the mouth of the Blanco River, a 16-year-old Mexican youth named Jesus Garcia joined them. He said the Indians in the region were on the warpath and they must travel carefully.

The party camped on what was known at the time as Stollsteimer Creek. Here they planned a devious course, slightly different from their intended route, in an effort to avoid the Indians.

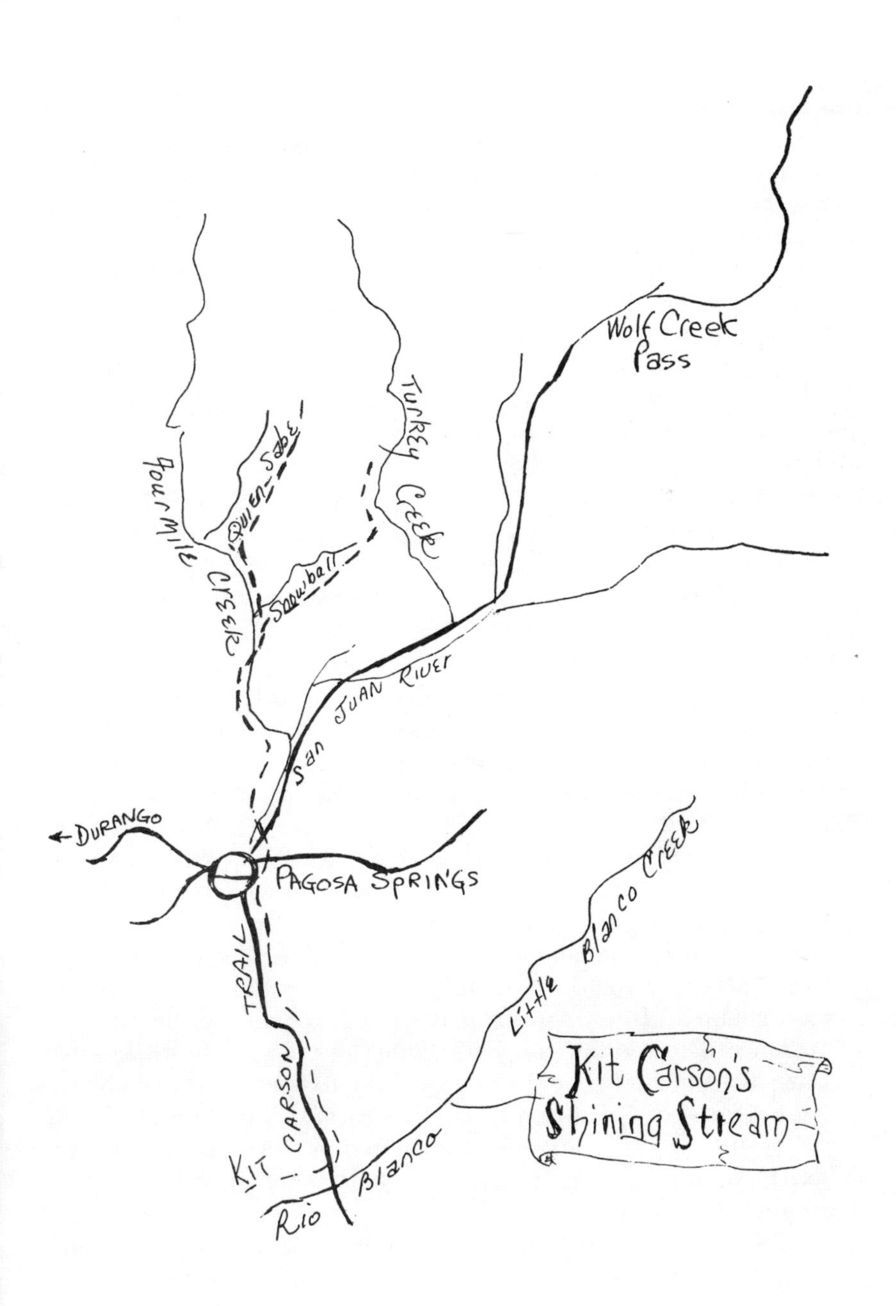
Wolf Creek Pass
Turkey Creek
Fourmile Creek
Quien-Sabe
Snowball
San Juan River
DURANGO
PAGOSA SPRINGS
KIT CARSON TRAIL
Little Blanco Creek
Rio Blanco
Kit Carson's Shining Stream

The next day they followed up the San Juan, passing east and south of present day Pagosa Springs, and continued along Four Mile Creek. The next day they continued up Four Mile Creek a short distance and then later reports claim they changed their course to follow up what they thought was Turkey Creek, although some members of the party believed they were still on Four Mile Creek.

That evening they camped in a small open park. It was Lieutenant Stewart's turn to do the dishes. In those days they washed their pans in the creek and then used the sand along the bank as a dishrag. In doing so, Stewart noticed small flecks of placer gold in the pan. Stewart panned as much gold as he could until dark, and then by the light of the campfire, he made careful note of the area in his little black book.

On reaching California, Stewart sold the gold for $87. It was more than he received in a full month in the army. In fact it was more than he received in three months, so he resigned his commission and headed back to Colorado. The trouble was that his little black book was destroyed in a fire. Still he was confident that he could find the spot again.

He spent much of the rest of his life hunting but didn't have any luck at all. At one time he found what he was fairly certain was the spot but discovered that a cloudburst had caused a flood which had resulted in a tremendous landslide and destroyed the little stream.

Kit looked for the little stream, too, whenever he was in the neighborhood. But generally he had too many other things to do.

This seems to be the most authentic story of the find. There are many stories told about it since, and just about every one varies from the other in some points. Almost every story gives a different date and destination of the party. Some say the trip was made in 1846, another says 1849. One story says the find was made when Kit Carson brought the news back to Santa Fe of the bloodless conquest of California by the Americans. The number in the party also varies considerably. A couple of stories say there were sixteen in the party, another says there were only Kit Carson, Stewart, and Archuleta.

Most stories agree that Stewart received $87 for his gold, although one report claims he only received $18. The location of the find varies somewhat from story to story. One story says the find was made on the Weninucha and another claims it was made over range in Antelope Park, near Creede.

At least we can feel certain that there *was* once a shining stream in southern Colorado and that Stewart and Kit Carson found it once . . . and lost it again.

27. JIM STEWART'S LOST TREASURE

Perhaps no story in southwestern Colorado has gathered more contradictory moss than the lost Stewart's lode. No doubt the reason is that no story has been more bandied about.

The similarities between this story and the Kit Carson tale should also be noted. It's quite possible some story teller many years ago took the Stewart story and gave it a big-name star to lend it prestige. However there are enough differences to merit separate writings.

Of all the stories told about this lost mine, the two outstanding locations seem to be either Antelope Park near Creede or northwest of Pagosa Springs near the site of the Kit Carson shining stream. There are strong adherents to both locations, so the reader can take his pick.

Not only the location varies, but everything else in the story does too, despite the fact that there is no doubt about its being a true story. The only problem is the thing began a hundred years ago. A true story can gather a lot of fuzz in that time.

I think we can settle on the name Jim Stewart, although he has been called Dick a time or two and the initials "R. E." have also appeared. And his rank has been both a lieutenant and captain. It's possible he was a leiutenant when the story started and a captain when it ended—he could have been a general in all that time.

The dates, too, have varied from 1846 to 1864, although the most promising date was 1852. So . . .

Once upon a time, in 1852, Lt. Jim Stewart, headed west from New Mexico to deliver the mail. Stewart was an army courier. His route was longer than most mail routes today. His destination was California.

On this trip, in addition to his guide, several traders and trappers joined him for the long journey. He set out on a route very similar to that taken by Kit Carson. The old Spanish Trail was the usual route between Santa Fe to California. Along the way, he, too, met a young lad and his name was also Garcia. Kit's lad was named Jesus Garcia, Stewart's was Mariano Garcia.

The message was the same from both of them—the Indians were on the warpath.

One story says the information forced Stewart to make a wide circle around the planned route, taking him as far east as Antelope Park. The other story said the worry over Indians caused only minor changes in the route. He followed up the Little Chama, over the Continental Divide, across the San Juan River, and along the Piedra River, to a point 40 or 50 miles northwest of present-day Pagosa Springs.

The discovery of the gold seems to be confused with the Kit Carson story, too. Some say Stewart found the sparkling sand while doing dishes one evening. A more popular version says his pack mule slipped while crossing the stream, dumping his mail pouch into the water. This happened frequently in the early west and the couriers knew just exactly how to handle it. They paused along the banks, spread the letters out in the sun, and waited for them to dry.

While waiting for Stewart the party set up camp a short distance ahead. While Stewart was waiting he panned some of the promising sand in the stream, letting the washings dry on a large leaf of skunk cabbage. It looked like good gold and he put it in his saddle bag. Before leaving the stream he made careful notes about the location in his little black book.

On reaching San Francisco, Stewart sold the gold for $36 (this is the most popular price, although the figure has varied all the way between $18 and $88) . Some stories say he hurried right back to Colorado, but most say he was unable to return for a couple of years. Nonetheless, he *did* return eventually—where he returned to, we're not sure.

Half the tellers say he built a cabin near the Colorado-New Mexico border, others say he took up residence near Antelope Park. Wherever his home was, he spent the rest of his life wandering all over the region. He found many of the old landmarks, or what seemed to him to be familiar landmarks, but he never found his shining stream.

Just about everybody in the neighborhood has a pet theory about where the mine is, or was, and what happened to it. Two theories about the latter stand out. One is that a cloudburst changed the route of the stream and washed away many of the old landmarks. Some believe that Indians were spying on Stewart when he made his discovery. After the Stewart party left, the Indians put logs and dirt over the spot in the stream and they changed its course and many of the landmarks to make sure the palefaces never found the site again.

Despite the fact that there are thousands of "experts" on the lost Stewart lode, and thousands more have looked for it, many "experts" using time-taking, thorough methods, no one has ever located the rich sand.

They say a lot of other rich mines were found during the search for the Stewart placer, mines all the way from Summitville to Telluride.

About the only other things this story proves is how confused a legend can get when too many people go to work on it.

28. MARK BIEDELL'S LOST LODE

Mark Biedell was an important man in the history of southern Colorado. He was a prospector, mining man, and town builder. At one time there was a town named Biedell after him, but it is a ghost town now.

Biedell was an honest man and highly respected, so the people in the neighborhood could well believe the story he told of his lost fortune.

In the early 1870's, Biedell built a feudal-like place on the Saguache River for protection against the Utes. One night three Frenchmen and a half dozen Mexicans stopped by his place. They said they were up from the Maxwell Land Grant on a surveying trip.

After they departed, Biedell didn't think any more about them

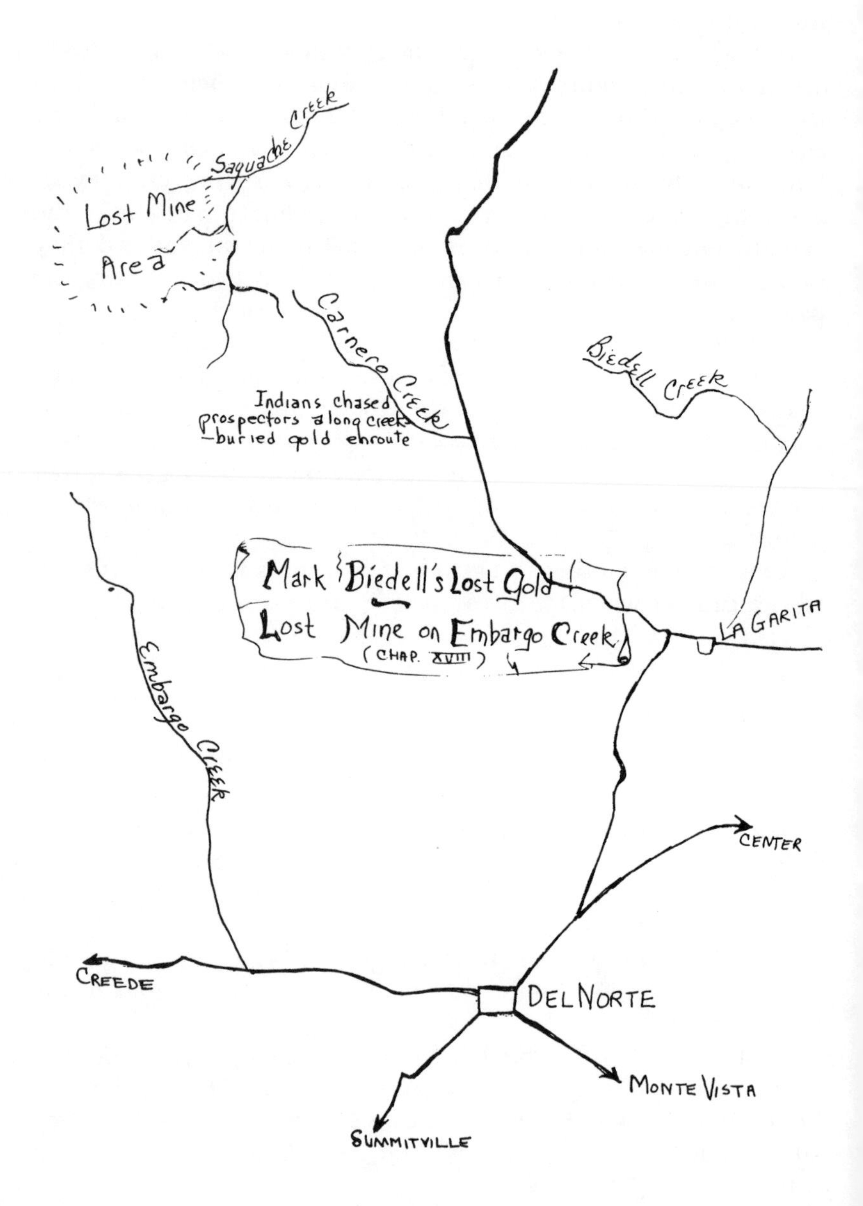
Saguache Creek
Lost Mine Area
Carnero Creek
Indians chased prospectors along creek —buried gold enroute
Biedell Creek
Mark Biedell's Lost Gold
Lost Mine on Embargo Creek
(CHAP. XVIII)
LA GARITA
Embargo Creek
CENTER
CREEDE
DEL NORTE
MONTE VISTA
SUMMITVILLE

until several years later when a lone Mexican member of the party stopped by. He told the following story:

He said the surveying party had followed up Carnero Creek and crossed over what they thought was the head of the Saguache. When they found some rich gold streaks, they forgot about surveying, set up camp and began digging. Everything went well for a few weeks until a band of Utes bore down on them. They grabbed up the gold they had mined and closed down camp in a hurry. The chase followed down the Carnero. When the Indians started closing in, the surveyors buried the gold dust, fearing it would go worse with them if they were caught with the loot.

They marked the spot of the buried gold dust with three mounds of dirt and a blazed tree, and made a careful map of the area, and then left. Apparently they did all this with the Indians still hot on the trail, because the chase continued all the way down to New Mexico. Two of the Frenchmen were killed and the third died shortly after returning to civilization.

It wasn't until 1880 when the lone Mexican dared to venture back to look for the gold. He had the soiled old map with him.

Biedell, who knew the area better than any other, made the search with the Mexican. They found what they believed were the three mounds of dirt, but otherwise the map didn't work. They couldn't find the blazed tree and they couldn't find the gold dust.

The story has long been a favorite one in Saguache. At one time, in the 1880's or early 1890's, the town was almost deserted when a report hit town of the gold's being found. It was a false alarm. But the search for the buried gold dust and gold mine near the head of what may, or may not, be the Saguache River, continued to be a popular outdoor sport with the people of the region.

In the early 1890's some old workings were found up Goose Creek and some more were found along the Cochetopa. There are those who think the surveying party got confused and actually crossed the range and found their gold in those streams.

It's not often a surveying party gets this confused, however.

See Addendum, p. 281, for further information.

VII. *THE SILVERY SAN JUANS*

29. SPIRITS AND THE HIGHLAND MARY

Edward Ennis had a million dollars to start with. He lived in New York, on the income from his inheritance. But to Edward Ennis this was not enough. He wanted to make a fortune. In those days, gold and silver mining was the way to the quick money.

Previously, however, Ennis had become a spiritualist. He believed in spiritualism with all his heart and soul. As long as one believes in something that strongly, why shouldn't one put it to good use? Ennis figured spiritualism would lead him to a "lake of silver."

For a mere $50,000 fee, a New York spiritualist said the Lake of Silver would be found near the Divide in southwestern Colorado.

Ennis hopped a fast train to Pueblo. Here he hired a pack train and bought all the supplies he would need to gather in his fortune. In the early spring of 1875, Edward Ennis headed for the San Juans. Early in July he found the spot which he believed the

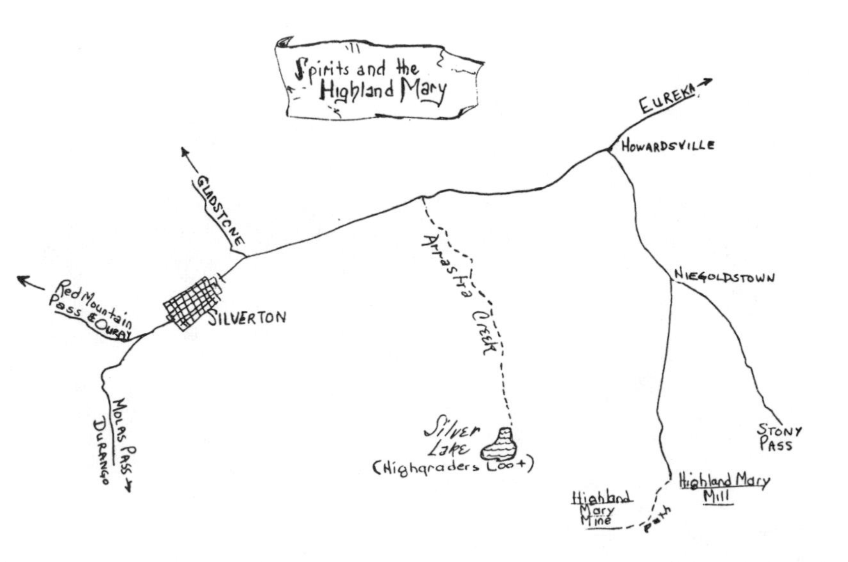

spiritualist had indicated. It was near the Divide about nine miles from Silverton, at the end of Cunningham Gulch.

Prospectors had swarmed into the area the year before with the signing of the Brunot Treaty with the Indians, but, because of the extreme isolation of the area, not too many of the claims had been greatly developed as yet.

Ennis quickly bought up about $30,000 in claims and hired the men to begin digging for the Lake of Silver. Confident in his quest, he also began building large, permanent buildings, even before the shaft had hardly cleared the surface. After the work was well begun, Ennis began building his lavish home.

He named his mine the Highland Mary, and it was destined to make mining history.

The spiritualist's instructions included methods for the sinking of the shaft. Ennis didn't make a move without the say-so of the spiritualist. Ore, good ore, was discovered early in the mining experiment. It assayed up to $7,500 a ton. It was shipped to Pueblo in 1876. Ennis accompanied the shipment. He directed all work to stop in the mine until his return and he continued on to New York.

He returned the following spring with more money and new instructions. The men were directed to stop working the ore they

The fabulous Highland Mary Mine, not far from Silverton. Some say the Ennis ghost still lives in the old shaft.

had uncovered and were told to begin tunneling through the mountain, where, Ennis said, they would find the Lake of Silver within 2,000 feet.

Ennis contacted his spiritualist through dreams each night. The spiritualist told him the direction to tunnel each day, and work did not begin in the morning until Ennis gave the workers the word. It soon became the most crooked mine shaft in the state. It passed by several good ore veins which were disregarded in the push for the Lake of Silver.

Ennis was warned—in his dreams—of water caves and was told as the tunnel neared each one. He passed his warnings on to his workers and they bypassed them. However, one such warning which Ennis telegraphed to his men in 1879 from New York, was ignored. And the men *did* puncture an underground water cave and several men were almost drowned.

Ennis pushed the work until 1885 when the tunnel had passed the 1,000-foot mark. A business failure of one of the companies in which Ennis had invested cut off his revenue. He had already spent one million dollars on his mine, and, although he and his men had found much good ore, he had only realized a few thousand dollars from it, far from enough to pay for the work and shipping expenses.

The court gave Ennis one year to raise funds to continue the work on the mine. Ennis tried desperately to raise the money, showing samples of some of the ore found in the Highland Mary. He was sure the Lake of Silver was only 600 feet away.

But try as he might he could not raise the money. For some reason potential investors were a little leery of him.

At the end of one year, Ennis was forced to sell the Highland Mary. The new owners went back to the beginning and began mining it through more orthodox methods. It paid big from the start, becoming one of the most lucrative mines in the area. At approximately 600 feet from where work had stopped under Ennis, the new owners uncovered what could be called a Lake of Silver. It was a body of almost pure silver.

Ennis died in 1900 in an insane asylum, penniless. Some local residents said he returned to the mine after his death. If one penetrates the deserted old mine today, he may find Ennis, Colorado's most unusual mining man, swimming in an empty Lake of Silver.

30. THE LOST UTE MINE

The history of the Lost Ute Mine, one of Colorado's greatest lost treasures, dates back to 1760. Ancient records in Taos and Santa Fe tell of the Spanish working the mine. It is believed located on Ute Creek, about thirty miles northwest of present-day Pagosa Springs.

For years, during the late 1700's, the mine was worked each summer by Spaniards from Taos. Because of hostile Indians and Spanish robbers, the rich ore was often hidden at intervals along the trail from Taos to the mine.

In 1780, seven men were working at the mine when they were attacked by Indians. Five of the seven were killed. The first two

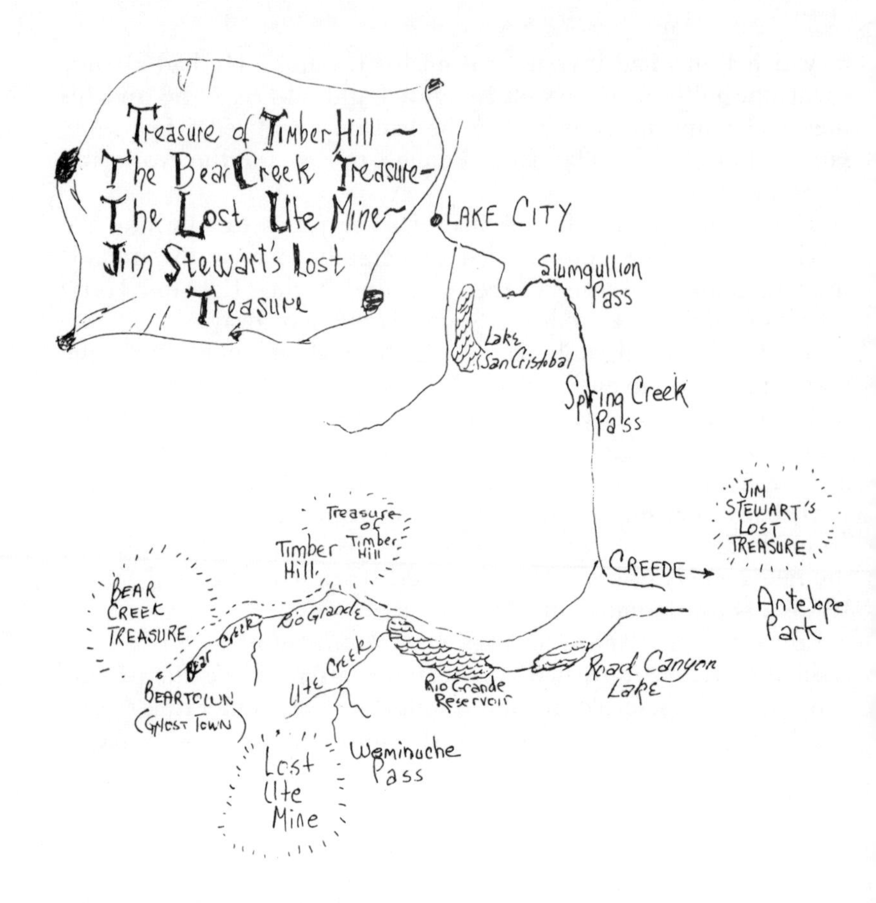

killed were left at the entrance of the mine. Their skeletons have guarded the entrance ever since.

Since that time, the two survivors, their descendants, and scores of others have attempted to find the mine, but it has never been located.

In the 1890's a young Frenchman appeared at the ranch of Jack Pearson in the lower Pine River Valley. The stranger became known as La Sombra—the shadow—because he was always off by himself, slipping around.

La Sombra was around those parts for a good many years and nobody was sure of what he was up to until 1934 when the Frenchman, on his death bed, told his story.

He said he had been searching most of the time for the Lost Ute mine, which, he said, had once been worked by his grandfather. With La Sombra when he died—of consumption—was a rough and time-worn map of the Ute Creek area. La Sombra was buried among the Indians near Taos.

Previously, two Mexicans, Doneciano Aguilar and Candido Archuleta, had told of finding the mine with two skeletons in an underground passage. Since the legend of the Lost Ute had grown to such proportions no one ever believed it would be found—such legends just don't end that way. So Aguilar and Archuleta were laughed at, and they refused to talk any more about it.

Aguilar was later involved in a murder and was imprisoned in New Mexico for life.

Archuleta, in his wanderings, met a wealthy young Spaniard who claimed to have been a descendant of one of the survivors of the original miners. Later, Archuleta found some markings that were supposed to be the key to the location of the Lost Ute, but he could never find the Spaniard to verify the markings.

In 1911, a well-equipped expedition was formed to search for the mine, but it was never located.

Jose Garcia, a well-known figure in the San Luis Valley, searched for the mine for several years, as did Ed Speel of Pagosa Springs, but they, and others, had no luck.

In the middle 1930's, there was much excitement in the region when two skeletons were found on Starvation Creek. But these were later identified as two members of Fremont's ill-fated fourth expedition and had no connection with the Lost Ute.

In 1938, two men, who were careful not to have their identities known, found a $40,000 gold cache two miles south of Ute Creek. It may have been one the ancient miners hid so many years ago.

But the mine itself, and perhaps other such caches, are still waiting to be discovered.

31. THE BEAR CREEK TREASURE

There is another lost mine in the same area as the Lost Ute mine . . . and it goes one skeleton better. One might forthwith conclude that they are the same stories told by men of different educational levels. It's possible, but in just about every respect the stories are different.

In 1905, an old prospector walked into Durango with a heavy bag of highly concentrated gold ore. He sold his gold and bought some supplies so he could go back up into the mountains and work the mine he had found.

He was a talkative old man, as are many of the wandering hermits, once you get them going. He said he found the mine in a well-developed stage. There was a tunnel shaft, although the timbers were rotted and old. He said there were sacks of ore in the entrance and evidence of plenty more good ore to be mined.

But the most unusual part of the old mine were its inhabitants.

Just inside the mine, guarding the entrance, were three skeletons. The prospector said there was no evidence around of how and when they died. Actually, however, although this was not a typical mine entrance by any means, it was not so unusual to find skeletons in mines. Many a mine became a tomb due to rock or snowslides. Many a miner was trapped inside a mine by Indians or bandits or claimjumpers.

Anyhow, the old prospector was more interested in the gold than in the background, and, after telling his strange story, he headed back into the hills . . . never to be seen again.

In 1918, a man by the name of Pedro Martinez came into Durango with another bag of rich ore and told the same strange story. But before he was able to return to the gold mine, he died in the flu epidemic of that year, and the location of his mine died with him.

Twenty years later, in 1938, a sheepherder showed up with some of the gold and with the same old story. Before he could get away, the good people of Durango organized a search party and had the man lead them back into the mountains. But the man was more at home leading sheep than prospectors. He became confused and never did find the mine. In fact, the search party almost became lost.

Durango is waiting for the next person to come into town with rich gold ore and the story of a lost mine in the Bear Creek area, guarded by three lonely skeletons.

32. NEWTON'S LOST GOLD MINE

During the depression many an unemployed man set out to make his fortune by prospecting for gold and silver.

One of this army of latter-day fortune hunters was an earnest young man who stumped into Newton's Cafe in Durango one day. He told Newton that he had studied rocks a little and would be willing to split any and all of the gold and silver he found in return for a grubstake.

Newton took an instant liking to the youth and agreed on the deal. So, hopes high and loaded down with supplies, the young prospector headed for the mysterious mountains.

Two weeks later the boy returned and proudly plopped down a number of fascinating rocks onto the counter. He said he knew where there were tons more just as pretty.

Newton, the youth, and several other customers admired the shining rocks for a spell. Then an old prospector pushed through the crowd. He inspected the rocks for a moment. Then he began to laugh.

He said the rocks sparkled with iron pyrite, better known as "fool's gold."

The crestfallen young man disappeared and was never seen again. Newton threw the rocks up on a shelf in the cafe as a reminder of the time he thought he had a fortune. Anyhow, they were still pretty rock specimens.

A few weeks later, a mining engineer noticed the rocks while eating at the restaurant. He asked to look at them. After a moment he said it was some of the richest ore he had seen.

Newton, still not convinced, had the rocks assayed. They checked out at better than $5,000 a ton.

Newton still has half interest in a gold mine, but his partner, the one who knows where it is, has long since disappeared.

33. THE TREASURE OF TIMBER HILL

Timber Hill was a well-wooded section of the once-busy stagecoach and ore wagon run from Silverton to Del Norte and points east. It's still well wooded but the road and the traffic have long since disappeared.

The legends remain, however.

There were many tales of lost treasures in the Timber Hill area. Two of the most popular concern ill-begotten gold.

One concerns two fellows named Soapy Robinson and Buster Reede. To these young men, even high-grading was too slow. While working in an Ophir smelter, they worked out a pretty good scheme to make off with a few of the boss' gold bars. One night Reede was able to throw five of the bars out of the window into the waiting arms of Soapy Robinson. At the time the five gold bricks were worth about $65,000.

The two men pulled the job at the end of a week end shift, so the theft wasn't apt to be discovered until the men came to work on Monday morning. By that time, Reede and Robinson figured they would be out of the country and out of reach of any and all pursuers.

The bullion weighed 200 pounds. Adding that to their other gear meant a pretty good load for their three scrawny burros, but they figured they needed everything for the long, hard trip ahead.

They skirted around Silverton, down Cunningham Gulch and over Stony Pass, and down into Lake City country, following fairly closely the stage road to Del Norte. Everything went well until they got to the down side of Timber Hill. Here, one of the burros gave out. He lay down on the trail and refused to get up. The two men decided to make camp here and give the animal a rest, hoping it would be ready to hit the road in the morning. But, as luck would have it, snow started falling during the night. There was still a good 50 miles ahead of them before they would reach civilization, and they didn't have any time to waste. They awoke early, planning to hit the trail by daylight. However, they found that one burro had died during the night.

The two men called a quick board meeting and decided that the only way out of their dilemma was to bury four of the gold bare in a safe place and head east as fast as the two remaining burros could carry them. The profit from one gold bar would easily carry them through the winter, and they could return in the spring for the rest of the loot.

They buried the four bars close to the trail so they couldn't miss them on their return. They also cut an odd-shaped blaze on the tree nearby and noted down all the landmarks there were to identify the spot.

The men got out just ahead of the worst part of the storm, sold their bullion in Pueblo and split the money they received. The money they got for this one brick was more than either of them had ever seen in their lives. The possession of it was the one thing that fouled up their plans and turned the four gold bars they left behind into a lost treasure tale instead of a successful business transaction.

Soapy was a wild character down underneath. His new wealth afforded him the opportunity to give vent to all the wildness he had saved up during his lean years. During one of this extended drinking sprees, he was shot down and killed in a barroom brawl.

The money afforded Reede another opportunity which he too took advantage of. He had always wanted a cattle ranch. With his share of the money he saw the opportunity to buy one. Which he did, figuring he could return for the rest of the bullion in the spring and greatly add to his spread. He soon discovered, however, that cattle ranching ties a man down so he can't go gallavanting off any time he felt like it.

This didn't bother Reede too much. He figured it would be safer to wait a year or two anyway. And his business was doing alright, it wasn't as if he needed more money. Being a man of some standing now led to something else that really put a crimp in his plans. He got married. We know what that does to a fellow.

In fact, it wasn't until 1926, some 40 years after the gold was buried, that Reede, now 70, decided to return for it. He did so more for the adventure than the need for money. And a man does hate to go to his reward leaving some chips on the table.

Needless to say, the country had changed immensely in the intervening years. The old road from Del Norte to Silverton was little used, no more than a vague trail in places. The giant Farmers Union reservoir now covered much of the area along the way.

Reede rustled up some professional assistance to help him in his quest. He and his guide did find many of the old landmarks along the way but, try as they might, they never did find the blazed tree and the treasure site. Reede spent as much time looking for the treasure as he figured he could afford, and then headed home. Before he left, however, he told two or three other people about the buried bullion, being careful not to go into too much detail.

These people told others, and they told others, and that's how the story grew. Those who have searched for the treasure since, have turned up traces of the landmarks mentioned by Reed. One fellow even found what he thought was the blazed tree. But Reede never returned again so nobody knew exactly where the bullion was in relationship to the tree.

No doubt, many a fortune hunter has walked over, around and about the buried bullion without even knowing it.

Another well-known story of lost treasure on Timber Hill takes advantage of the fact it was a popular hangout for highwaymen. Many a rich ore wagon from Beartown, a scant ten miles away, and from the Silverton side of the mountains, rumbled over the hill enroute to Del Norte or Pueblo. Heavily-wooded Timber Hill was ready-made for ambush and escape.

One time three particularly rich wagonloads of ore out of Beartown headed up Timber Hill. Wary of the bandit road, three scouts rode ahead of the shipment to scout the way.

About half way up the hill, the scouts were ambushed, two were killed and the third one escaped to dash back and tell the wagon crews. The wagon crews quickly dumped two of the wagons in a hastily chosen hiding spot, but before they could dump the third wagon, the bandits were upon them and the wagon crews and the third scout were killed.

The bandits rode off with the remaining wagon of ore, not waiting to scoop up what had been dumped on the ground. A few days later the animals were found dragging two empty ore wagons along behind them. There is no record of the rich ore dump ever being found, however.

34. THE CRAZY SWEDE'S LOST MINE

J. T. Boyd was a well-known mine manager in the San Juan area. He first heard of the Crazy Swede's Lost Mine in 1906. He looked for it off and on, himself, for several years. In fact, in 1940 he hired a plane and flew over the entire area taking pictures for later analysis.

But he never found the elusive mine.

Boyd was staying at the St. Elmo Hotel that winter of '06. One day during a snowstorm, the "Swede" came to the hotel carrying a heavy gunny sack. Boyd worked with the Swede at the Camp Bird Mine and was on good terms with him.

The Swede was excited and couldn't wait to open the sack in Boyd's room. The sack weighed about seventy pounds and was full of ore chunks weighing from five to fifteen pounds each.

It was the richest ore that Boyd had ever seen. After his working at the Camp Bird, that's saying a helluva lot.

It was solid, pure calaverite with hardly a speck of anything else in it. The ore was malleable and black with moss on one side, demonstrating that it had come from the surface.

The Swede danced his excited little jig and said he was going to make old Tom Walsh, millionaire owner of the Camp Bird, look like thirty cents.

The ore was melted down and brought in $7,300—pretty good take home pay for seventy pounds of ore.

The Swede was confident he could find the place again although the circumstances surrounding the original find were somewhat hectic. He told Boyd he had been caught in a blizzard between Ouray and Lake City, some of the cruelest country in the whole cruel state. When things got so bad he couldn't see the trail, the Swede was finally forced to take refuge in a cleft of rocks. Here he found the ore vein. The Swede whacked off a few samples to while away the time before the storm cleared.

The earliest day possible, the next spring, he took off for the hills. He looked all summer. When the snows came again, the light-hearted Swede was now filled with doubt. During the winter he went over all the old trails in his mind. He cursed the mistakes he had made. And always the rich vein was there, beckoning him.

He continued the search next summer, the summer of 1908. As the days and the weeks wore on, the futile search became more desperate. The lure of the lost gold blinded the old Swede. His mind wandered more and more into the golden cleft of rocks while his body followed one dead end after another.

Finally, the mind and the body lost touch altogether. The babbling old Swede was committed to the state hospital at Pueblo. He died a short time later.

Boyd took up the search in 1909. In a stream in the general locality of the Swede's lost mine he found a shining pebble. It brought $15. Pretty good for a pebble. It encouraged Boyd to keep up the search.

He followed up the following year.

Eventually, however, he realized the search was becoming uppermost in his mind, and he forced himself to return to his other life before the golden cleft made a babbling idiot out of him, too.

But Boyd continued to look off and on over the years, always taking care not to let the thing get the better of him. During the years of searching he found several areas that looked promising, but none of them was very good compared to the Swede's lost treasure.

For a final look, Boyd hired a plane and took pictures of the entire area, and had the pictures blown up. It seemed like a good idea, but nothing came of it. The pictures didn't come close enough to the Crazy Swede's lost mine.

35. THE LOST MINE ON OAK CREEK

Around 1863, two venturesome California prospectors made their way into Ouray country, then very much in the possession of the Indians. The two men followed up Oak Creek onto the flats on the west side of the creek. They recalled seeing the Uncompahgre Valley unfolding below them on the north and the Continental Divide to the south and to the east.

They worked cautiously, prospecting one moment and scouting for signs of Indians the next.

Eventually they reached a small spring where they spotted some

promising gold float. They traced it to rich quartz nearby. That night they slept in a cave so they couldn't be seen by the Indians.

The next day they searched some more, seeking the mother lode. Searching and scouting for Indians, sleeping in caves until they finally found the source of the rich metal . . . a ledge of almost pure gold.

From the point of the discovery they could see the Indians in the valley far below them . . . but they went to work, carefully.

They chopped down several nearby trees for boarding. Working as efficiently as they could without attracting attention, they dug the ore and stored it.

It so happened, however, that winter was fast approaching, their food was running low, and they still hadn't been able to accumulate much ore. The time was coming when they should be making their way back.

Finally, in desperation, they built a fire against the ledge and stoked it until the wall became red hot. Then they dashed cold water against the rocks. The process resulted in securing for them about 100 pounds of ore. They pulverized this and were amazed at the results . . . some of the finest gold they had ever seen.

The rich ore, they decided, was too good to pass up in spite of the constant threat of Indians. They made plans to get more supplies and work through the winter.

But fate was against them. An ember of the fire they had set had caught on an evergreen. Unbeknownst to the two prospectors, the wood smoldered until the smoke was seen by the Indians.

Fortunately, the two men became aware of the situation in

Looking up Oak Creek from Ouray. White House Mountain is in distant center and Twin Peaks are at right. Daring prospectors claim to have found a rich golden ledge up the creek.

sufficient time to get a head start. They escaped into New Mexico just ahead of the Indians, losing one of their two burros.

Their narrow escape cooled their desire to return in any big hurry. Eventually they became involved in other things and parted ways.

Forty years later, an old man in Shasta County, California, lay dying. A young stranger took mercy on him and attended to his needs.

Finally, as death approached, the dying man told the youth of the lost mine. He gave the young man a tattered map and told him all the details he would need to find it.

The next year, the youth appeared in Ouray and outfitted himself for prospecting. He set out for the hills alone, following the map and the directions carefully. However, he soon discovered that many of the landmarks had changed in the past forty years.

He found no tunnel and no signs of work.

It didn't take him long to realize that finding something in the rugged mountains was not as easy as it appears. He returned to town and hired an experienced prospector, told him the story and showed him the map.

The two of them headed into the mountains. For weeks they searched, following every possibility on the map.

They did find some gold.

But it wasn't the golden ledge . . . lost so many years before.

36. THE LOST TRAIL MINE

The story is well known in the San Juans. It was printed as truth in an 1892 newspaper.

It's about two experienced prospectors whose luck was running thin on the eastern slope of the Rockies. They had heard of the rich strikes made in the San Juans. So, in the early 1870's, they packed up their supplies and headed over the Divide.

When they crossed the last high range into the San Juans, the weary prospectors paused to drink in the marvelous view.

There were the rugged peaks of the silvery mountains on all

Majestic and rugged Mount Wilson, in center, scene of the mysterious circumstances surrounding the "Lost Trail Mine." The near-ghost town of Ohpir can be seen far below in the valley. *U.S. Geological Survey photo.*

sides. There was a beautiful green valley far below. And straight ahead was majestic Mt. Wilson.

A mountain as beautiful as that must contain precious minerals. With new hope they aimed for the magnificent peak. They passed down through the valley. They headed up the narrow canyons of Mt. Wilson.

Finally, they found a likely spot. They pitched their camp and went to work. In no time at all they found rich ore. They knew low grade ore wouldn't pay in such a remote spot. They were sure this was worth it. They worked all that summer, storing their ore in preparation for the return trip.

When the air turned cold and the first lazy snowflakes fell, they loaded what was left of their supplies, and what gold they had accumulated, and headed back over the Divide.

As they had expected, the ore brought a good price. Such a good price, in fact, that some of the other unluckier prospectors became curious. But the two old prospectors had been around long enough that they parried all questions, saying no more than that they made their strike in the San Juans.

After a satisfying winter, the two prospectors packed up their supplies and headed back over the Divide.

They were never seen again.

The two men were almost forgotten until about ten years later when human bones were found scattered over a small park high on Mt. Wilson. Near a cabin in the park were found the remnants of a sampling outfit, identified as the one belonging to the two prospectors. In the cabin were found good ore samples.

Death is no stranger to the rugged mountains, but no one could ever explain how the bones became scattered over the park. Possibly the two men were killed by Indians, or a snowslide. But evidence at the scene didn't support either theory.

Another mystery was the missing mine. It was never located. The trail to the mine could well have been erased by time and weeds. But not even a prospect hole was found within practical distance of the camp. Of course, a mine entrance could have been destroyed by a rock slide.

Any one of a hundred things could have happened.

VIII. *FOUR CORNERS' GOLD*

37. BURIED TREASURE IN BULL CANON

The State of Colorado joined in the search for the buried treasure in Bull Canon, laying claim to it, but even the State of Colorado couldn't find the treasure. No one else has found it either. It's still there . . . someplace.

The treasure was hidden by "Indian" Henry Huff, well-known hermit in Bull Canon, rugged country about eighty miles from Telluride. Huff was a real Indian. He was a pioneer prospector and mining man in that area and was a cattle rancher at the time of his death in 1917, when our story begins.

Huff lived in a rude cabin in a desolate section of Bull Canon. He was a hermit and lived a hermit's life except for the fact that he was in partnership with Carl Akers, his one and only friend. Huff didn't believe in banks although they say he had plenty of money. He led a miser's existence and hoarded his gold. The amount of his hoard can only be guessed, but it is a recorded fact that he added $5,500 to it a few weeks before his death. He had this money in his possession from the sale of a large herd of cattle. He also had an unknown quantity in gold dust which he received from the sale of several old mining claims.

On May 11, 1917, at three o'clock in the morning, Indian Henry Huff was shot by one John Keski, after a long quarrel. Witnesses to the shooting, which took place at Keski's cabin, were Mrs. Keski,

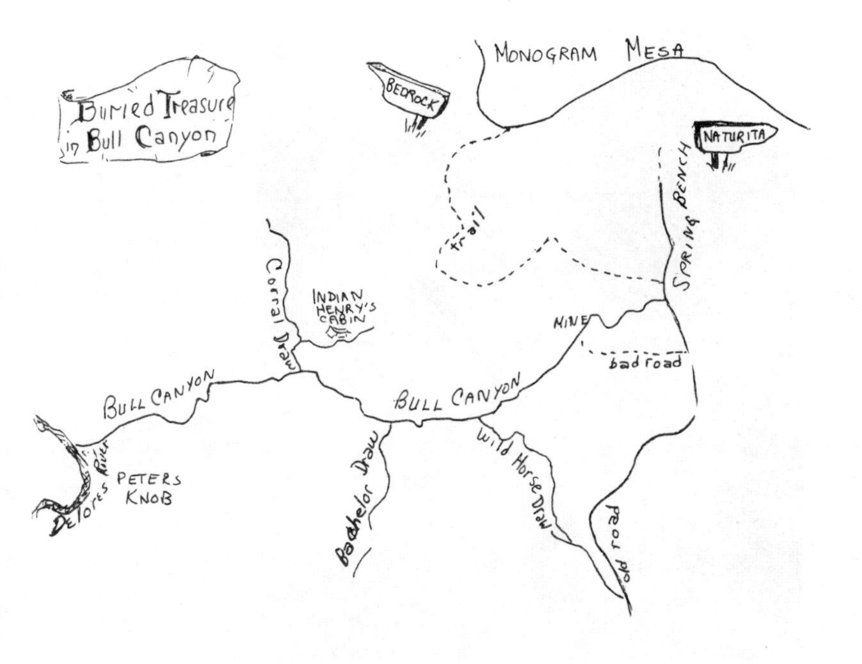

her two children, and Carl Akers, Indian Henry Huff's "one and only friend." Versions of the shooting differed widely. Keski and his wife claimed it was self-defense. Akers said Keski planned the shooting all along and invited Huff to his cabin just for that purpose.

That's neither here nor there. The important part of the story followed the shooting as Huff lay dying in the cabin of the man who shot him. The Indian dictated his will orally to Mrs. Keski.

For many years the oral, or nuncupative, type of will was formally recognized just about every place as long as there were witnesses—and there were witnesses here.

At the time, however, this type of will was not honored. It went out in Colorado a short time before this incident. Thus the state claimed heirship to all that was left behind by Indian Henry Huff.

In dictating his will, Huff was quoted as saying: "I want Carl Akers to have all I've got as he's the only one I ever had in the world." Included in the possessions given Akers were Huff's three mules, but Huff had warned, "ride two of the mules as the

Indian Henry's cabin in Bull Canyon. Somewhere nearby is the buried treasure the old hermit left behind, but even the state was unable to find it. *U.S. Geological Survey Photo.*

Indian markings in Mesa County, similiar to those found near Dove Creek, which has been interpreted by one old timer as showing where a famous Spanish treasure is buried. The story, however, is not as well-developed as the unidentified girl viewing the markings. *Colorado State Publicity Department photo.*

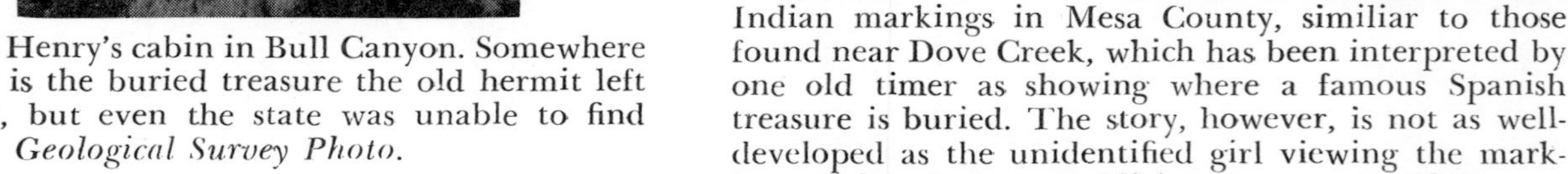

pleasure of the owner warrants, but do not ride the red one, as it will kill you."

But before Huff could finish dictating the will, he died. With his last breath he attempted to tell where his hoard was located but he was unable to do so.

Oldtimers say the treasure could be buried near the Indian's rude cabin, or anywhere in Bull Canon. Indian Henry Huff knew the canon better than anyone and consequently knew the best hiding places. The state and many other people in the region searched for the treasure trove, or troves, for several months after the shooting. Much of the area around and under Huff's cabin was dug up, but no gold was found.

Many, many people have wandered up the lonely canon in the long years since. If they ever found the treasure they made no public announcement. It's doubtful if any of it has ever been unearthed. Indian Henry Huff knew the best place to hide it, and it will take another Indian Henry Huff to find it.

38. THE LOST JOSEPHINE MINE AND THE GOLDEN JESUS

One of the best known legends around the Four Corners area is the Lost Josephine Mine and the Golden Jesus. Actually, it is two stories in one, of buried treasure and of a lost mine. To further complicate things, the location, or locations, of the stories could be just about anywhere in the Four Corners area. Many believe the mine is in the La Plata Mountains in southwestern Colorado. Just as many firmly believe it is located in the La Sal or Henry Mountains in southeastern Utah.

Tellers of the tale are even farther apart on the location of the Golden Jesus.

The story begins in New Mexico almost 200 years ago, shortly after Father Escalante made his trip through southwestern Colorado in search for a route to the Pacific. This was in the 1770's, about the time of our Revolutionary War.

According to legend a group of Spaniards from Santa Fe followed close on the good Father's heels. Their purpose was not

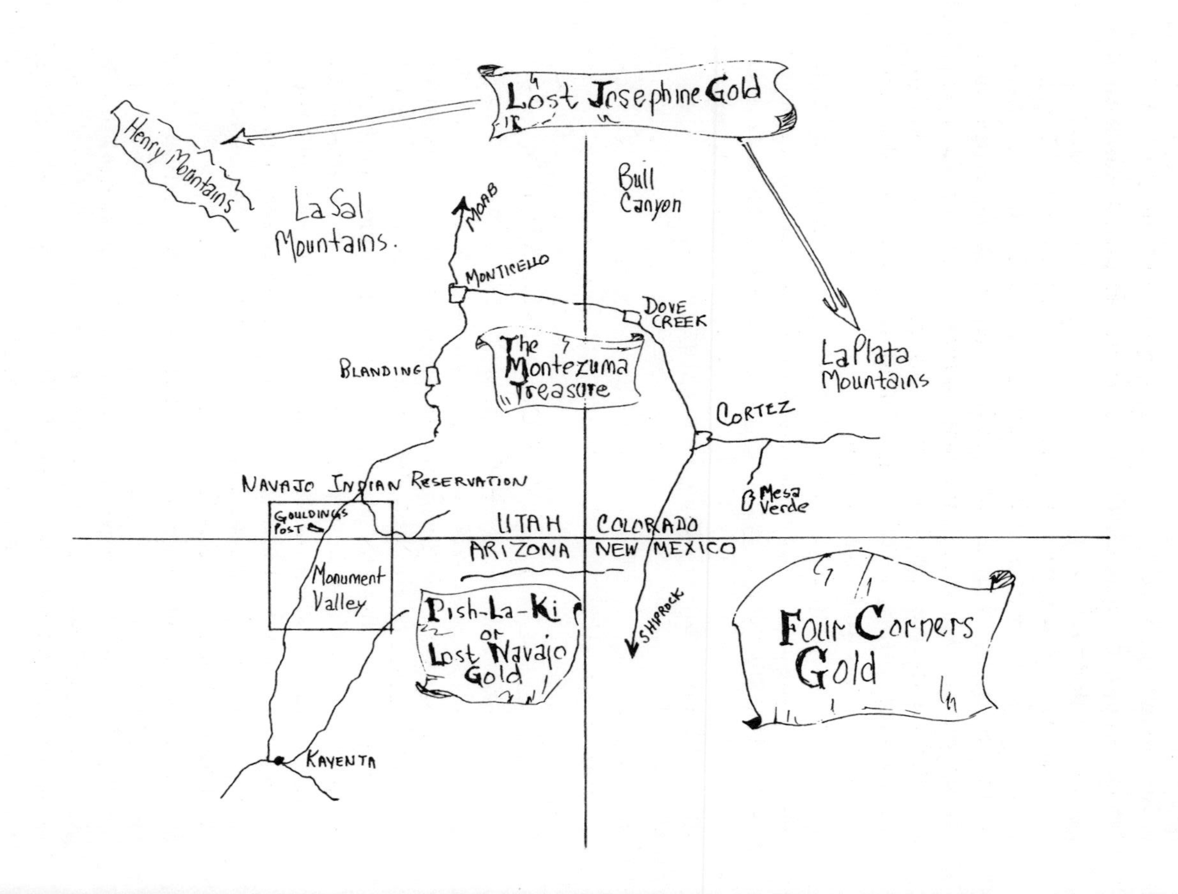
Lost Josephine Gold
Henry Mountains
La Sal Mountains.
MOAB
Bull Canyon
MONTICELLO
DOVE CREEK
La Plata Mountains
BLANDING
The Montezuma Treasure
CORTEZ
Mesa Verde
NAVAJO INDIAN RESERVATION
GOULDINGS POST
UTAH
COLORADO
ARIZONA
NEW MEXICO
Monument Valley
Pish-La-Ki or Lost Navajo Gold
SHIPROCK
Four Corners Gold
KAYENTA

nearly so noble as his. They were in search of gold. And, according to the legend, they found it—in the La Platas or in the La Sals. They called their mine the Josephine Mine.

The Spaniards set up shop and began mining their gold with good results. However, after several weeks and just before they were set to return to New Mexico for the winter, they began to argue over the distribution of the gold.

Finally, to settle the argument, they melted all the gold down and cast it into the image of the Christ Child . . . a Golden Jesus, to be presented to the Spanish court.

That settled, they began their journey back. But shortly after they started the Indians set upon them. Their own lives meant nothing but by any means they had to save the Golden Jesus from the pagan savages. So they drew straws. The two winners were to escape with the Golden Jesus, while the others held off the redskins. However, the two with the Golden Jesus soon found their way too rugged and slow with the cumbersome idol. So they hid the precious statue in a cave, made a careful map of its location, and scampered on back to New Mexico just ahead of the Redskins.

After such a close call, the escapees were too frightened to return for their treasure, but they preserved their maps. Some stories say they never returned, others claim they did return but couldn't find either the Golden Jesus or the Lost Josephine Mine. A well-known tale says they did return and they did find the golden idol, but were ambushed by Indians before they could remove the statue from its hiding place.

This begins the stories of jinxes connected with the statue. And this begins also the confusion that seems to exist between this buried treasure and the Lost Montezuma Treasure. There are many stories told down through the years of a lonely party, or an individual, coming upon the one treasure or the other just before meeting a violent end. Most of the stories claim it to be Lost Montezuma Treasure but some claim it to be the Golden Jesus. Like the babbling, haunted, old prospector who died shortly after reaching civilization, but not till after he mumbled something about seeing the golden statue.

There is another story of a man dying of fright after viewing the statue somewhere in the wastes of the Four Corners area. Old timers attached the death to one or another of the legends going at the time. There are also tales of the earth's opening up and swallowing those who had the audacity to view the treasure. One wonders, however, how these tales got back to civilization.

Most stories put the Golden Jesus and the Lost Josephine Mine in the same general location. However, it is possible that the buried idol could be a greater distance from the mine, anywhere along the trail leading back to Santa Fe from the La Platas . . . or the La Sals.

More authoritative stories are told of the search for the Lost Josephine Mine. Many concentrated their search in the La Plata Mountains, and it seems more logical that they should. There was vague reference to Father Escalante himself finding precious metal in or near these rugged mountains. The Spanish named the mountains for the silver they believed abounded there. Years later, many good mines were located here. Perhaps the Yankees never did find the legendary Spanish mine; yet it's quite possible that the claim they worked had been worked by the Spanish hundreds of years before.

Nonetheless, there are many who believe that the Lost Josephine Mine is in the La Sal or Henry Mountains in southeastern Utah. Many searched here, including two old prospectors who passed on one of the most interesting and believable stories of the search for the Lost Josephine.

The story was told in recent years. It concerns Al Hainey, a newsboy around California for many years. In his younger days, around the turn of the century, Hainey was a prospector of sorts. In 1900 he happened to run across a man named Frank Olgean, who claimed he was a descendant of one of the original miners. Olgean said he had one of the maps that had been passed down from generation to generation. Hainey figured, with his experience and Olgean's map, the two of them could find the mine.

According to the map, the mine was located in the Henry Mountains, and that's where they headed. After several weeks of searching they found an arrow marker. Following it in a straight line, they came to a cave. On the back wall of the cave was a lengthy description on how to find the mine. Part of the inscription said that there were three large round mounds split open like halved apples. By sighting through these and lining them up, they could see the exact location of the mine. They followed the instructions and found the location. Here, they said, they found a small smelter, some ashes, slag, charcoal and other vague evidence of ancient work, but the only ore they found was trachyte. It seldom contains any gold, but they tried it out with their crude wilderness methods and . . . sure enough . . . it didn't contain any gold.

They combed the area thoroughly, but didn't have any luck. Olgean eventually gave up the search and became a sheepherder. Hainey made a few more trips into the area but the results were always the same. Finally, he scooped up a couple of trachyte samples as souvenirs and headed west to his newsboy career.

On a hundred different street corners during the next thirty years, Hainey mulled over his lost fortune, wondering what he had done wrong, wondering why he was selling newspapers instead of living in a palace.

It took him thirty years to come up with answers. He went home and dug through his many mementos of yesteryear until he came to the samples of trachyte. He took them to an assay office and they showed up to $50,000 of gold per ton. Hainey immediately packed his knapsack and began hitchhiking to Utah. A few days later he dragged himself, half dead, into a sheep camp belonging to Harry Ogden. The mountains were in sight, but Hainey was not prepared for the trip and couldn't go any farther. He had only a few pennies, only the clothes on his back, one ragged blanket, and only what cooking utensils he found in a dump.

Ogden fed him and gave him his own bed. After a couple of days the old man felt well enough and appreciative enough to tell Ogden of his quest. Ogden told Hainey to rest up for a couple more days while he, Ogden, went into town to get supplies which they needed for the expedition.

Ogden was gone for two days and when he returned the old man was gone. Ogden set out in search for him, but the gold-hungry newsboy was never seen again.

There have been vague tales since concerning a bewitched old man wandering aimlessly about southern Utah. A few skeletons were found in the neighborhood, but one can't be sure if any one of them was Hainey's skeleton. Some think that if his skeleton is ever found, it will be found in the cradle of the treasure that plagued his life.

39. THE MONTEZUMA TREASURE

The Montezuma Treasure is perhaps the most elusive of all lost treasures of the West. Mayhap there is no such treasure at all, but, instead, an accumulation of fragments from other lost treasure stories molded into one good representative lost treasure.

Everything about it is vague, just under the surface, just beyond reach. Its creation, location, stories of its being found, are all contradictory, far-off rumors.

There are stories of the great Indian tribes of Mexico moving their treasures north for protection, shortly after the invasion of the Spanish. The vast Montezuma treasure is said to be hidden somewhere to the north, its location known only in Indian legend and symbols, the location of which are also unknown.

There are also stories of the Spanish, through stealth, through torture, and other means, locating the treasure, moving it from its original location to another. These stories tell of the Spanish being killed to a man, taking the secret of its location with them to the great beyond.

From this shadowy beginning stem the stories of the "Montezuma Jinx." The stories of death and destruction meeting the isolated few who located the treasure down through the years are the most vague stories of them all. But they carried throughout the west, adding to the legend and the mystery of the Montezuma Treasure.

Some say rumors of the Indians moving their treasure north helped inspire Coronado to travel north seeking Quivira.

But the closest the legend comes to documentation is in tales of adventure of Cortez. In his history of the conquest of Mexico, Cortez tells of acquiring the estimated seven-million-dollar treasure in 1520 A.D.

However, the finding of the treasure by Cortez is vague, too. Where he located it, what he did with it, and if he hid it again, where, are unknown.

Rumors had the riches in gold plate and ornaments in the Colorado mountains, more specifically, the Sangre de Cristos. Often the Spanish Peaks, or the Spanish Caves are mentioned in the legend—demonstrationg how the Montezuma story is often involved with other legends.

Arizona also lays claim to the Montezuma Treasure, and it is involved with one or more other legends in that state. New Mexico has cause to fix the limits of the legend within its boundaries. No doubt, Utah might find reason to believe the vast treasure lies somewhere in the mysterious land in the southern reaches of that state.

A few years ago, a self-styled expert on the legend claimed that details of the treasure are told in the mysterious symbols carved long ago in a cave near Dove Creek, Colorado.

The expert said the symbol, corresponded to the Aztec Calendario Piecho del Sol, discovered in 1792 and now in the Mexico City National Museum.

The expert, whose identity is unknown, said the symbols are compass point carvings and indicate a ring of seven mountains and the location of the treasure is marked in relation to the mountains. He claimed the seven mountains match those in the Kanab, Utah, area, and the location of the treasure would then be in Colorado, in the Four Corners area.

Apparently his claims were not conclusive enough to stir up further investigation. Nothing more was done about it, and the expert became just another character in the limitless legend.

Mysterious symbols have been found near Dove Creek, and other places. Perhaps they do tell the story of the Montezuma Treasure. Perhaps they don't.

40. THE PISH-LA-KI OR LOST NAVAJO GOLD

One of the most famous lost treasures in the southwest is the Lost Navajo Treasure, known in scientific circles as the Pish-La-Ki, a corruption of the Spanish and Indian meaning "white money."

Many stories surround the legend, not the least of which is the belief that the treasure is jinxed and whosoever is fortunate, or unfortunate, enough to locate it, may well be doomed.

The location of the gold is on the Navajo Reservation in northeast Arizona, near the Four Corners area where Utah, New Mexico and Arizona come together with Colorado. Rumors of gold here

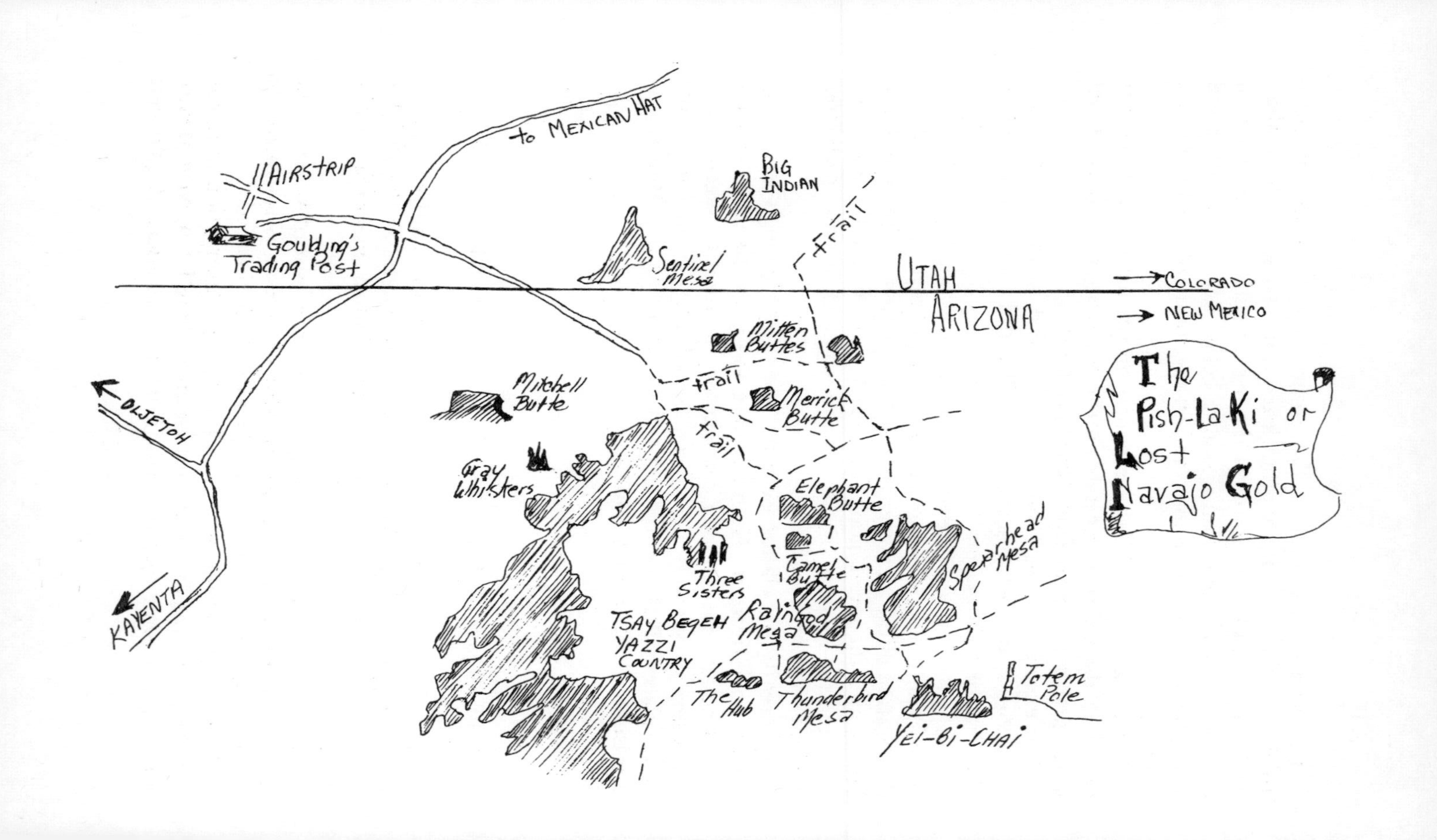
The Pish-La-Ki or Lost Navajo Gold
to MEXICAN HAT
AIRSTRIP
Goulding's Trading Post
BIG INDIAN
Sentinel Mesa
trail
UTAH
ARIZONA
→ COLORADO
→ NEW MEXICO
Mitten Buttes
Merrick Butte
Mitchell Butte
OLJETOH
KAYENTA
Gray Whiskers
Elephant Butte
Camel Butte
Spearhead Mesa
Three Sisters
Raingod Mesa
TSAY BEGEH YAZZI COUNTRY
The Hub
Thunderbird Mesa
Totem Pole
Yei-Bi-CHAI

began with the first history of the area. The Navajos, in legend, would sell nuggets and other golden trinkets to neighboring tribes. The Spanish heard about it. It might have been this rumor which sent Coronado on his wild goose chase toward Quivira.

The Spanish, they say, did find placer gold here and looking around for its source, they found a ledge of sparkling gold and silver. They roasted the metal in a rude furnace producing matte. It was taken in this stage to New Spain (Mexico).

When the Spanish left, the long string of prospectors began. Fortune hunters, high-hoping hobos and the like that toured the Four Corners area, and other places as well, in the search for the treasure.

One of the more unusual aspects of this legend is the fact that so many claimed to have found it. But, in this case, finding the treasure was not a sign the finders lived happily ever after. In fact, those who found it were lucky to live at all.

Two noted searchers and "finders" of the gold were Merrick and Mitchell. Jack Merrick was a Colorado prospector who decided to buck the Navajo jinx. He obtained a grubstake in Colorado and disappeared into the mountains. Months later he showed up in Durango with a goodly load of silver ore which assayed at better than $800 a ton. He said he had found a rude, ancient furnace near the silver, and some gold.

Before heading back into the mountains, Merrick met a twenty-one-year-old youth named Mitchell, who had recently come west to seek his fortune. Merrick took an instant liking to the youth and took him on as partner. The two men set out.

This was in 1880.

Months passed and Durango received no news of the two men. Finally, word got out through the Indian underground that the two had been ambushed and killed by Indians.

A well-armed posse from Rico and Durango set out to locate them.

The posse went to Navajo Chief Hoskininni, who had escaped Kit Carson's roundup of the Navajos in 1863. Hoskininni said he had heard of the murder of Merrick and Mitchell, but denied that the Navajos had anything to do with it. He said the Utes had ambushed the two men at night.

Hoskininni led the posse to two skeletons eaten away by coyotes.

and vultures. The posse buried the men near two lonely buttes that now bear their names.

Their work done, the posse wasn't above looking around for itself. They questioned, or attempted to question, several Indians. The chief's son, Hoskininni-Begay, told them that the mine did exist, but, he said, only seven Navajos knew where it was. He didn't say, or didn't know, who the seven were.

The posse couldn't find any gold or silver, or even any evidence of it. This wasn't even gold and silver country. Minerals of any sort were rare here in this bleak land (uranium wasn't known then).

In 1882, a prospector named Charles T. Johnson formed a party and retraced the route of the posse. In looking around, he became separated from the others. While climbing over some rotten logs he lost his footing and fell down a steep incline. After he had collected his senses he found he was in an old mine shaft, the ceiling of which had apparently caved in under his weight. He saw a large vein of white quartz and was sure it was rich in gold.

His shouts eventually brought the others in the party to the rescue. Johnson got back to civilization and told his strange story.

Then, his part of the story ended. Johnson disappeared. It was never known whether he and his companions found the treasure again, or anything about him.

Another well-known story comes from Prescott, Arizona, where a priest showed up one day looking for this same gold. His, too, was a strange story.

He said he heard of the gold from a man in a Denver hospital. The dying man said he and two others had taken $75,000 in gold from a placer mine in Navajo territory, and that they had fled the scene just ahead of the Indians.

They chose a long, difficult route in order to avoid the redskins. They traveled south through western New Mexico, crossed the Mogollon mountains, followed the Gila River to the Verde, and finally reached Prescott.

Along the way two of the men contracted malaria and died soon after. The sole survivor suffered wounds in a brief skirmish with the Indians. Fearing for his life, he buried the gold under a boulder near a stream at the foot of a mountain. The stream flowed into a small valley somewhere near Prescott. The old prospector never returned for his gold, and on his deathbed, begged the priest to find it and build a hospital.

The priest never found it.

Harry Goulding said the mine does exist—and he ought to know.

Goulding owned and operated the Goulding Trading Post much of his life and lived among the Navajos. Although he never spent any time searching for the mine himself, he estimated its location in the extreme northeastern section of Arizona, or southeastern Utah, near the Four Corners.

Goulding said he first learned of the mine from an Indian named Hosteen Yazzi, who visited the trading post often. Convinced that the Indian was accurate in his knowledge, Goulding, one day, offered to finance a prospecting search by Yazzi. At first, Yazzi refused, but sometime later, when Yazzi's family was sick and he needed money, he agreed to make the trip.

Goulding outfitted the Indian for a three-week trip. Soon after Yazzi left, however, the weather turned cold and damp. Goulding became concerned. His concern mounted as time passed and still no word from Yazzi.

Goulding was just about ready to form a party to search for Yazzi when the Indian stumbled into the trading post, cold, hungry and frightened. He had no supplies, he was soaked, shivering and half dead. He muttered over and over that the gods of Pish-La-Ki were angry. He said the gods brought on the bad weather and wanted to destroy him for attempting to disturb the treasure.

The story of Pish-La-Ki was recounted in a Denver newspaper in 1915. It prompted the most publicized search for the lost mine.

This one was led by Colorado State Representative James O'Rourke. He rounded up a few experts, purchased the most modern equipment, and all the supplies they would need. The party set out on April 18, 1915.

After several weeks of careful combing of the Four Corners area, the group finally found some gold nuggets. A short time later they came to a pile of stones which they believed marked the location of some 200 pounds of silver matte left by the Spanish at least 100 years before.

But they didn't have time to dig out the treasure.

The isolated Indian villages at first had just grumbled at the trespassers. But the longer the palefaces continued, the more the natives became restless. Finally, they banded together to drive the strangers out. Most historians claim the Indians merely intended to throw a scare into O'Rourke and his party, but they did more than that.

The party was chased into Box Canyon where four of the party were killed in a rock slide. Two others barely escaped death, receiving serious wounds. The rest of the party was held captive for forty-five days while the Indians wondered what to do about them.

Finally, they were turned loose, but only after they had lost all taste for treasure.

The Indians still don't cater to much trespassing by palefaces. A few years ago a Navajo chief even refused to discuss a plan offered by Colorado Governor Steve McNichols to run a road through Four Corners. The road is being built now.

One wonders how steam shovels and earth movers will fare with the gods of Pish-La-Ki.

41. THE LANDLADY'S LOST SILVER

A recent story of a lost mine was recounted in 1958 by Virgil Hutton. Hutton and his friend Jack had just returned from Alaska and had taken rooms in Fruita.

One day while rewiring the attic, the two of them found an unusual stone and carted it down and asked the landlady about it. She said she had knocked the stone off a ledge a few years before while cutting Christmas trees in a canyon northeast of Fruita. She was attracted to the rock and brought it home with her. She put it in a fish bowl, but later thought it might have minerals in it that might harm the fish so she had put it up in the attic and forgotten about it.

Hutton and Jack had the rock assayed and it ran better than $200 a ton.

They told the landlady the results of the assay and she said she believed she could find the spot in the canyon again.

The following Sunday they took off. They went as far as they

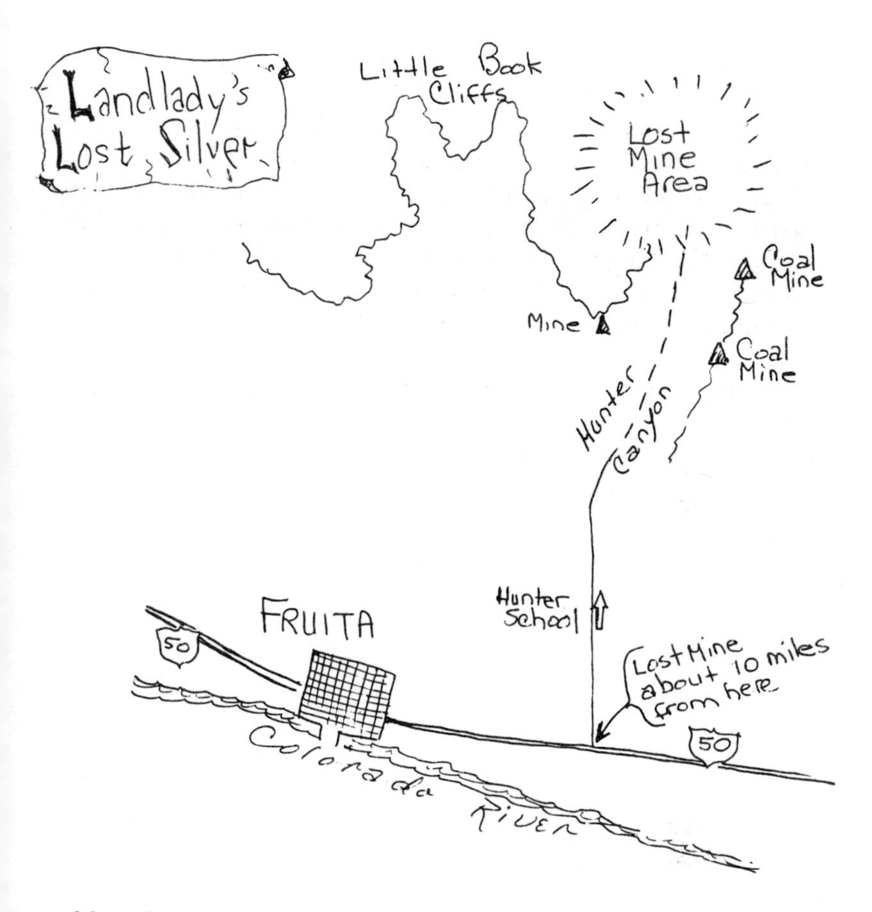

could go by auto. The landlady had an appointment that afternoon so they turned back before reaching the spot, planning to return the following week end.

But a couple of days later it began to snow and it continued for three days. It looked like the beginning of winter. They weren't able to return until the following spring. Meanwhile, however, the landlady had a stroke and wasn't able to go back with them.

But she gave them all the details she could remember about the place.

She said the ledge was high up and the whole side of the mountain "sparkled like a million fireflies." She said the Christmas tree party went up the canyon on mules in the early morning and got out with their Christmas trees before nightfall. They had eventually reached an area where there were plenty of evergreens on the right side of the canyon. They went up a hill to the edge of a rim where she found the rock. From this point they could see two small valleys of evergreen pine and spruce trees.

Hutton said it sounded like chimney ore of the calcopyrite and sugar quartz variety. Needless to say, he and his friend spent many a week end looking for the lost silver but they never found any.

Almost everyone in Colorado collects pretty rocks at one time or another for one reason or another. Backyards are full of pretty rocks.

How many of them belong to some far-off lode?

IX. *BROWN'S HOLE*

42. THE BAD MEN OF BROWN'S HOLE

The desolate and mysterious Brown's Hole region in the extreme northwest corner of Colorado is a natural breeding ground for legend.

The first white men, the fur traders, very early found this section an ideal meeting place. Brown's Hole abounds in game and there were many caves and protected areas against the weather and the Indians. So many trappers were making Brown's Hole their winter quarters by 1837 that Philip Thomsom and William Craig established a trading post in this wild region.

Fort Davy Crockett was built on the Green River bottom in a grove of cottonwood two miles above the entrance of Lodore Canyon. The mountain men were just about the most rugged hombres ever to come west, little different from the wild game they hunted. Many took Indian squaws for brides. Fort Davy Crockett was a brawling, boozing and boisterous place. It was called "the meanest fort in the west."

The post fell into disuse after a few years. But before the mountain men had left completely, the desperados began to come. Ideal for trappers, the place was even more ideal for renegades. The many fortified lookout points, the impregnable areas, made

The magnificent and mysterious country in Dinosaur National Park in the extreme northwestern section of Colorado. The park includes Pat's Hole, the scene of a lost mine. Just north of Dinosaur are the "Fabulous Diamond Fields" and Brown's Hole, where Butch Cassidy and the other bad men hung out. *Colorado State Pulicity Department photo.*

pursuit almost impossible. If a posse did venture into The Hole, there were many escape routes that were difficult, if not impossible, to follow. A short ride would put the escapee across the state line and out of the sheriff's jurisdiction.

For many years few posses or lawmen dared venture into The Hole, while many of the toughest men in the west made their home here. They all were here at one time or another, the horse thieves, the rustlers, the bank and train robbers, and every other fugitive from justice the early west produced.

About the first lawmen to enter The Hole were three different posses from Colorado, Utah and Wyoming that converged upon Harry Tracy and David Lant shortly after they escaped from the Utah prison in the 1890's. After their capture they were taken to Hahn's Peak. They escaped jail again, were captured and taken to the Aspen jail, where they escaped again. Lant disappeared but Tracy cut a path of blood and terror through the Northwest before he was shot down in Wyoming.

The west's most notorious bounty hunter, Tom Horn, made his bloodthirsty way through Brown's Hole around the turn of the century. They say the cattlemen paid him as much as $500 to $750 per head for a rustler. Horn usually warned his victims of his presence. Many escaped in terror, many didn't. The bodies all bore Horn's trademarks, not the least of which was a single bullet hole between the eyes. Horn was said to have killed three men in Brown's Hole during his brief visit. Many another renegade fled the area on hearing of the bounty hunter's presence.

But perhaps Brown's Hole's most famous residents were Butch Cassidy and his gang. This was one of Butch's two or three favorite hideouts. He made many a sortee out of Brown's Hole, to rob a bank or a train, and then to dash back.

He was a classic western outlaw. He never went in much for killing, but he apparently bluffed enough people so that he became one of the most successful men in his line of work. He was a jovial fellow who lived life to the fullest. One couldn't help liking him. Even the lawmen liked him. He always insisted on paying his bills, even if it was with stolen money. He made many a "special trip" out of The Hole just to pay a bar tab or a grocery bill. Whenever he or a member of his gang shot up a bar, the tavern owner was usually reimbursed for the damages.

Many of the legends about Brown's Hole stem from Butch and

Famous family portrait of Butch Cassidy and the "Bad men of Brown's Hole." George L. Parker, alias Butch Cassidy, is seated at the right. With him, standing, left to right are Will Carver and Harvey Logan; seated, at left, Harry Longabough, and Ben Kilpatrick, center. *Denver Public Library Western Collection.*

his gang, known as "the wild bunch." It was believed he often buried or otherwise hid his loot after a robbery. A legend or two makes use of the theory that Butch was unable to find the hiding place again.

One story is noted in history. Elza Lay, one of Cassidy's lieutenants, buried his share of the $30,000 the gang got in the Wilcox, Wyoming, train robbery. Lay left a very detailed map of the hiding place with his girl before he left on another foray. Legend makers say he didn't return for the money, but it is doubtful that this is true. Lay later became a highly respectable citizen. No doubt, the reformation was financed with stolen money.

There is another vague tale of the Wild Bunch leaving about $50,000 in loot from a Wyoming train robbery somewhere in the Powder Springs area, just east of Brown's Hole. At least, a few other underworld characters believed the story had enough sub-

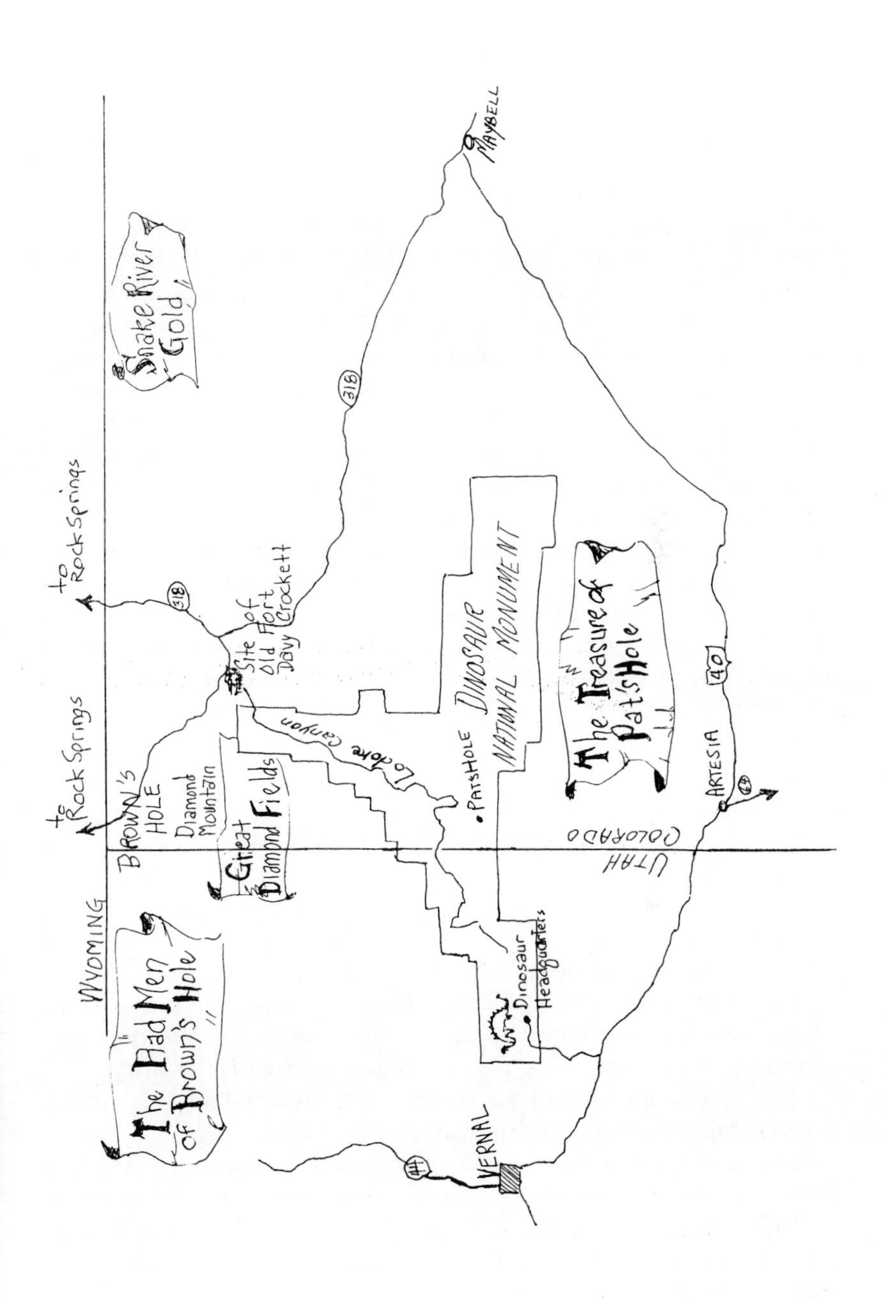
WYOMING
The Bad Men of Brown's Hole
BROWN'S HOLE
Diamond Mountain
Great Diamond Fields
to Rock Springs
to Rock Springs
318
Site of old Fort Davy Crockett
Lodore Canyon
Snake River Gold
318
MAYBELL
DINOSAUR NATIONAL MONUMENT
PATSHOLE
The Treasure of Pat's Hole
40
ARTESIA
64
COLORADO
UTAH
Dinosaur Headquarters
VERNAL
44

stance to search for the loot. There is another such tale of the Wild Bunch leaving some loot around the old town of Alma, New Mexico, another gang hideout for a time.

As with many another bandit gang in the west, stories of hidden and uncollected loot followed in the wake of the Cassidy gang. Generally, it would follow that if a gang worked so hard to get it, they wouldn't care to leave it behind. But anything's possible.

Things got a little too hot for Butch after the turn of the century and he skipped the country. He was next heard from in South America, following the same line of "work" he followed here. He was reportedly killed at San Vicente, Bolivia, in 1909, although many people in the west couldn't believe the news.

There were reports throughout the west, long after 1909, that Butch was seen in one of his haunts or another.

Brown's Hole legend doesn't stop with Butch Cassidy. It grows here in profusion, setting the tone of the whole region. Not very far away in Wyoming was the setting for the Famous Lost Cabin Mine, and just south of Brown's Hole, in Colorado, was the site of the Great Diamond Fields, one of the west's greatest tales.

Another story in Addendum, p. 281.

43. THE GREAT DIAMOND FIELDS

Rumors of the great field where vast deposits of diamonds, rubies, emeralds, sapphires and other precious gems lay scattered around preceded its discovery by several months.

The rumors started in 1872. Nobody was sure where they came from, who started them . . . just a rumor here, a vague report of a finding there. And soon the west was ablaze with the story.

The precise location of the treasure field was not known. It was always some remote spot far from civilization.

The first general location to emerge was northeastern Arizona. It was a logical beginning. Just three years before the report flashed around the west that Major J. Cory French, agent for the Navajo Indians, had found large quantities of diamonds and rubies scattered over the surface of the ground near the pueblos of the Moquis, about 300 miles from Santa Fe.

Shortly after this location was named, a man known as Phil

Arnold, a stranger in town, was interviewed by the editor of the *Laramie City Sentinel.* From this interview the fantastic story begins. Arnold's words electrified the country, caused an excited new burst of westward migration, disrupted the financial structure around the world, and . . . well, a few other things.

Arnold announced himself to be the discoverer of wealth in precious stones "which surpassed the wildest extravagances of the Arabian tale of Aladdin and the wonderful lamp." He said some Indians had shown him two large, rough diamonds three years before and then guided him to the spot where they were found. He had been accompanied by an old California miner named Captain Slack.

Arnold said he and Slack had worked the diamond fields for two full years, keeping their work strictly secret. Eventually, however, they figured the operation was too big for two men alone and took on two other Californians as partners. The newcomers, Arnold said, mined their claim for only thirty days and took out what they estimated to be two and one-half million dollars in precious gems. Arnold related that the two men had deposited about half of their store in the Bank of California.

Arnold said the largest diamond he had found to date in the fields weighed 108 carats, for which, although it was uncut and unpolished, he was offered $96,000.

Arnold divulged the fact eventually that his was not a haphazard operation, that through carefully channeled negotiations he had formed a company with himself at the head and some of the wealthiest men in the country in the organization. Some of the names he mentioned were the Rothchilds, General McClennan, S. L. M. Barlow, and others known to be some of the richest men in New York and San Francisco. When these great men had satisfied themselves as to the genuineness of the precious stones, two and one-half million dollars in stock had been issued and quickly sold. Three thousand acres of land had been surveyed and claimed as the property of the corporation. Since the west and particularly northeastern Arizona was already being overrun by diamond hunters, Arnold said he had hired 100 men in San Francisco who were due soon to stand guard over the claim.

Arnold was reluctant to pinpoint the diamond field, but the *Sentinel* editor indicated that remarks made in the interview led him to believe that the rich field was on Flax Creek in the San Luis Valley (in Colorado or New Mexico).

Arnold indicated that the corporation's claim by no means covered the entire diamond area. In fact, Arnold surmised that a much larger area was involved and a richer claim than his might well be found there.

The story published in the *Sentinel* was picked up in newspapers throughout the country, creating a flash of excitement throughout this broad land equal to, if not surpassing, that of the California gold discovery and the Colorado gold rush in 1859. The original story was followed almost daily with wild reports of other discoveries, some so fantastic as to try a person's credulity.

Every social level was involved in the excitement and the wagon trains poured forth from the east. Diamond stocks couldn't be printed fast enough to keep up with the demand.

Along with the daily stories of new finds there were a few stories charging Arnold and his ilk with fraud. William N. Byers, erstwhile editor of the *Rocky Mountain News,* went so far as to claim the excitement was a result of nothing more than a carefully planned and skillfully carried-out swindle.

Such journalistic warnings were much like washing windows in a dust storm, however. Many more people believed the claims of important people, including millionaires and public officials—the attorney general of the United States, a member of the cabinet, several senators and a former governor of Colorado.

Late in 1872 an event occurred that removed all doubt as to the truth of the diamond fields. A man named Crossman, a resident of Chicago, came to Denver from New Mexico. He said he traveled through the diamond field and took the liberty of picking up a sample. He produced a rather large, although rough, stone and allowed it to be examined by a Denver lapidary, who pronounced it genuine and valued at about $5,000. The stone was forthwith sent to Chicago and the windy city's top jewelers supported the original finding except to estimate the value of the stone at $8,000.

Other stones were produced and were likewise pronounced real. Some went on display in Denver.

But for the remainder of 1872, nobody got any closer to the fantastic fields. In fact, their location, which had never been pinpointed by any of the men involved, began to change.

It shifted from Arizona, as originally believed, to the San Luis Valley of Colorado, as suggested by the editor of the *Sentinel,* down to northern New Mexico, and then again back up to Colorado, the southwestern part. Another report brought a new rush to the old town of Shakespeare, in southwestern New Mexico.

Armed men and crazed prospectors chased the elusive field wherever it went. And while the frantic search continued, speculation was just as frantic. The San Francisco and New York diamond corporation had quickly sold its two and a half million dollars in stock and was hard-pressed to issue more to meet the demand. The rich and the poor wanted in on it. Haphazard and fly-by-night diamond companies were formed, the stock was instantly sold out, operators made fortunes . . . and often flew the coop. Inflated prices were offered, and usually accepted, for any unusual-looking stone that came along. A report was circulated that a large sale of the diamonds was transacted in London. Another report got around that the New York-San Francisco company had already brought in a large force of Central American Negroes and Mexican peons to work the fields, because they were afraid to use local miners. Ex-Governor Gilpin delivered a lecture to a sell-out crowd in Denver, tracing the geological formation of the Rocky Mountains, demonstrating how it was only natural that this formation should produce precious stones and that through the geological processes it followed that the richest deposits were naturally in the Colorado Rockies. Specifically, he named the San Juan mountains of southwestern Colorado as the logical habitat of the precious stones. Thus, for awhile, the location of the fields switched to the San Juans.

This location was verified a few days later when a letter was received in Denver from a citizen of Fort Angelo, Colorado, who said the community was greatly excited over the visit of a Dr. Wallens and party who had just come from the diamond fields—in the San Juans—and who carried two gunny sacks full of rubies and sapphires and lesser emeralds.

About the same time—December of 1872—a Captain John Moss of California said he had traveled through the fields and that a man could pick up gems worth up to $5,000 in one day. He said he had talked to two men who realized $30,000 in two days' work. He also reported that he was in Santa Fe when an expert from Tiffany's in New York pronounced a ruby found in the fields as worth a quarter of a million dollars.

Then, things came to a head—it couldn't go on forever.

About the time the New York-San Francisco company was preparing another stock issue of twelve million dollars, a report appeared in a San Francisco newspaper. The report was by Clarence King, an eminent geologist. He said he had had occasion to examine some of the gems and that he doubted their value and that he placed a question mark upon the whole setup.

The diamond titans were taken aback. They hired another expert, Henry Janin, to verify the richness of the fields. The tour was conducted by Arnold and Slack, the original discoverers. They took Janin not to Arizona, nor northern New Mexico, nor the San Luis Valley, nor the San Juans in Colorado, but to an isolated spot just south of Brown's Hole in the extreme northwestern corner of Colorado on the Colorado-Utah border. (The site is sometimes put across the line in Utah.)

Arnold and Slack led Janin through the fields, and sure enough, Janin found several stones peeking through the surface. He returned to San Francisco, verified the genuineness of the stones, and claimed, for all the world to hear, that the story of the diamond fields was true. He concluded his published report by saying that, in his opinion, any investment in the stock at forty dollars per share, or at the rate of four million dollars for the entire property was a safe and attractive one.

For his services, Janin was paid a generous sum and allowed to buy a large block of stock at only ten dollars per share, which he promptly turned around and sold for forty dollars each. For his short stint he realized more than $30,000.

But, despite Janin's report, more and more experts began to raise doubts. The corporation leaders, now becoming a little wary, let out some more stock, but carefully, and they endeavored to get more verification on the fields. In the next few weeks, other experts journeyed to the site. Some reports verified the initial report, others were vague.

King, however, was not satisfied. In fact, after examining some more of the gems, he became more and more unhappy. Finally, he decided that there was no other way to rest easy than to go and see for himself.

Janin accompanied King on the jaunt, and the jaunt was a jolt.

Through careful examination and some mature deduction, King became convinced that what gems there were in the fields had been planted there, and that Janin had been duped by being led over just the right trail by Arnold and Slack so that he would find the right precious stones.

The diamond world came tumbling down with King's return to San Francisco. The corporation manipulators attempted to suppress the report as long as possible to give them time to unload as much of their investment as they could.

But the real clincher came in the case with published reports from London which said two men named Buchanan and Arundell had made several purchases from various London jewelers. The purchases consisted of a good many rough, uncut, sometimes impure, and scrap stones, used by jewelers for cheap rings and bracelets and other related uses. The men, it turned out, purchased a few fairly good stones, too.

The bursting of the bubble, for a short while, was as ferocious as its inflation. Millions of dollars were lost . . . from the major manipulators on down to the penny-pinching small stockholder. One of the manipulators committed suicide, others were ruined. Janin's reputation fell to zero.

Curiously enough, most of the wrath fell on the big manipulators. The original perpetrators, Arnold and Slack, were almost forgotten. Since they had planned everything else so well, it only follows that they planned this, too. It was estimated that they had cleared over a half million dollars on the deal.

And while all the diamond capitalists were falling and the fury fell upon them, Arnold and Slack silently stole away. Arnold turned up at his home in Elizabethtown, Kentucky, shortly before his death in 1879.

Nobody ever heard of Slack again.

44. TREASURE OF PAT'S HOLE

A Uintah Indian told the story to prospector Pete Madison.

The Indian said two miners once spent the winter in the isolated Pat's Hole region of Dinosaur. The two men worked the entire winter in spite of the snow, to prepare for an all-out mining venture the following spring, and to accumulate enough gold dust to buy supplies.

As spring neared they began to run out of supplies so they decided to take the rest of the winter off and run into Salt Lake for the necessary food and equipment. They had accumulated about twenty-five pounds of gold and they loaded it into their knapsacks and set off.

Just after they crossed the Utah line, however, they were set upon by a band of outlaws. The miners put up a gallant battle but were eventually done in. The bandits were disappointed at the small take, but they dutifully covered the evidence of their crime, burying the miners in a shallow grave near a ledge of rocks.

Madison checked into the story and after a long search he found the bodies of the miners. He was less lucky in Pat's Hole. He searched now and again for quite a while but never did find the workings of the two men. It's quite possible that they obscured the workings to prevent it being found while they were gone.

Pat Lynch, the longtime hermit of Pat's Hole, knew the area better than anybody. There was no evidence that he ever found any gold, but, then, maybe he wasn't looking for it.

45. SNAKE RIVER GOLD

During the Civil War a party of government engineers, teamsters, packers and guards were engaged in defining, with monuments, the 41st parallel, that later became the boundary line between Colorado and Wyoming.

One evening the party camped on the headwaters of the Snake River. One of the party found peculiar-looking float that sparkled with a wealth of various colored minerals. However, none of the party was expert in things of that sort and since the nearest assay office was hundreds of miles away, there was nothing the finder could do but throw the stone in among his souvenirs and forget about it.

About a year and a half later, after the party had returned to

Washington, a member of the party ran across the ore quite by accident, and had it assayed just for a lark.

The assay showed it contained about 1,600 ounces of silver per ton, with some good gold and copper. The owner thought such ore was well worth another trip out, after the war.

It just so happened, however, that the finder was killed while serving in the army on the Potomac.

But after the war, a friend rounded up two more men and set out with only a vague idea of where the float was found. To add to their problems, the Indians were riled up at the time and the men had to keep on the alert for them. The area was a source of dispute between the Shoshones, Blackfeet and Sioux to the north and the Utes and Arapahoes of the south.

The three-man party soon realized they couldn't find the place themselves, so they hired old scout Jim Baker. They searched the area off and on for several years but didn't have any luck. Finally they gave a sample of the float to Baker and told him to keep on looking and if he discovered anything to let them know in Washington.

Baker kept the sample with him to the end of his long and active life. Whenever he was in the neighborhood of the Colorado-Wyoming border he spent some time looking for similar-looking rock, but he never found it. It became just another lost mine that the famous scout knew about.

It's possible the location was found in later years as there were some workings on or near the headwaters of the Snake. If this particular location was ever found we can only guess.

46. JIM BAKER'S LOST MINE

One of the greatest mountain men of them all, Jim Baker, was a great story teller as well. He had many lost mine stories, but history notes that he was never corrupted by the possession of much of the shining stuff.

One of his favorite stories concerns a fabulously wealthy mine lying somewhere between Steamboat Springs and Hahn's Peak in northern Colorado.

Jim Baker, one of the west's greatest scouts, had his share of mine tales. *Denver Public Library Western Collection.*

He said a piece of gold float was given him by a group of 49ers heading for California. They told Baker that they were in too big a hurry to reach California to dilly-dally making a fortune in Colorado.

The 49ers said the float was found on the range of mountains south of Hahn's Peak, a certain distance up a hill from "the broken hands of a wagon."

Baker found the broken hands of the wagon but never found the outcroppings. He said there was evidence of rockslides on the hill and they might have covered up the spot.

Baker said he spent a lot of time looking for the gold which he claimed would have been "one of the great mines of the world."

But we wonder how hard he looked—he was so busy being a mountain man.

47. THE ELK CREEK TREASURE

In the spring of 1866, at the time of the Hahn's Peak excitement of northern Colorado, a party of four prospectors set off from Alma to the New Eldorado. They traveled through wild, uncharted territory, full of hostile Indians.

One day they stopped and unpacked the burros for dinner on a small creek, a tributary of Bear Creek. One panned the creek just to keep in practice. He found some gold. He traced it to a small dry gulch a short distance above their camp. They followed it to the source, a rim of rock crossing the gulch.

They dug a hole in the bedrock and found very rich gravel. The four forgot dinner and began mining.

They cut two cottonwood forks and an alder pole, the latter being held up by the forks. The forks were propped against a prominent ledge of rocks on the banks of the river. Over the frame they stretched a wagon-sheet.

That was just about all they had time to do.

Just before sundown a band of about twenty Utes, led by Colorow, rode down on the camp. Colorow killed all the animals and took the men prisoners. After taking possession of everything the men had, he marched the four to the Continental Divide and

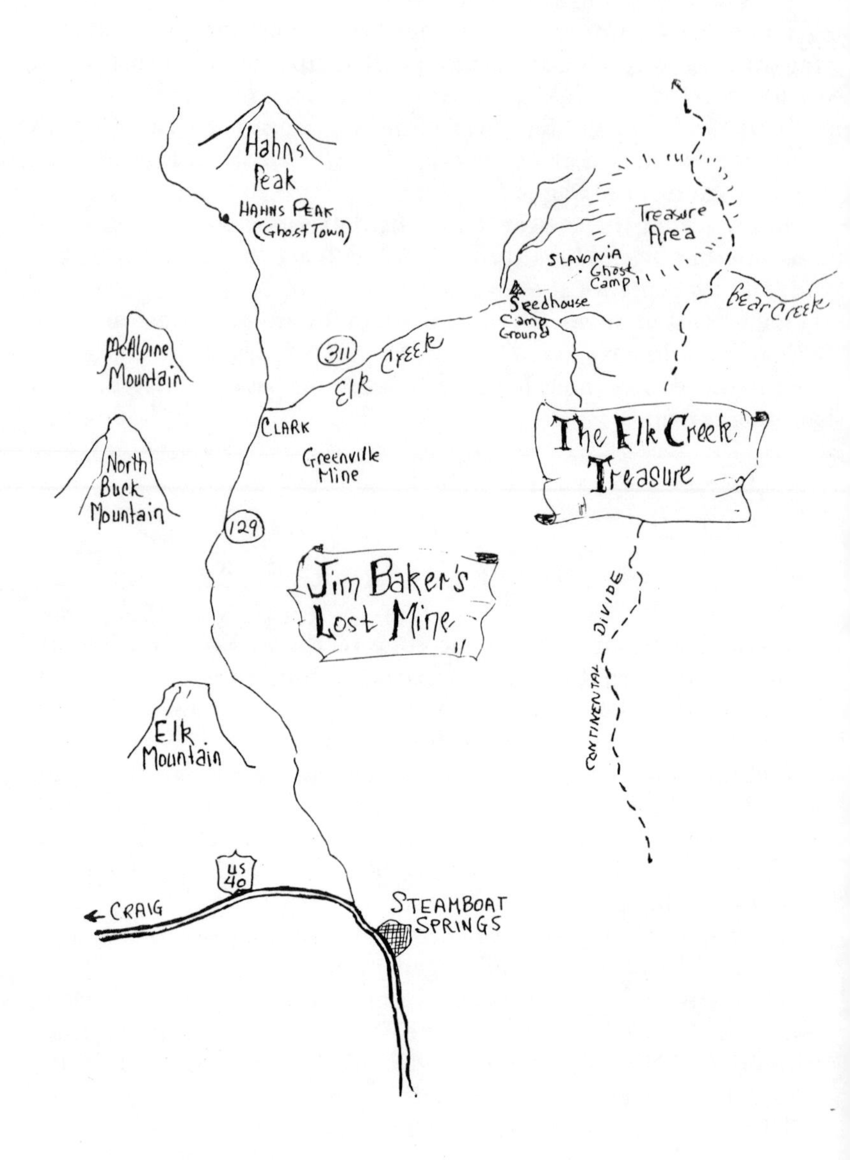
Hahns Peak
HAHNS PEAK (Ghost Town)
McAlpine Mountain
North Buck Mountain
Elk Mountain
311
ELK CREEK
CLARK
Greenville Mine
129
Jim Baker's Lost Mine
Treasure Area
SLAVONIA Ghost Camp
Seedhouse Camp Ground
BEAR CREEK
The Elk Creek Treasure
CONTINENTAL DIVIDE
US 40
← CRAIG
STEAMBOAT SPRINGS

told them to go and never come back if they valued their scalps.

The four made their way to Laramie where two of them were killed in a gambling quarrel. The other two drifted to Denver where one took sick and died.

The last survivor, a Frenchman, finally wound up in New Mexico, where he told one and all of "his" lost mine. He finally talked himself into another expedition.

The Frenchman said, besides their makeshift shelter, the site was marked by an old hickory rifle cleaning rod, left by the original party. He estimated the site as about ten miles east of Hahn's Peak, near the Divide and on the headwaters of the Elk River.

The problem was that the second expedition set out in 1879, the year of the big Indian scare in Colorado. Colorow was the leading figure in the scare. He set fire to many of the forests in the north-central section of the state. Most of the landmarks and trails were burned beyond recognition. The Frenchman found what he believed was a site of one of the camps of the original expedition, but look as he might, he never found the final camp, and the mine.

The party searched through the summer and finally gave up, all except old prospector "Pony" Whitmore. Pony, who told the story, searched for the mine until his death in 1884. The story may or may not be true, but Pony believed it, and Pony was real. His grave is marker number three in the Steamboat Springs cemetery.

X. *GORE RANGE GOLD*

48. OLD FRYING PAN GOLD

This is another one about a lost mine in the Gore Range. The story is told by W. A. Scott, a long-time Colorado prospector, one of the very many who found exactly nothing.

He joined the thousands of wandering silver miners thrown out of work by the panic of 1893. With him was "Gold Pan" Jake, one of the first to wash gold in California Gulch back in 1860. The two were wandering aimlessly. They crossed over Tennessee Pass, heading north, but with no particular destination.

The second night out they made camp on the Eagle River near the site of Wolcott. They finished their supper and sat back to enjoy their pipes when a stranger wandered into camp.

After a few pleasantries the stranger told them about the lost mine. In the fall of 1876, he said, he was a freighter in Breckenridge. One night a man came in with two burros carrying four sacks of ore which sampled "up in the thousands."

The whole town became excited about the gold. They surrounded the finder with questions and made many offers to buy into the lode. He would only say he found it near Rabbit Ears. He said he was going to his home and would return in the spring. Maybe, then, he would tell them where it was.

By the following spring a number of prospectors were loaded up, waiting for the stranger to come and lead them to their fortune. But—and naturally—the stranger never showed up. When the loaded-up prospectors were tired of waiting, they set out for Rabbit Ears on their own. They never found the rich lode, nor had anyone else found it up to that time.

After the story was told and after the stranger had left, Scott and Gold Pan Jake decided they might as well join the army of men that sought the Rabbit Ears gold.

Scott and Jake set out the next day—this time with a destination. They were headed over the range to the headwaters of the Muddy, a short distance from Rabbit Ears. The next day they made camp over the crest of the range on Grizzly Creek. They looked over the area and eventually found evidence of some long ago placer workings, a dilapidated cabin, a decaying sluice box. Nearby they also found a trace of yellow metal. The following day they followed up the find, searching for the source. About noon, they stopped for lunch in a small cleft of rocks cut into the side of the canyon.

While they were eating they noticed a place above them where the bank had broken away. On closer inspection they found evidence of earlier work, some digging and some quartz piled up. They cut into the wall with their picks and soon came to a solid formation and exposed a well-defined crevice containing about eighteen inches of the same quartz that had been piled up on the bank.

They were positive it was the same kind of quartz which had been brought to Breckenridge nearly thirty years before.

The ore seemed thoroughly oxidized and decomposed and no gold was visible. But they were sure it was there.

They gathered up the best samples and took them back to camp to test. They crushed it and washed it . . . but found no gold, only a few grains of black sand. They tried all the samples with the same results.

They were both disgusted . . . so disgusted they didn't say anything for the rest of the day.

However, the next day, Scott woke up with new heart. He realized that a fortune can't be found in a day. He set out to continue the search while Gold Pan Jake moodily lolled around at camp.

Scott looked all day with no luck. He returned to camp about 3 o'clock in the afternoon to find Jake talking to another prospector.

Jake was telling the prospector their sad story and showing him a couple of samples. The prospector looked the samples over carefully and said they looked good. Scott and Jake told him the samples looked good to them, too, but didn't test out good.

"Why not try roasting it?" the prospector said.

Scott said the ore was too thoroughly oxidized already and only required panning. The prospector said that was a mistake. He said that about half the ore that looks oxidized, isn't.

Scott and Jake were willing to try anything so they roasted the ore according to the prospector's directions.

He told them to pulverize the ore, then to moisten it thoroughly with diluted sulphuric acid, and then place it on a hot fire and keep dampening it and adding salt.

After it was completely roasted, they took the solution to the river and panned it.

To their amazement there were some sure signs of tellurium at the bottom of their pan. Tellurium is a rare metal which often contains gold and/or silver.

The prospector asked them if they had staked their claim. Jake lied and said they had.

So then the prospector took them to the frying pan in which they had roasted the samples. The roasting had not only roasted off all the scum on the pan but had seared off part of the pan's original surface.

That was their tellurium.

The prospector chuckled to himself and was guffawing loudly as he headed off.

Scott and Jake were stunned.

All they had to show for their trouble was a clean frying pan.

49. GORE RANGE GOLD

The Gore Range is an ideal setting for lost mine stories. The country is cut from a tedious pattern. Heavy evergreen and undergrowth cover the area, landmarks are few, and one moun-

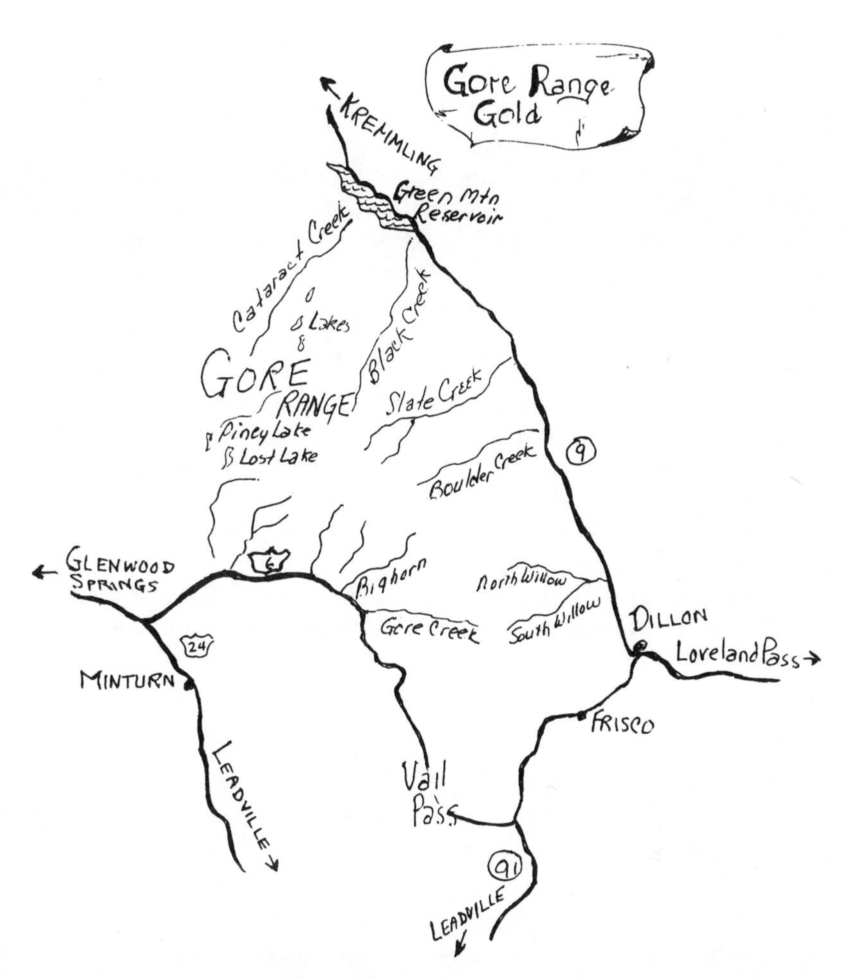

tain, one gulch, one clearing is twin to the one nearby, and the high mountains are very rugged and there are many rock slides.

The range is named for Sir George Gore, whose fabulous hunting train camped here during his two-year hunting trip in the middle 1850's. The Irish nobleman led a party of fifty including secretaries, stewards, cooks, fly-makers, dog-tenders, and so on. His wagon was fitted out similar to a Pullman car and included a well-stocked wine cellar. Gore hunted alone from 10 A.M. until dark, although he employed some of his help to chase game his way.

He bathed after each hunt. He spent many an evening reading

Shakespeare or the Bible to his guide, Jim Bridger. Bridger, one of Colorado's most colorful mountain men, could neither read nor write, but they said he enjoyed Shakespeare although he doubted some Bible stories.

The chronicler of the expedition claimed Gore killed forty grizzlies, 2,500 buffalo, dozens of elk, deer and antelope, plus large quantities of small game. After the hunt, Gore attempted to sell his outfit, but eventually became so fed up with efforts of buyers to cheat him, he dumped the whole thing in the Missouri River.

The first stories of lost gold in the Gore Range came from this expedition. Louis Dapron, foreman of the expedition, reported that a member of the party found gold near the camp one day. On seeing the gold, Gore ordered Dapron to break camp immediately and move on, saying:

"This is gold but I did not come here to seek gold! I don't need it. This is a pleasure trip."

After the hunting trip, Dapron returned to the Gore Range to search for the spot again. After several futile assaults on the range he gave up the search.

Indian Gold in the Gore Range

Stories of Indian gold in the Gore Range began circulating shortly after the Gore expedition.

Early settlers in the area reported that the Ute Indians often brought gold ore down from the mountains to sell to traders for sugar, coffee and tobacco. A well-known Middle Park pioneer named King reported trading a pound of sugar for two pounds of gold ore.

The Indians were always asked where they found the gold and they would always point vaguely toward the mysterious mountains of the Gore Range. Many men attempted to follow them back to the source of their treasure, but one can't follow an Indian in the mountains. Many men searched the Gore Range for the Indian gold, but none found it.

Perhaps the Indian gold was from the Golden Ledge of the Gore Range. In fact, most or all of the stories of the lost ledge in the range may be about the same thing. Most of the stories tell of a ledge of similar appearance, but they are recorded separately. We will tell them separately, keeping in mind, however, that they may all be about the same lost gold mine.

The Lem Pollard Story

During the early years of Colorado territory, General Bela M. Hughes traveled through the Gore Range in search of a shortcut through the mountains to Salt Lake City.

Along on the trip was a youngster named Lem Pollard. One evening, while out hunting, the boy ran across some "pretty" rock. He chipped off a piece of it as a souvenir.

Treasuring the rock for its beauty more than anything else, Lem carried it around for several years, until someone noticed it was gold ore.

After Lem discovered he had been carrying gold around all these years, he went back and tried to find its source. But too much time had passed, his memory played tricks on him, and so did the Gore Range.

Lem took time out from his search to become clerk of Grand County. He stayed clerk for several years. The old timers around there knew that if old Lem wasn't clerking he was out searching the Gore Range for some long-lost gold.

The Hill Story

In the 1870s, a trapper named Hill stumbled down out of the mountains, with a bad case of "mountain sickness" and some samples of gold ore.

He died a short time later, but before he headed west, he told his friends his story.

He said he was camped at the head of Morrison Creek. Near here, one day, he accidentally stumbled on an immense ledge of free gold which cropped for some distance above the surface of the ground. He attempted to tell the location as closely as he could.

After Hill's death, the ore was assayed and measured $15,000 to $20,000 in gold per ton.

The men attempted to find the source after that, but the directions were too vague and they were unable to find the ledge. They searched for it off and on for several years without any luck.

In 1879, their search was complicated by the landmark-erasing fire.

The Franz Story

This one was told by George Franz of Clark in the late 1930s. Franz prospected through northern Colorado for some fifty years. But before he ever came to Colorado he had heard of the Lost Golden Ledge in the Gore Range. He read about it in the *San Francisco Examiner* in the 1870s. The story was one of the attractions Franz found in Colorado.

The newspaper story told of a man who left Georgetown, bound for Salt Lake City.

He had camped his first night out under a protective ledge in the Gore Range. The ledge sparkled strangely in the light of his fire. The next morning he investigated and found that the ledge contained gold.

The man broke off several samples and continued on his way. In Salt Lake City, the ore was assayed and showed $10,000 in gold per ton. The man continued to San Francisco with every intention of hurrying back to the Gore Range. But in San Francisco, he had a stroke and was unable to return. However, he drew a detailed map for two friends.

The two men journeyed to Colorado only to find that most of the landmarks in the Gore Range were destroyed by a fire set in 1879 by Colorow and his band of Ute renegades. One of the map landmarks was the cabin of Charlie Nieman, long-time sheriff of Hahn's Peak.

Nieman's cabin had been destroyed in the fire.

The John La Foe Story

This story comes from the gold fields of Nevada. It is told by John La Foe.

La Foe says he and a party set out from Cripple Creek around the turn of the century. While camping in the Gore Range, they found good free gold. But before they had time to get a mining camp set up, it began to snow. The men were forced to move on. They wound up in Nevada where they became involved in various enterprises, became rich, and did not feel the need of coming back.

However, they sent a detailed map of the gold's location to friends in Colorado. The Colorado friends searched long and hard for the gold, but found nary a sliver.

The Horace Pullen Story

In 1896, Horace Pullen, originally of Council Bluffs, Iowa, was hunting in the Gore Range.

He got a good bead on a deer and let fire from his rifle. He winged the animal but it ran off. Pullen chased the wounded deer for several miles. He didn't get a second shot, but he did soon discover that he was very much lost.

While trying to find his way back to his cabin, he stumbled on an outcropping of "peculiar looking" rock. Pullen had no knowledge of minerals but he was struck by the peculiar beauty of the rock and couldn't help noticing its difference from its surroundings.

He chipped off a few samples, but since it was getting dark, he didn't make camp here but hurried on his way.

He finally found his way out of the Gore Range and returned shortly thereafter to Denver. Here, he showed the rock samples to some friends who saw immediately that it looked like gold ore. Pullen had the rocks assayed and they showed about $17,000 gold to the ton.

Pullen hurried back to the Gore Range, but he was only able to search a few days before it began to snow. He set out as early as possible the following spring and searched, and searched and searched. He even tried to get himself lost again, but he couldn't find the gold.

Finally, in desperation he went down to Toponas and organized a party of surveyors. They began at the edge of the area and ran lines across at every 200 feet, although the region was densely wooded. By 200-foot sections, they combed several miles of the range—to no avail.

Even later, Pullen hired experienced prospectors and again he combed the area.

All in all, he spent several hundred dollars and several summers in the search, but didn't find a thing.

50. THE RABBIT EARS TREASURE

In 1947, young Bill Keplinger and his father went fishing in northern Colorado. Like many a fisherman they sought an isolated stream, unpopulated by fellow sportsmen. A short distance off Highway 40 on Walton Creek they came to a narrow, almost inaccessible canyon. With some difficulty, the two men climbed through the canyon mouth. A short distance up the canyon they came to a small clearing beside the creek.

Here, they found evidence of ancient mining activity. There was a man-made ditch which at one time had extended nearly 100 feet, there were the ruins of an old cabin, a prospect hole here and there, and a few tree stumps.

They later told local authorities about their discovery. After further research into the matter, localites believed the workings were the twice-lost mine of George A. Jackson.

Shortly after Jackson's famous find on Clear Creek—that began the mining era of Idaho Springs—he took to the hills in search of greener and less populated pastures. Jackson and a companion entered Middle Park and crossed the range on the westward border. They found gold in Buffalo Park, but no water to sluice it and besides the Indians were threatening, so they continued on along the top of the range, panning on either slope. They kept to the high country to avoid Indians.

After several miles, still quite a distance from Rabbit Ears Peak, they panned a little gold in a tiny stream off the Yampa River. They followed the creek down about three or four miles when they came to a small sand bar which sparkled with gold.

Jackson said he could see Rabbit Ears Peak and judged it to be five or six miles away.

Jackson and his companion returned to Georgetown in the spring of 1868 and organized a party of ten men. As soon as the

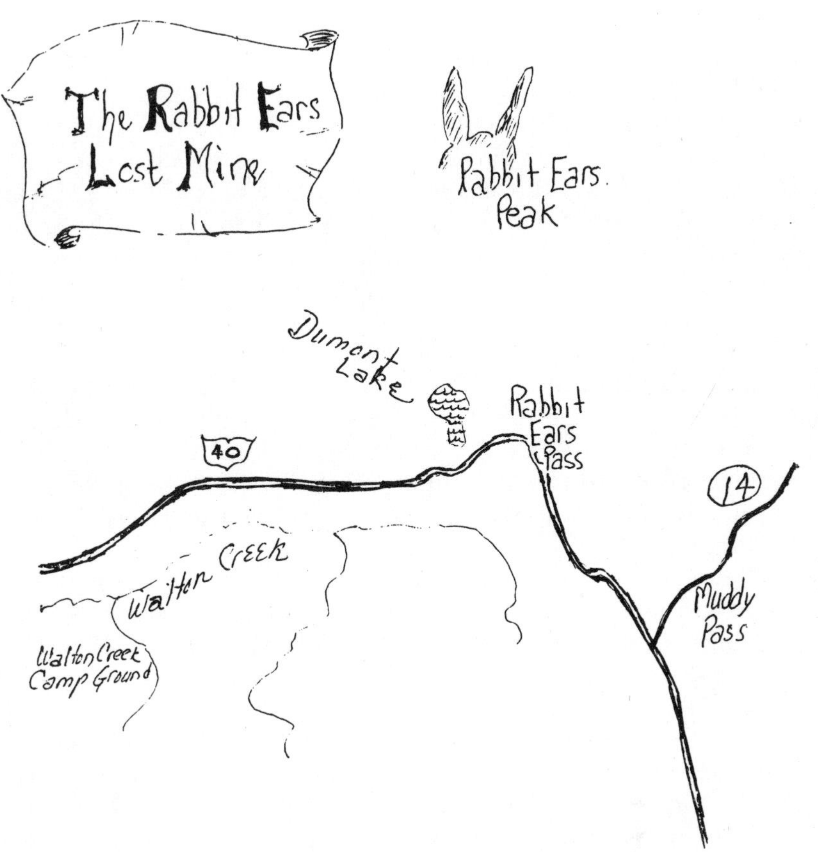

snow was off the range they returned. They built a cabin and a corral for animals. The men made a sluicing ditch about 200 or 300 feet long, whipsawed some lumber and made sluices. Jackson cut his name on a tree at the corner of the cabin.

The men worked here for about three weeks. In that time they mined between $9,000 and $10,000. They put it in buckskin bags and buried it in the corner of the cabin.

However, after three weeks when the men were just starting on another run, about 100 braves, led by the bad Injun Colorow, swooped down on them, separating the men from the cabin and horses. Two men were killed in the battle and another one was wounded so badly he died shortly after reaching civilization. The rest of the men scattered. Many of them were from Illinois and they kept on going . . . right back home.

As far as Jackson knew, he was the only man from the original party still around. Jackson was an adventurer and the Indians couldn't frighten him for long. Shortly after he had returned to Georgetown, he and another man he had taken on as partner, headed back to the diggings. But they hadn't traveled far when it began to snow. It continued to snow and Jackson and his partner were forced to turn back, after deciding to head out again as early as possible the coming spring.

But, alas, that was the winter Jackson accidentally shot and killed himself while pulling a rifle from his wagon to shoot a coyote.

His partner, however, thought he could still find the workings by what Jackson had told him. He set out in the spring. He arrived in the gold area only to find that Colorow had set a torch to much of the woodland around. All the landmarks were burned down. He searched long and hard, but couldn't find what he was looking for.

The man made another try as late as 1912, taking an oldtime guide with him. They did find some workings on Harrison Creek but didn't find a trace of gold about. They also found evidence of some gold on Walton Creek but hardly enough to make it worth their while. They finally gave up in disgust.

The mine was forgotten for several years until Rap Peck, former supervisor of Routt National Forest, ran across some old workings on Walton Creek. Peck was a great one for history, and since he knew of no mining in this area, his curiosity was aroused. His long search for an answer finally put him in contact with the former partner of Jackson, who was then living in San Francisco and was well along in years. The partner told Peck the story in a letter.

Peck returned to the scene and verified the fact that it was Jackson's old diggings. He even found the last three letters of Jackson's name carved in a burnt stump of a tree. Peck searched through the cabin thoroughly, however, and found only debris, no evidence of the buckskin bags and the gold.

Peck eventually lost interest in the workings and later moved to Grand Junction.

The workings were again forgotten until the Keplinger fishing trip in 1947. The Keplingers didn't find any gold either.

Perhaps, as many believe, one of Jackson's original party didn't return to Illinois after all, but came back for the gold instead. It wouldn't have been such a dirty trick. After all, that's what Jackson was planning to do.

51. LOST TREASURE ON SLATE MOUNTAIN

Some of the mass of humanity that answered the cry of "Gold in California" in 1849 drifted through Colorado enroute, sifting the waters and the sands for the precious metal.

One such party was from Illinois and was led by a man known in history as "Buck" Rogers. Their vigilance was rewarded by the discovery of good gold near Glenwood Springs. Some of the party were still too blinded by the glitter of California to tarry and they pushed on, but Rogers and five others remained.

They established what may well have been Colorado's first Yankee gold camp near their treasure spot. By wintertime, they had amassed between $60,000 to $100,000 in gold dust, storing it carefully, and continuing their work.

When provisions ran low the men drew straws to see who would go for supplies. Rogers won. He took $500 from the kitty and set off. It was a tortuous trip but he managed to get back to civilization all right. However, once there he celebrated with an extended binge rather than face the long, cold trek back.

After a few weeks of this his conscience began to gnaw him and he bought what supplies he could with what money he had left, and headed back into the mountains. When he finally arrived at the spot he discovered a huge snow and dirt slide had completely buried the camp—the men, the gold and all.

Rogers never recovered from the sight. He became a broken babbling drunk. In his wanderings he finally arrived in California a few years later, and there he told his story. Many didn't believe it. They called it the ramblings of a drunkard. But many others vouched for its truth. Scores of fortune hunters believed it enough to join the search. Some have even lost their lives in the quest.

Forty years after the original incident, a miner stumbled into the stage station run by Arthur H. Fulford, who also served as marshal of Redcliff.

The miner said Rogers kept notes on the ill-fated mining enterprise and the notebook fell into his hands after Rogers' death in California. The miner came to Colorado, and, following the notes in the notebook, soon found the snowslide area. After digging here and there for several days he finally came to a man-made tunnel where he found fragments of tools, human bones and pieces of ore, all thrown together by the slide.

The miner was sure he had found the right spot, so he covered up all evidence of his find and headed for Redcliff to get equipment and supplies.

He showed Fulford the ore samples to verify the tale. Since the miner was penniless, Fulford had little difficulty in persuading the old man to take him on as partner. They began to make plans for the mining expedition.

But before they could make the trip, the miner was shot and killed in a barroom brawl. Fulford searched the miner's cabin and

Landslide country at the head of Brush Creek in the Gore Range. This is the country in which Buck Roger's treasure is buried and in which many persons have seen the illusive gold ledge of Gore Range. *U.S. Geological Survey photo.*

found some evidence of where Slate Mountain was located. He set out for the mountain by himself.

But he never made it. He was reportedly killed in a snowslide on New Year's Day in 1892. His body was never found.

About ten years earlier, a prospector clumped into a Denver saloon and ordered drinks for the house, paying the tab in gold dust. The more he tippled the more he talked. Eventually, he confided to the bartender that he had discovered Slate Mountain.

A short time later the bartender became ill and in payment for the doctor's bill, he told the medic about the location of Slate Mountain.

The doctor was said to have searched for the mountain time and time again, but he never found it.

Directions for finding the treasured location are common knowledge around Glenwood Springs and Redcliff. Wild tales are told about where the directions came from. They may well be the figment of someone's imagination. Nonetheless, Slate Mountain is in the general neighborhood, so here are the directions:

"Go along Eagle River to the mouth of Brush Creek. Follow the creek five miles to the forks. Take east branch about five miles until you come to a shift of rocks coming almost to the water's edge. Follow dry gulch running north until you come to four large trees standing close together with the bark all taken off. About two feet around it, turn due east and go directly up the hill until you come to a small hole dug in the ground. Continue on until you come to another hole, and then a third hole. This line is also marked by blazed trees on both sides. From the third hole turn due north about 200 feet and from the last blazed tree you will see three tall trees standing in a triangle. The trees have their tops broken off about 30 feet up. This is about 300 feet from timberline, and the vein runs north and south on the place described."

XI. *OVER THE RANGE*

52. THE DISAPPEARING CLIFF

In 1890, Carbondale prospector Joseph Johns was hunting deer on nearby Muddy Creek when he came upon a small cliff, the side of which had been bared by a rock slide. Always the prospector, hunting or not, Johns climbed over the rock pile looking for mineral specimens on the mountain face.

After a short time Johns came upon a well-defined vein of what seemed to be very promising gold quartz. He chipped off several pieces until he had a full load. Then he staked his claim and headed home, not bothering to take too much notice of the surroundings. Since the cliff was by far the most dominant feature of the landscape, he was certain he would have no trouble locating it again.

On returning to civilization, Johns had the samples assayed and found the ore ran to $5,000 in gold per ton. A short time later, all rigged to dig his fortune, Johns returned to the scene of his strike—at least, what he thought was the scene of his strike.

It wasn't there, at least he couldn't find it.

Johns searched the entire area, carefully and desperately. No luck. He searched it again and again. By nightfall he was dead

tired and nearly out of his mind, but slowly the clear, crisp night air calmed him and he was able to plan a practical course of action.

To make a long story short, he searched methodically for the cliff the next day, and the next, and the next. . . .

After a couple of years, Johns took W. L. Girdner and B. B. Hills into his confidence. For the better part of twenty years the three of them tramped Muddy Creek and all the other creeks in the area looking for the cliff of gold. In 1911, when Johns was eighty years old, he made his last search for the cliff he had lost twenty years before.

Girdner and Hills searched long after that. There's no record of their ever finding it. Perhaps when they got too old to look any more someone else took up the search. Perhaps someone is still looking for the lost cliff on Muddy Creek.

53. LOST COPPER MINE ON MEADOW MOUNTAIN

Around the turn of the century, W. Porter Nelson returned to Aspen from Salt Lake City. He told of the "richest copper mine in the state" lost somewhere in the Crystal River Valley of Colorado.

Nelson said he met a man in Salt Lake who had prospected the Crystal River in the early '70s. Before the Indians chased him out of the valley he discovered a fabulous copper ledge. He said the ledge projected from a vein of great wealth of almost pure copper, with only a little gold and silver. The man told Nelson that the ledge was exposed by a giant landslide which ploughed a great gulch from high up on the side of the mountain, across a slope and down to the course of a small mountain stream. The stream had as its source a lake set in a cluster of cedars and aspen trees at the base of a particularly high mountain peak.

The fellow said the outcrop uncovered by the slide was located about 150 yards from the junction of the gulch and the stream, at a point about three-fourths of a mile from the lake.

Although the ledge showed almost pure copper, the man did not become particularly excited about it since copper wasn't worth so much at the time. At the turn of the century, however, copper had come into its own.

Nelson figured the ledge was probably on the southwesterly slopes of Snowmass Mountain at the upper end of Meadow Mountain near the head of Lost Trail Creek.

Nelson was looking for backing to finance a prospecting trip. He said he had promised the man in Salt Lake part of the profits if the mine was found.

There were some good copper properties which had been discovered a short time before on Meadow Mountain. The Lead King Mine was the best mine and was considered one of the best copper properties in the state at the time.

Perhaps the Lead King or some other mine was the lost mine known to the man in Salt Lake City. Or maybe the fabulous copper ledge hasn't been found yet. Perhaps it was covered over again by a later landslide.

All we know is that Nelson never found it.

54. THE ABANDONED MINE ON CONUNDRUM GULCH

During the 1880s, two men, owners of valuable property in Conundrum Gulch, between Aspen and Redstone, found themselves with nothing to do for an afternoon. Having never taken the time before, the two men decided to look around.

Climbing from Conundrum Gulch, they finally arrived at a ridge which separates Conundrum from Maroon Gulch. They looked down into beautiful Maroon Gulch and eventually their gaze fell upon what seemed to be a large cavern of unusual appearance.

They decided to investigate.

The nearer they got, the more the cavern took on the appearance of a man-made mine. It was. There were a slag pile and a

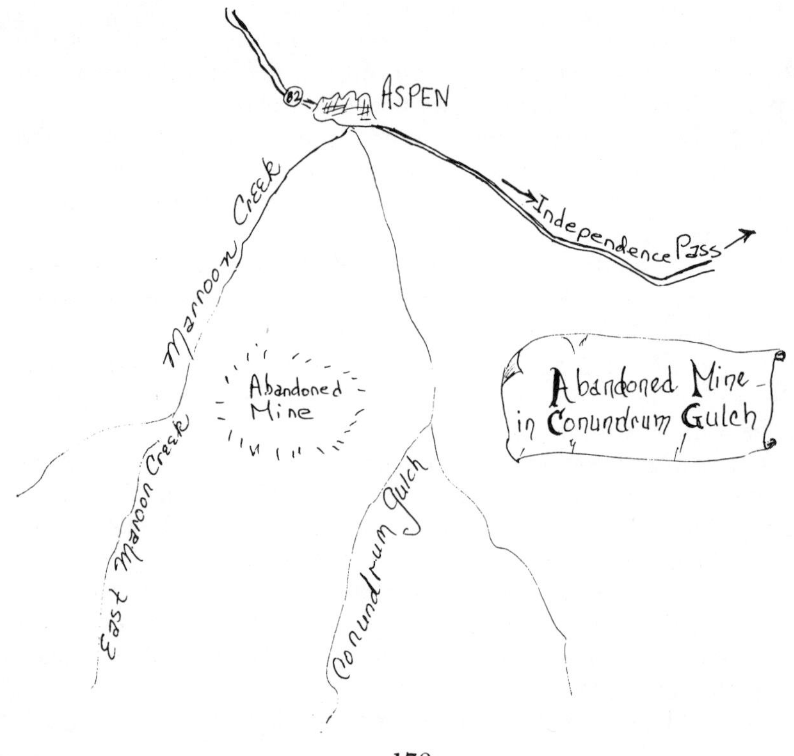

few old rusted tools lying around the entrance. There were several sacks full of ore within the shaft entrance.

The sacks were so rotten that they fell apart at the touch, but the ore was most promising.

The two men excitedly staked a claim to the property and immediately began making plans to take over and work the mine. The fortunate find they made was uppermost in their minds, but, even so, they did pause for a moment and wonder at the secrets the mine had to tell. Who, one day, had made the fabulous strike and spent his time working the mine?

And, above all, why would anybody abandon such promising property?

The two men never did find out.

There was no claim on the property and it did become a very valuable asset for the two finders.

55. THE TREASURE OF THE CEMENT CREEK CAVES

When Mother Nature leaves unfilled holes around in the Good Earth it's strange enough to begin with, and what she has done to these holes over the centuries adds to the strangeness. Ancient tribes, when not living in these caves, filled them with gods or legendary monsters. The legendary potential of these holes in the ground has continued down through time, but modern man, much more materialistic than his ancestors, has filled these caves with stories of treasure.

Almost any cave worthy of the name has some legend about it which concerns buried treasure.

The high mountains of Colorado are filled with caves. Spelunkers estimate that there are more than 70 caves in the state, but they would be the first to admit that many more might still be found. Only in recent years, led by the Colorado Grotto of the National Speological Society, have these Colorado caves begun to tell their stories.

A cave is defined as a hole deep or large enough so that a part of it is in complete darkness. The most, and the most interesting, caves are found in the Sangre de Cristos and in the Glenwood

Cement Creek caves and overhang. It may well have been these very "caves" inspected by the Denver scientific expedition nearly 100 years ago.

Springs area. There are other good caves here and there. But many of the stragglers do not qualify to be listed as caves. These are called "grottos." Some of Colorado's most interesting holes in legend are misnamed. For example, the Italian Caves near Julesburg and the Spanish Caves near Buckskin Joe are listed as grottos by the spelunkers.

Another group of grottos misnamed are the Cement Creek Caves. Time and water have worn many holes into the cliffs along the creek. Our story concerns itself with the deepest and best-known of these.

In the summer of 1883 a Denver committee was sent to visit the Cement Creek Caves in Gunnison County to look for fossils and mineral specimens for an upcoming exposition. Cement Creek empties into East River at a point about six miles south of Crested Butte. Its source is in a gulch through which passes the

Red Mountain Trail, one of the earliest and most used trails of the early prospectors. Newer highways were in wider use at this time, but Red Mountain Trail was still a busy highway between California Gulch north of the range and Washington Gulch on the southern side.

These particular caves are about a mile and a half from where Cement Creek and East River join. There were, and are, three entrances to the caves which open in the face of a cliff about 100 feet high.

Among the members of the committee were Pat Daly and Matt Hayden, who told the story of the treasure of the caves. They showed pure gold dust to prove their discovery.

The two large openings were all but inaccessable, but a smaller opening, on the eastern face of the cliff, was available to the group by climbing to the top and then down on a shelf.

Looking from a grotto on Cement Creek. *Photos taken by the Geological Survey in 1885.*

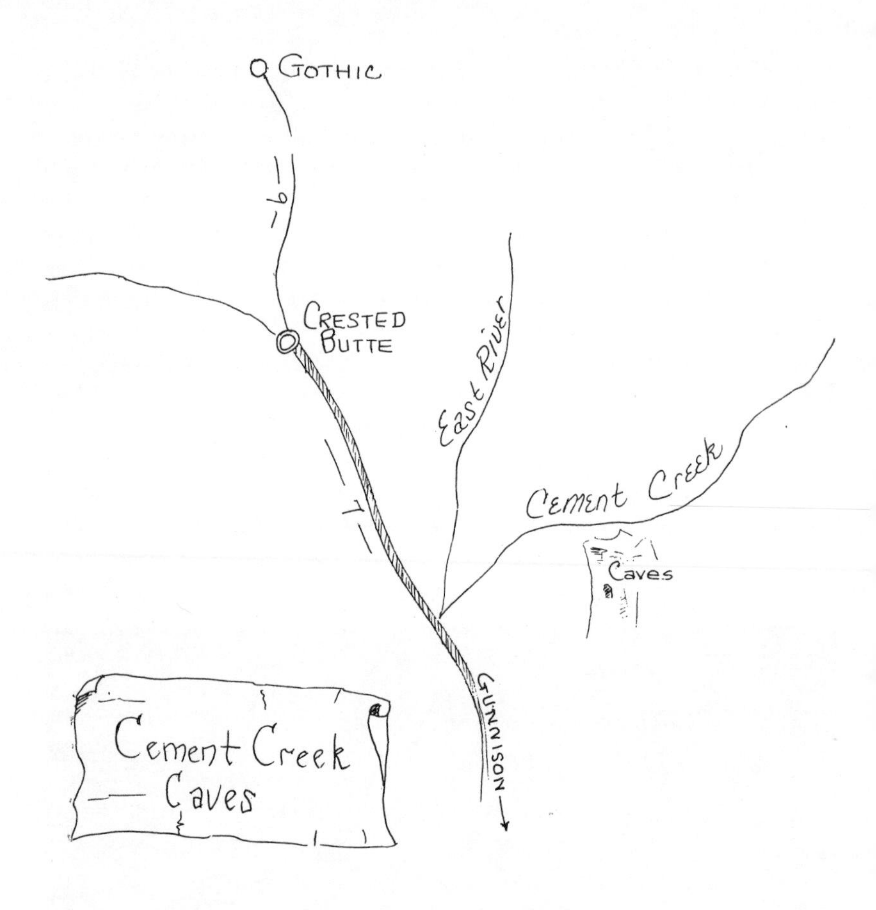

Making their way through a small passage, the investigators soon found themselves in a large vault which had apparently been a refuge for wild animals down through the centuries. The floor was thick with dust, excrement and bones.

Daly uncovered a small section of the floor with the drill he always carried with him. When he hit bottom, he gave it a couple of taps and heard a hollow sound. Supposing it to be the vault below, Daly thought little more about it.

The group decided to investigate another opening about fifty feet from the ground, but after shimmying around the cliff they found it was out of reach. Returning to their camp, however, Daly and Hayden decided to return alone with ropes and hooks and explore the other opening.

The next day Daly let Hayden down to the opening from the top of the cliff. The moment Hayden reached the cave, he let out a shriek, and called up to Daly, "For God's sake, come down here."

Daly let himself down in a hurry. There, near the entrance of the cave, was a skeleton of a man. Its bones were shriveled and some had been eaten by worms and rats. Water oozed from the side of the cave and over the ghastly scene.

When Daly and Hayden recovered from the sight, they looked further and found the floor around the opening strewn with pans, kettles, gold pans, picks and shovels, two or three cap and ball revolvers and two rifles.

They lit torches to search deeper. The floor of the cave seemed to go down while the roof remained level. Considerable slime from the water covered the passage, making traveling difficult. After about 150 feet they came to a wall. Feeling along the wall, they eventually felt a draft of fresh air and found a small opening about two feet in diameter. They worked their way through this, a distance of about ten to twelve feet. Daly pasted postage stamps at the end of the passage so they would be able to find it again.

There were two rooms adjoining the vault. The adventurers selected the one to the right, and after several more passages and leaving several more stamps, they found themselves in the same room they had been in the day before with the rest of the group.

They were about to make their way out of the cave when Daly remembered that the floor had seemed hollow and that this would be as good a time as any to discover why.

With little trouble he found the spot he had previously cleared and he scraped off a larger area around it. Eventually he discovered that the floor covering was actually a large gold pan turned bottom side up. The two men cleared all around it and then turned it over.

Under the pan was a doe skin cut to cover a hole in the floor. They lifted the skin and the sight startled them as much as had the skeleton guarding the entrance to the cave.

There was a small excavation filled with sparkling gold nuggets, gold dust and U.S. coins. At the top on one side of the opening was the picture of a beautiful girl who appeared to be of Mexican descent. On investigating the gold, they found that much of it had apparently been in buckskin bags and money belts that had rotted and turned to dust, or which finally fell to dust at their touch. The latest date on the U.S. coins was 1860.

The two men speculated that the caves were used as a hide-out for robbers, or one robber—the one found at the entrance—who preyed upon prospectors and miners traveling the Red Mountain Trail.

Daly and Hayden laid claim to their find and didn't share any of it with the other members of the committee.

56. THE LEGEND OF SNOWBLIND GULCH

The Legend kept men looking for gold in the Tomichi region all through the 60s and 70s and might be partially responsible for the good finds made around North Star and Tomichi, near the western foot of Monarch Pass.

According to the story two prospectors, off the beaten track, located some gold here in the early 1860s, years before other mining ventures in this area. The men carefully set up a long tom sluice and other equipment needed for mining. According to the legend they washed out a pound of gold per man per day.

But in their eagerness to take out as much gold as possible before winter set in, they remained here just a few days too long. Winter caught them on the way back and they became snowblind in the heavy snow, lost, and were killed by Indians.

Years later when gold was found in this region, evidence of early mining activity was found alongside a stream, including an old sluice box, flume and an old whip saw.

57. BURIED TREASURE ON ROUND HILL

There are two stories of buried treasure on Round Hill, about ten miles from Poncha Springs and two miles beyond Poncha Pass. They may be the same although it is doubtful. Enough people have believed both stories to mark up the hill with their digging.

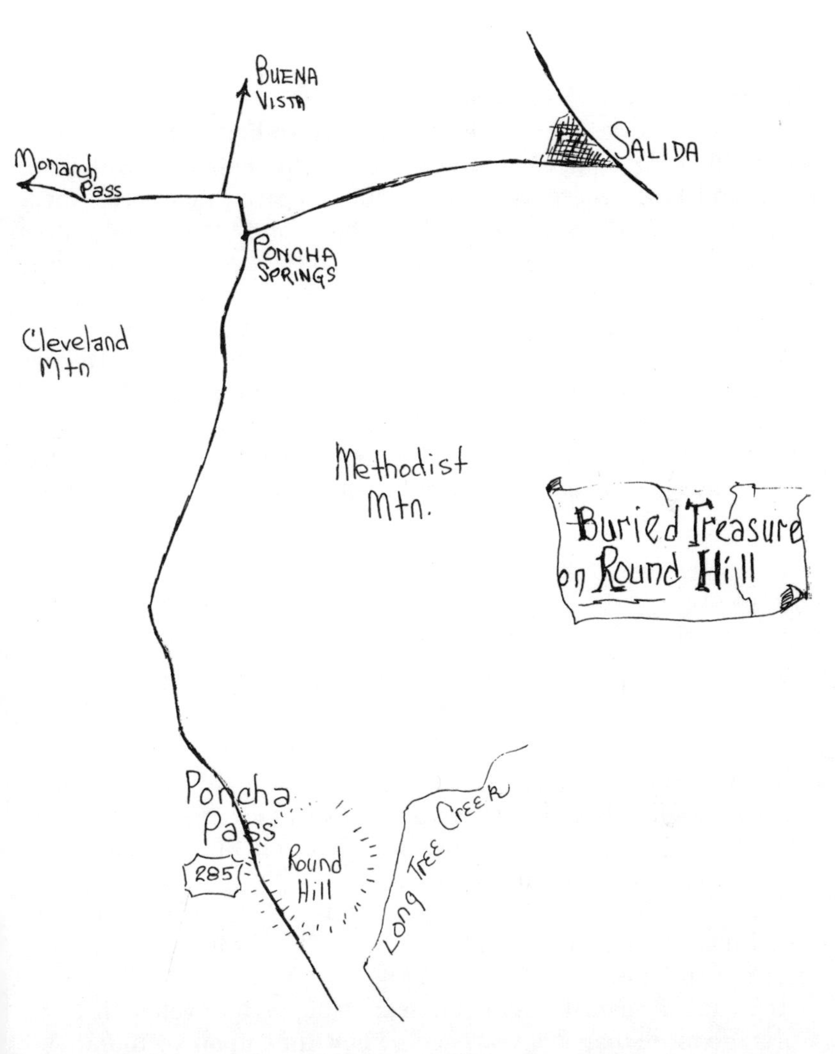

Local legend has it that a miner, many years ago, buried a donkey skin filled with gold dust on the hill. Some say he did so just to lighten his load and hurry on to civilization. Some say he just wanted to hide it so he would know where it was when he wanted it. Whichever the case, he never returned and the donkey skin full of gold is still there.

A more authenticated story concerns four miners who worked the San Luis neighborhood and who wandered off one day to make their own fortune. They made a good find—somewhere in the southwest. At the end of the mining season they headed back to Denver with a pack train loaded with gold.

But on the way they were attacked by Indians. Two of them were killed right off. The other two fought their way to the top of Round Hill, where they dug in and prepared themselves for a long siege. They put up a valiant fight and it was only after several hours of fighting that they decided the best thing to do was to hide their gold. Subsequently, one of the miners was killed and the other was desperately wounded and left for dead.

Despite his wounds, the last survivor made his way to Denver to die. Before he died, however, he told of the buried gold.

The story was printed as true in an 1877 *Rocky Mountain News* which said the rude fortification used by the two embattled miners was found near the summit of Round Hill . . . but no treasure.

58. THE SPANISH PRINCESS TREASURE ON MT. PRINCETON

They say it's only legend, but the people around Salida believe in it. Enough so that they take up the search now and again. They say a couple of people have lost their lives on the perilous chalk cliffs of Mt. Princeton in the quest.

The way they tell it, the treasure was well-known among the Spanish in Mexico years and years ago. The story drifted north with the Indians.

It seems a Spanish legion in search of gold traveled through Colorado more than 200 years ago. They came upon an Indian village while the braves were off hunting game. The conquistadores raided the teepees of all the valuable trinkets.

Shortly after they left the village, however, the braves returned and set out in pursuit. The chase covered a wide area of rugged Colorado country, but the braves were gaining.

Finally, to lighten their load, the Spaniards buried two muleskins bulging with Indian trinkets somewhere in the Chalk Cliffs area on the southern face of majestic Mt. Princeton. Soon after

The Chalk Cliffs of Mt. Princeton. Legend says an ancient Spanish treasure is buried somewhere on the precipitous ledges. *Colorado Historical Society photo.*

that the Indians caught up with the Spaniards and slaughtered them all.

It would seem that the story of the buried treasure would die with them, but they claim the hoard was mentioned in ancient Spanish documents. The specific documents, however, have never been named.

Nonetheless, it was a well-known story in 1912 when veteran Colorado prospector Thomas Summers took up the search. He came into Salida one day and said he had solved the riddle of where the treasure was buried but he needed financial backing to get the treasure out.

He said he had spent a long time browsing through many old Spanish documents and maps until he finally found a chart that told of the location. He said the Spanish inscription said: "Measurement is taken from the face of the Spanish princess which is a face in the mountain resembling the countenance of the beautiful royal highness."

Summers also showed a picture of the Chalk Cliffs and outlined the face of the Spanish princess. Those who have been able

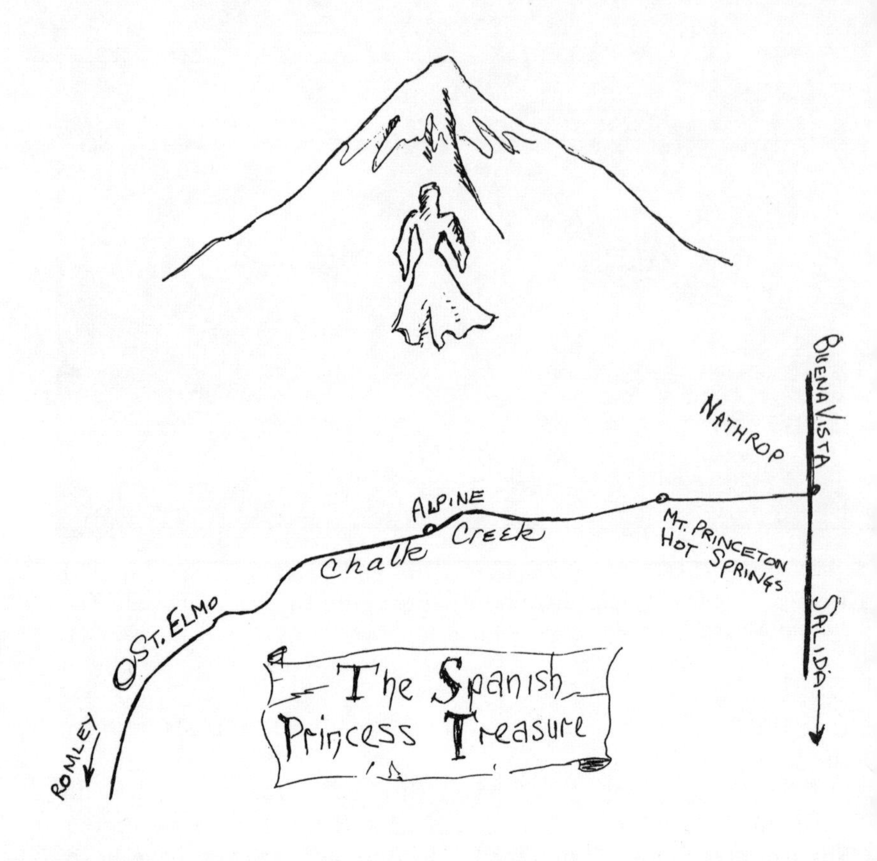

to find the face on the cliffs say, however, it is anything but beautiful.

Summers never did find the treasure. None of the many others who have searched for it have found it either.

XII. *FABULOUS LEADVILLE*

59. THE SEARCH FOR LOST GULCH

Within days of the Russell discovery near Central City in 1859, the narrow little gulch was jammed with gold seekers. At night it was marked by campfires that cast eerie shadows against the nearby hills.

One night, into the glow of one campfire, a stranger appeared. As he warmed himself and imbibed of the hospitality of the prospecting party, he told his story.

He said he had been prospecting over the Divide when he became lost. For five days he wandered around aimlessly without anything but bark and wild berries to eat. While trying to find a way out of his predicament, he stumbled across a sparkling outcropping of gold. To prove his story, he produced several large gold nuggets. The nuggets were larger than anything found along the gulch now lit by hundreds of campfires.

The other men around this one particular campfire attempted

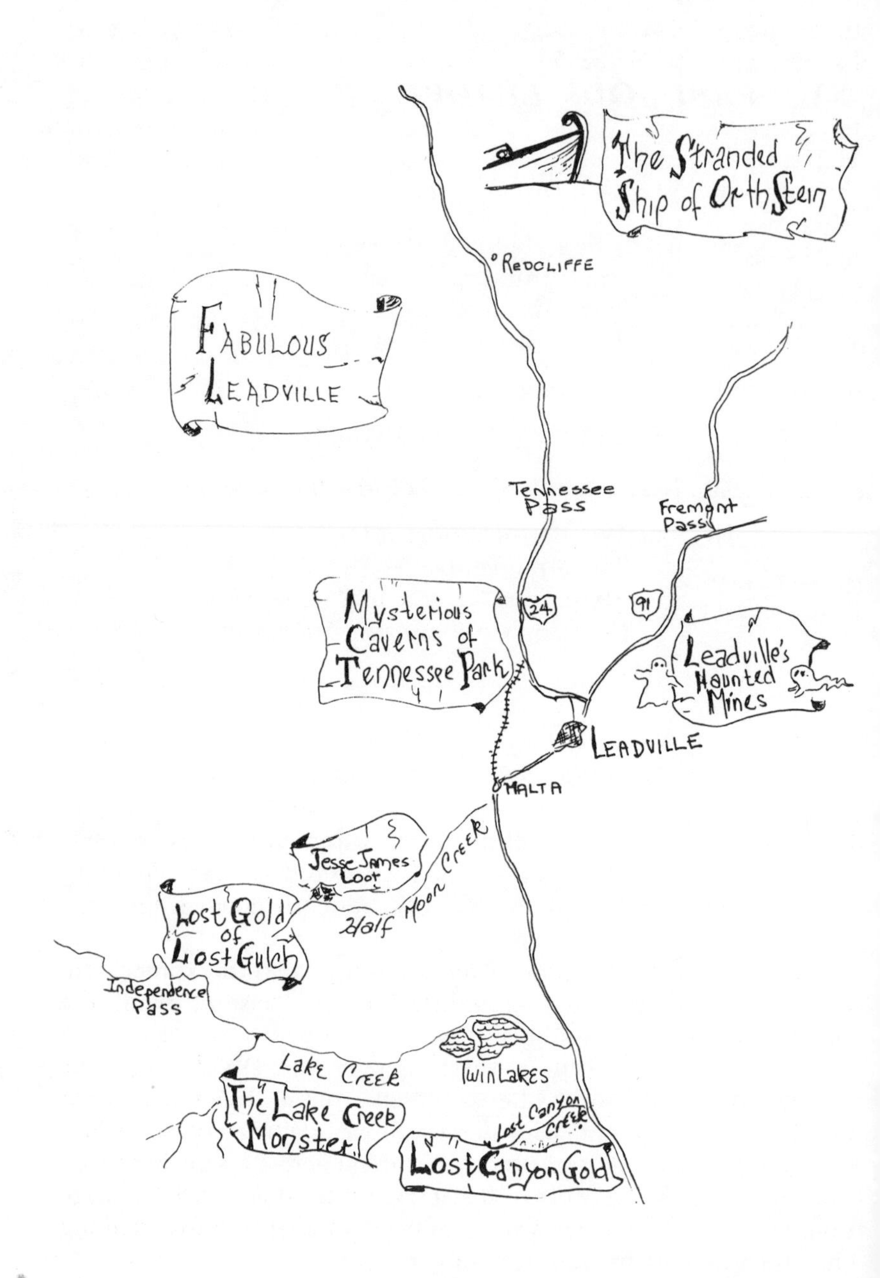

The Stranded Ship of Orth Stein
Redcliffe
Fabulous Leadville
Tennessee Pass
Fremont Pass
24
91
Mysterious Caverns of Tennessee Park
Leadville's Haunted Mines
Leadville
Malta
Jesse James Loot
Half Moon Creek
Lost Gold of Lost Gulch
Independence Pass
Lake Creek
Twin Lakes
The Lake Creek Monster!
Lost Canyon Creek
Lost Canyon Gold

to persuade the stranger to lead them to his find, but he would have none of it. He said he had considerable property back east and that he merely came west for the adventure. However, he had never dreamed of the hardships that that adventure would entail. He said he would gladly tell them, as closely as he could, where the gold was located, but that he had enough of the west.

He said he made his find in a gulch between Twin Lakes and the headwaters of the Arkansas River. He drew them a crude map from memory.

The party set off next day for Twin Lakes. They searched for months in all directions, but they found no trace of the rich nuggets they had seen.

That might have been the end of our story had not the party made another important discovery. The names of the prospectors were said to be S. S. Slater, George Stevens, Ike Rafferty, James Miller, Rufus Alvord, Abram Lee, and John Currier.

And their discovery was in California Gulch. It brought about the first stampede over the Divide and raised the curtain to the Leadville story, the most fabulous one of them all.

60. LEADVILLE'S HAUNTED MINES

When men burrow into the bowels of the earth, they bestir the devils and demons sleeping there. It is expected. It is an accomplished fact.

The helmet lamps cast eerie shadows in the pitch black caverns. The wind screaming through the drifts, the water dripping, the work and talk in a distant shaft, the wood creaking under the strain, the clanking of a pick on hard rock. The earth itself unleashes its mysterious sounds to blend into the ghostly harmony.

The ghosts are the men who died in the mine accidents who return to haunt the mine for good or evil. Hermits that lived out their lives in the mine know no other home, even after death.

Of course, there were the mines that weren't really haunted by ghosts, but by live people for a reason. The fired miner, the brother of a miner killed, who returned to punish the owner. There were the hired ghosts of a nearby mine owner who wanted to purchase the adjacent diggings cheap.

These artificially haunted mines don't count.

And then, of course, there were the "Tommy Knockers."

The Tommy Knockers, cousins to elves and second cousins to leprechauns, came to Central City with the Welsh miners. Once here they multiplied rapidly and spread throughout the state. Tommy Knockers hid in empty mines or deserted shafts. Some miners claim to have seen the little fellows, but that was generally after a drink or two too much of Taos Lightning. Generally Tommy Knockers kept out of sight . . . but their presence was felt.

To Welsh miners, and others, every untraceable sound in a mine was made by the Tommy Knockers. Every time a pick was mislaid or a helmet candle went out, it was the Tommy Knockers.

Believing in Tommy Knockers, however, was the easy way out. There were honest and true ghosts . . . as every miner knows.

Mines throughout Colorado were, and are, haunted. Any mine worth its salt had a ghost or two.

The long-deserted caverns hidden by the lonely, whispering night, echo, scream, or shriek the stories of their youth. Skeptics need only to spend the night in one to be converted.

Leadville, Colorado's most active mining camp, had the most notorious ghosts. Many of the mines here were haunted when they were very young. Surely, they are haunted still.

The Shrouded Woman

Of course, miners believed in ghosts more than most people did. The ghosts grew in their minds as they worked the dark, lonely corners of the earth and as the threat of death hovered over them. With the ghosts grew all sorts of jinxes and superstitions they couldn't afford to disregard. The most prominent superstition was in regard to a woman's entering the mine.

So certain were the miners that a woman's setting foot in a mine would bring trouble that many miners refused to work after a woman entered. Frequently a mine became worthless due to a woman. After she entered, it was jinxed and haunted. For this reason, women were rarely allowed near a mine. But still, somehow, they entered.

Many of the ghosts were women—to a miner, the worst kind.

Many a mine was haunted by a woman's sobs, her shrieks, her screams. Most miners refused to work in such a mine.

The first Leadville mine haunted by a woman was the New Discovery.

The apparition of an unearthly female wearing a fluttering shroud appeared frequently to the miners of the New Discovery. She first appeared in the spring of 1879. Many of the miners, on seeing her, drew their pay and never returned. Some of the braver men attempted time and time again to capture her. But when they closed in on her, the shrouded woman spat at them, and then vanished, with her rustling shroud.

She became so well-known, her story even appeared in a New York newspaper. Before long, however, Leadville became too busy to bother with the ghost and her appearances became less and less frequent. She was seen from time to time, however, and when things got less busy, and when other fellow ghosts made their appearance, she was on hand much of the time.

She was in on the death of the New Discovery. They say she was quite happy about the whole thing—if ghosts can ever be happy.

They say she still dwells in the forbidden chambers of the New Discovery. Perhaps, if you penetrate the old mine far enough, you may meet her. Even if you don't, you will still feel her presence.

The Mikado Ghost

One may not consider the ghost of the Mikado a legal-type ghost since she was man-inspired. But even after the truth was known and man stopped manipulating her, she remained. Once a mine is haunted, you can't un-haunt it just like that.

The Mikado woman was more brazen and more nerve-wracking than the ghost of the New Discovery. Even though she wasn't always visible, her weeping and wailing were heard. She even went so far as to lay her clammy hand on the shoulder of an unsuspecting miner or two, who generally high-tailed it out of the mine without looking, or coming, back.

The Mikado woman first made her appearance in the early 1880s. Her strange voice-like wails were heard drifting through the shafts and through the drifts. When a miner, braver than most, investigated, he would suddenly come upon an ill-defined figure shimmering menacingly in some dark spot as the light from the candle shone upon it.

The wails, the clammy hands, the visions were enough for most miners. It was getting so bad that the owner, W. R. Chadburn, was finding it impossible to get help.

Then the truth came to light.

It came out that the grotesque figures and the wails were man-made, by pranksters who wanted to scare Chadburn, who was a firm believer in spiritualism.

It would seem that the truth would put a stop to the strange goings-on at the Mikado. Not so.

Even after the pranksters had called off their eerie dogs, the woman remained in the Mikado. Her wails continued, many a miner ran from the mine after her clammy hand rested a moment on his shoulder. Some miners even saw her. They often heard her fiddling with the mine buckets and cages.

The reputation of the mine greatly interfered with the work there. Time after time they tried to prove that the ghost was man-made, but it never was proved after that first time. Once a group of skepical workmen, armed with revolvers, systematically searched the mine, thinking they would find practical jokesters. They found nothing.

Scoffers at the time, and since, have explained away the ghost many ways . . . they think.

They say the first man-made ghost left the miners with over-tense nerves and over-active imaginations. They also claim that the Mikado was especially well-ventilated and that the weird sounds were caused by miners on other levels laughing and joking, their sounds gaining eeriness as they sifted through the vents.

Perhaps these practical men went to their graves confident they had solved the riddle. But you and I know better. The most practical men in the world, no matter how hard they try, can't explain away an honest-to-goodness ghost.

The Gallagher Ghost

The Gallagher Ghost in the Moyer Mine was Leadville's most famous. He hindered the work all during the history of the rich mine. His story reached such proportions they are still spinning

The rip-roaring town of Leadville as it looked in 1882, the era of haunted mines, lost mines, Jesse James, and Orth Stein, the "mad journalist." *U.S. Geological Survey photo.*

yarns about him. There's hardly anything Gallagher hasn't done and isn't likely to do in the future.

Actually, Gallagher was just one of the many ghosts of the Moyer Mine, and a latecomer at that. In fact, they say he wouldn't have gotten himself into the position of being a ghost if he had heeded the warning of the other ghosts in the mine.

They say the original ghosts were twelve men killed in a mine cave-in during the early years of the mine's history. The cave-in was so bad that they never did get the bodies out. These were good ghosts. They usually showed up just in time to scare a miner or so away from a disaster area. One or more of the apparitions would show up to move miners back from an upcoming cave-in, or would scare a miner away from falling down a shaft, or something like that.

Take Johnny Cumfrey, for an example.

Johnny was a trammer in the Moyer. One evening, just before the shift change, his tram eased to a stop by some unknown power. Johnny immediately felt the presence of someone or something hovering over him. A conscientious trammer, however, Johnny leaned over the tram to see what was wrong. The feeling became so overpowering that he suddenly raised his head. There, staring him straight in the eyes, not a foot away, was a leering, pallid face "intense with woe and agony." The face was attached to a stooping figure with arms outstretched as if clutching for some support to keep it from falling.

Johnny froze for a moment, and then dashed right through the apparition and out of the mine.

There are two versions of what happened next, the popular version and the factual version. The popular version says Johnny was talked out of quitting and went back into the mine to where his stalled tram was. He found his tram buried under tons of dirt

A ghostlike sulphide formation in the Moyer Mine near Leadville. Such a formation, seen by a lonely miner, may have seemed like a spectre in this haunted mine. *U.S. Geological Survey photo.*

and stone. Johnny would have been crushed under the whole mess had he not heeded the ghost's warning.

The truth was that Johnny did draw his pay and quit, but after a few days he thought better of it and went back to work. The first day back he fell down a mine shaft, nearly lost his life, but escaped with a broken leg, which he wouldn't have broken, they say, had he but listened to the ghost.

Former State Senator Gallagher was part owner of the mine and he didn't cotton to all this nonsense about ghosts interfering with the work there. He thought better of it when he went in to the mine himself and saw a ghost firsthand. The ghost stepped in front of Gallagher and gave the senator a warning-like sneer. Gallagher paused a moment as just about anybody would upon meeting up with a ghost. But no such flimsy thing could scare off a senator and a mine owner.

So Gallagher walked right through the apparition . . . fell down a sixty-foot mine shaft and died.

From then on Gallagher was top ghost at the Moyer—a big shot in life and a big shot in death.

Only Gallagher wasn't as good as the other ghosts. Some say he had high ambitions and became embittered that a mine shaft should cut his life short. Anyhow, he was a mean ghost.

Many miners saw his image after that, leering and sneering, with a pick in his hand. He scared people out of the mine just to be mean. They saw him riding down a bucket in the elevator shaft making with that hideous laugh of his. They heard him threaten his enemies, and cursing friends and foes alike.

That's as far as the facts go . . . the legend is endless.

They say a miner would get lost in the mine or miss the elevator at the change of a shift and would be found the next day with a pick—Gallagher's pick—stuck in his head. There were no facts to corroborate the story, but nonetheless, few miners went alone into the mine, and they always made sure they caught the elevator at the end of the shift.

One story goes that the lift man one evening had just finished bringing all the men up from work and was about to leave the mine himself, when he heard three bells. This was unusual since one bell signaled a miner wanted the box lowered and two bells meant to raise it. The lift man went down anyway, and there at the bottom was a forgotten miner with a pick imbedded in his skull.

It got so it was difficult to get workers for the Moyer—and next to impossible to get night watchmen. One brave soul, more to show his courage than to get a paycheck, took the job.

The next morning he was found at the end of one of the shafts digging through the dirt with bloody fingers and muttering "I've got to find that light," over and over again.

Later, during one of his more lucid moments, he told his story. He said he was standing near the entrance of a shaft when he saw a light, seemingly coming from the other end. He went to it only to find the light was back where he had been before, or down another shaft. He chased the thing all that night, and finally figured he had it cornered when they found him the next morning.

Many years after the Moyer had closed down, some boys broke into the mine offices. In the shambles they found a complete record of every man who had ever worked at the mine. In addition to the vital statistics there were statements on why they quit. There were the customary ones about low pay, poor working conditions, or moving to another town, but one of the most frequent reasons mentioned on many of the file cards was, "afraid of the shaft" or simply, "the Gallagher Ghost."

61. LOST CANYON GOLD

Lost Canyon begins about three and one-half miles down the gulch from the present site of Granite. The story of the lost mine here gave reason for the name of the canyon.

It was in this rough, tractless country some prospectors became lost in 1860 while returning from Gunnison country. More hungry for gold than civilization, the men decided to make the most of a bad situation, and they did a little prospecting.

They were rewarded with nuggets "the size of eggs."

The group reportedly took out $60,000 in gold in a few short weeks, leaving just before winter entered the scene.

The prospectors eagerly trudged up the canyon the following spring. They searched the primitive land the entire season but never did find the spot that contained "nuggets as big as eggs" again. Many another prospector searched the canyons down through the years, but it wasn't until twenty years later that some more gold was found in Lost Canyon. It was good gold but the nuggets weren't as big as eggs.

62. THE LOST GOLD MINE OF LOST GULCH

In 1878, a man came into Leadville with a pack of very rich gold ore which he sold to Berdell and Witherell for a large sum of money.

He lived quietly in Leadville during the winter, was very secretive about the source of his gold, and, as much as possible, kept to himself.

Very early the next spring the man slipped off. He was not heard of nor much thought about until late the same summer when his body was found on Independence Pass by Frank Brown, manager of the Farwell properties in Independence—and the first man who tried to navigate the Colorado River, losing his life in the attempt. Brown said the body was uncovered by the thawing of a huge bank of snow at the head of Lake Creek. The victim had apparently been on his way to the town of Independence when he was caught in a late spring snowslide.

When the death of the man was known, the story of his pack of rich gold dust was recalled. Various clues came to light. For instance, some other prospectors remembered seeing the man prospecting in Lost Gulch, a branch of the Roaring Fork. Putting all the clues together, oldtimers in the area believe the stranger's gold find was on Lost Gulch. The gulch was searched from one end to the other but no evidence of his work was found.

Perhaps the gold is still there and the evidence of its existence was well hidden by the stranger who lost his life in a snowslide enroute to his gold mine.

63. JESSE JAMES LOOT IN HALF MOON GULCH

They claim Jesse James participated in the great Leadville excitement, making it more rip-roaring than it already was. They say old Jesse was just about everywhere in the old west. People down in Gunnison country claim he was even down there for a spell. And wherever there was a holdup of one sort or another,

Jesse was an automatic suspect—no matter where he was at the time.

But some people claimed to have seen Jesse and members of his gang around California Gulch. They also believe he indulged in his favorite pasttime there—holdups. His hideout was said to be Half Moon Gulch, one of the state's most delightfully mysterious strips of land.

Many a legend is woven about Half Moon Gulch, a short distance southwest of Leadville. The legends involve jinxes, murder, gold ledges and what-have-you. The wild beauty of the gulch includes a rushing mountain stream overhung by cliffs, lined with shrubs and pine trees, caves and wild mountain lions, and giant bears.

There were many stories of prospectors that entered the forbidden spot and never returned, becoming virtual prisoners of the canyon.

It was an ideal hideout for renegades . . . and for Jesse and his gang. Prospectors who dared enter the canyon and *did* return swear that Jesse and his look-outs spied down on them from their vantage points in the high ledges which jut out from the canyon wall; that Jesse's armed sentinels paced back and forth along the ravines and in front of the natural caves.

We know there were many more holdups in the Leadville neighborhood than there should have been. Whether Jesse played his part or not, he was blamed for a good share of them. There was a price on his head and armed vigilantes on the lookout for him. They say things got too hot for old Jesse and he flew the coop in a big hurry. They added that he left in such a hurry that he didn't have time to gather up all his loot. He left some of it in Half Moon Gulch, they say.

As the years went by, more and more prospectors ventured into the mysterious canyon. Good gold discoveries were made and some mining was done. But nobody ever found any Jesse James loot.

Jesse wasn't famous for leaving loot behind. Maybe he didn't leave any behind. Maybe he did.

64. THE WONDERFUL WORLD OF ORTH STEIN

Leadville had everything every other boom town did, only it had it in more lavish quantities. It drank more booze, spilt more blood, had more haunted mines, jinxes, lost mines, shady ladies, big-time gunmen, millionaires who went busted, than just about any other single mining town in the world.

And Leadville had Orth Stein. He didn't exactly cause the Leadville boom, nor the bust. But he fit beautifully into the Leadville character between the two.

Stein drifted into Leadville in 1880, posing as a doctor. He was successful in uncovering interesting facts on what he called "Indian Doctors." Later, when hired as editor of the *Leadville Chronicle,* his exposé was successful in driving many a quack out of the boom town.

Stein was one of the state's greatest crusaders . . . and he usually aimed at men in high places. Ineffective Mayor J. F. Humphreys was one of his favorite targets:

"Mayor Humphreys is rather slightly built, not very heavy. He can readily and safely stand on a very flimsy platform," or,

"J. F. Humphreys says he is a poor man. We all know he is a poor mayor."

Stein covered many a big story in Leadville. First of all he recorded the baby years of the fabulous boom town, the greatest silver camp of them all. His interview with the divorced wife of Charles Guitteau, the man who shot President Garfield, received national play.

But it is with his other stories, amazing stories, that we are concerned and as to why Leadville and Colorado remember Orth Stein. He played these stories straight, usually using names familiar in Leadville. He named real places and his detailed, descriptive sentences made them read like documents. Many of them were rewritten in newspapers throughout the country, and all of them became permanent legend in Colorado.

Stein played the stories as far as they could possibly go, with as many follow-ups as he could get out of them. Then, while the slightly suspicious public was catching its breath, he would come out with something else, changing the focus and locality.

Some believe that it was his vivid imagination that caused Orth Stein to leave Leadville so soon. But the truth was that his primary occupation, other than writing, was getting into debt. He left Leadville quietly in 1882. He reappeared a short time later in Kansas City and took a job on the *Star* under the name of John Bell.

In 1883 he was charged with the murder of George Fredericks, a variety theatre manager who vied with Stein for the affection of Mattie Hartlein, "the fallen dove." His first trial ended in his conviction and he was sentenced to death. But he won a stay of execution, another trial, and finally acquittal.

After that, Orth Stein drifted into oblivion. Perhaps he took another job on another newspaper somewhere under an assumed name. And again was writing the kind of stories that once turned Leadville on its ear.

The Stranded Ship

Orth Stein foisted this story upon the world in early 1880, shortly after his arrival in Leadville. It was picked up and reprinted as true in newspapers as far away as New York.

It tells of two prospectors, Jacob Cahee and Louis Adams, grubstaked by Denver, Leadville and southern Colorado speculators, who were prospecting in an area near Red Cliff, so remote and so primitive that it is doubtful it had ever been seen before by man. The two men had dug a shaft in what looked like good dirt. After digging through about thirty feet of wash, they were about to give up on the spot when they struck a lime formation stained with iron and evidently not in place.

Thus encouraged, they continued digging with new vigor. About fifteen feet further they hit a hollow sound. Believing they were nearing a subterranean passage or gallery, they secured themselves to the top of the shaft by ropes and continued cautiously.

After a few more feet the earth gave way and the two men found themselves suspended in a large, irregular cave, some 240 feet long and about 180 feet wide at its broadest point.

They had fallen into one end of the cave so they had little difficulty in swinging themselves against a natural stairway of granite boulders to one side. With miners' lamps they explored the sanded floor, and here and there they found huge crystals of quartz. Enormous stalactites hung from the ceiling fifty feet above; catching the feeble rays of light, they threw back myriads of rainbow hues.

The cave at first appeared empty, but finally they saw a huge dark object at one end. As they approached they saw, to their amazement, the object was the outline of some sort of sailing craft. They couldn't believe it, but close inspection proved it to be just that, only it was different from any ship they had ever seen or known of. It was about sixty feet long and about thirty feet wide. It lay tilted forward at an angle of about fifteen degrees over a rough pile of stones. The body of the craft was built of short lengths of some dark and very porous wood, resembling black walnut. Both ends of the ship wore moorish slippers and it appeared as if the vessel was intended to sail both ways.

The planking was apparently double-riveted on with nails of extremely hard copper, only slightly rust-eaten, and with heads cut or filed in an octagonal shape, while along the upper edge of the ship, eleven large rings of the same metal were found, evidently for the security of the rigging.

At the bottom edges of the craft, and running its entire length, were two keels some four and a half feet deep and six inches thick, hung on metallic hinges. They were fastened at the ends with rough copper rods, extending upward and bent over so as to attach to two masts rising from the upper edges.

The description of the outside of the ship was given in great detail. The whole ship was intact but the wood crumbled to the touch so the two men did not venture inside.

However, lying on the ground nearby, they found a gold instrument that bore a rude resemblance to a sextant. The only writing found was at one end of the ship about midway on the bow and enclosed in a metal ring. Here they found twenty-six copper characters riveted to the wood and bearing much resemblance to Chinese hieroglyphics.

No human remains were found, but the men did not preclude the possibility that some might be inside.

The men finally climbed up through their opening to the dark night outside. They built a campfire and were very silent, as men are wont to be when they awaken from a dream world or have visited the supernatural.

The next morning they lowered themselves into the cave once again, fully expecting it to be empty and to find that they had dreamed or imagined the sights of the day before . . . but the ship was still there.

After another inspection, they climbed back up again and eventually arrived at the cabin of a well-to-do miner, who owned thirty properties down the gulch. Cahee and Adams showed the cave to the mine owner and another expert from the city, to let them verify what they had seen.

The four men then tried to hide the opening of the cavern as much as possible, and vowed secrecy until such time as they could present their tremendous discovery to the world.

Stein said the only possible explanation was that "ages and eons, perhaps, agone, a vessel bearing a crew of bold adventurers tossed by the waves, then receding, left it stranded there. The awful upheavals and convulsions of nature, which we know so little of and can only be speculated on, pressed the face of the earth together and sealed it in a living grave. And this is but a groping guess, yet in what strange old seas the vessel sailed, what unknown, ancient waters pressed against its peaked prow, under what prehistoric skies it pitched, what man can tell?"

Mysterious Caverns of Tennessee Park

The world was still digesting the story of the ancient sunken ship when the following story appeared in the pages of the *Leadville Chronicle* under the by-line of Orth Stein.

This strange adventure happened to Stein himself as he traveled through Tennessee Park, a dozen miles northwest of Leadville.

While crossing a marshy piece of ground he was sucked into a "cyclopean cave." He found himself in a gigantic cavern of archways and hallways, leading in and out of dozens of chambers whose walls were lined with veins of mineral and from whose ceiling hung colossal stalactites.

In one chamber was a beautiful crystal lake. But the strangest sight of all was in another chamber where there were miners panning gold from an underground stream.

After wandering through other chambers he returned to this

Many a historian took Orth Stein's fabulous stories as the gospel truth. Many were reprinted in newspapers throughout the country and in the history books of the time. An example are the drawings of the "Underground Caves in Tennessee Park" which appeared in George Crofutt's Gripsack Guide in 1881. The above drawing depicts the Chronicle Rotunda and a man panning gold in the River Styx. The lower drawing shows a cross section of the cave and its opening. *Denver Public Library Western Collection.*

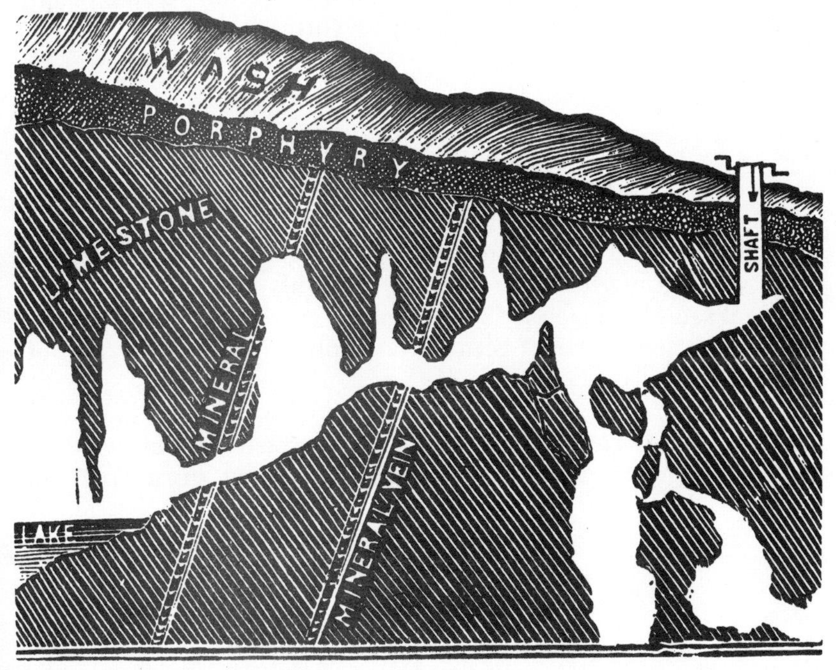

one and approached the miners carefully so as not to startle them. Although they were surprised to see him, they were friendly.

Stein talked the miners into letting him throw the caverns open to tourists while the miners retained the mineral rights. He rushed to Leadville to break the story and begin the publicity campaign. His glowing account listed several chambers to which he gave such names as the Chronicle Rotunda, the Bridal Veil, Lovers Leap, the Bottomless Pit, Serpents Glen, Beelzebub's Nose, Bessie's Boudoir, Lady Harris' Drawing Room, The Stein Gallery, The Davis Palace, and O'Connor Grotto (Charles O'Connor was a reporter on the *Chronicle*).

A follow-up story divulged the names of the discoverers and owners: Alexander Chisholm, D. A. Williams, Duncan McDonald, Hugh McClennan and Joseph Mivelle—all familiar names in Leadville. The story said that a Captain Cecil C. Morgan had taken out a $20,000 bond on the cave and was negotiating with London capitalists for its sale and full development.

This story was also reprinted around the country and was even mentioned as true in some early-day Colorado history books.

It created a large-scale stir in Leadville at the time. In fact, it caused such excitement that Stein ran a couple of more follow-up stories. Then Stein realized people were getting suspicious. So he turned his attention elsewhere. When it finally got out that the Tennessee Park Cave was a fraud, Stein had already led the people of Leadville into another exciting adventure.

Colorado's Abominable Snowman

Stein wrote many another story. He told of another cave under Long and Derry Hill, southeast of Leadville.

There was the Death Chamber on Capitol Hill, found while a man was digging for an outhouse behind his cabin. In the chamber was found a skeleton chained to one wall of the cave, reaching for the ancient remains of food on a plate just beyond the outstretched hands.

There was the skeleton of the frightening serpent found by miners in the Lake Creek area. The serpent was fifty feet in length and gave rise to many Leadville serpent stories that followed.

But perhaps the story that had the greatest following was the one about "The Lake Creek Monster," Colorado's Abominable Snowman.

This story appeared at about the same time as the Tennessee Park story. It said that several miners in the vicinity of Grizzly Peak had seen this strange animal—different from any animal seen before.

The creature resembled a man except for the extraordinary length of his arms and the long, shaggy hair that covered his body. The animal was usually seen at a distance and was originally believed to be but a myth or the figment of the imagination of an over-imaginative miner. The first miner who reported seeing the beast was hooted at, but eventually, when more and more people saw it, the story was believed.

The latest sighting was reported by two miners who came to a cabin on the east side of the mountain, occupied by a hunter named Lewis. The frightened and breathless miners told Lewis the following story.

They said they were working claims about three miles away when their attention was attracted by a peculiar moaning noise coming from a huge granite pile some distance away. They couldn't see anything so they climbed up on the pile. One man disappeared over the rocks. He had just dropped from sight when the other miner heard a shriek of terror.

The miner climbed down the rocks and ran to the cabin to get the rifle. When he came out of the cabin he saw his companion reappear "as pale as death and trembling so violently that he could hardly speak."

After the miner recovered from his fright he said he had seen the beast just on the other side of the rocks. He said it bore resemblance to a man but was more than half beast. His body was heavily built and looked somewhat like an orang-utan, with long and muscular arms.

It was his face that would strike terror into the hearts of the bravest of men.

It had an almost human countenance, but it was covered with coarse, brown hair. The face was made ferocious by a pair of eyes that glowed like coals, and the mouth had thin lips, between which a pair of long tusks appeared.

The miner said he was petrified with terror. And as he stood there the monster straightened, glared at him, stretched out his arms toward the thunderstruck miner and made the moaning sound heard before.

This aroused the miner who rushed over the rocks and back toward the cabin as fast as his legs could carry him.

The two miners, with their rifles cocked, went back over the rocks to investigate. At first they couldn't find hide nor hair of the monster, but they did find a rude animal lair of grass and brush, formed in a rough corner, and sheltered from the weather by a juncture of three rocks.

Finally, the monster was seen at a distance in a little clump of trees. They fired at it, but it quickly escaped on all fours.

Lewis, the hunter, was greatly interested in the story and followed the miners back to the spot. They scoured the area for several days. They did see the lair, they did find several half-human, half-animal tracks and they did believe they obtained several glimpses of the beast off in the distance. But they were never able to come within range of the monster due to its extreme fleetness.

The monster was reportedly seen off and on for several years after that. In fact, it's still not a good idea to travel the Lake Creek area alone, even today . . . especially without a loaded gun or a camera.

XIII. *BAYOU SALADO AND BRECKENRIDGE*

65. THE REYNOLDS GANG GOLD

Perhaps the most sought and least found buried treasure in Colorado is the Reynolds Gang treasure. Every now and again a Sunday feature writer makes the uncomfortable journey up Handcart Creek, follows up the research he did on the story (reading the stories of other Sunday feature writers), talks to the same oldtimers who say the same things they did the last time they were interviewed, and the writer journeys back down the hill shaking his head.

Historians down through the intervening 100 years are certain the treasure is there, although they never cared enough to put down their pens and go look for it. Some later historians claim the treasure was either a farce or not enough of a treasure to bear the title. Some mavericks believe some long-ago and well-informed person stole up the canyon and dug up the treasure . . . just to baffle future generations.

Anyhow, here are the "facts" available on the Reynolds Saga (or Fiasco) and you can judge for yourself if the uncomfortable trip up the gulch is worth your time or not.

Jim Reynolds, often called "Jim the Bold," was a swashbuckling young fellow when he strode into a corner of South Park with others who had been turned away by the miners at

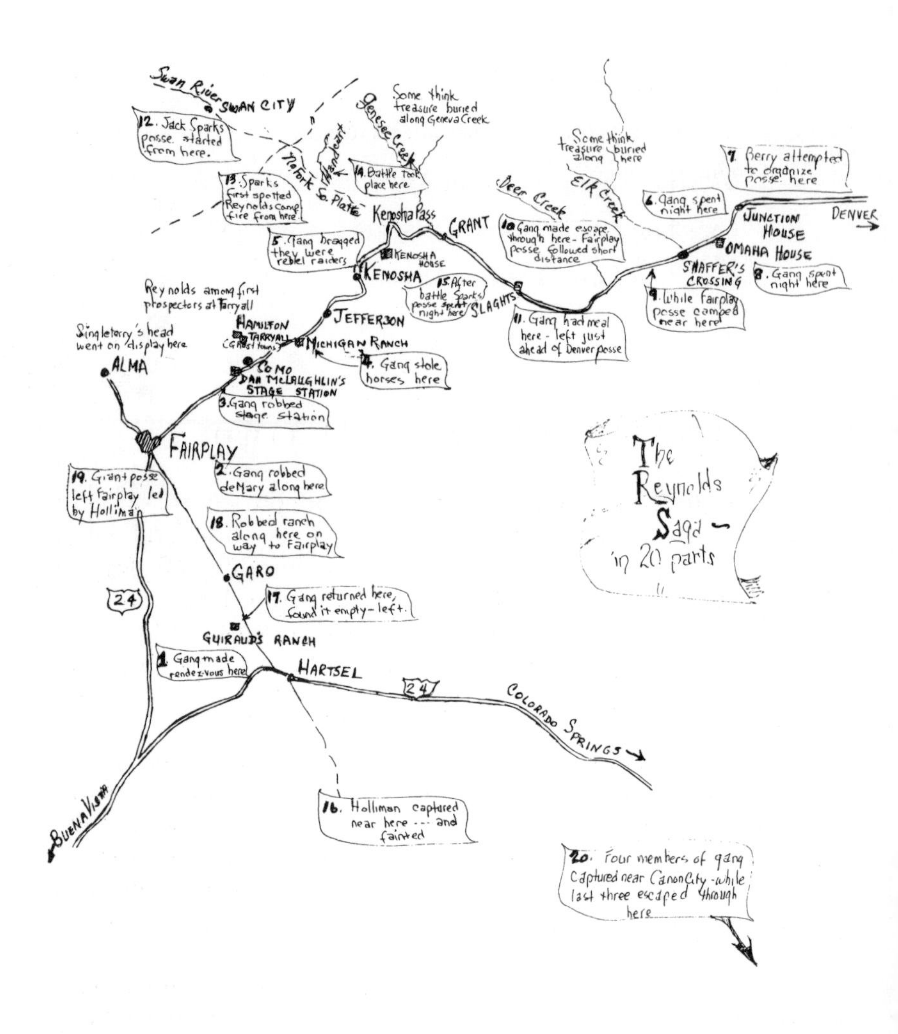

Swan River
SWAN CITY
12. Jack Sparks posse started from here.
13. Sparks first spotted Reynolds camp fire from here.
Some think treasure buried along Geneva Creek
Geneseo Creek
14. Battle took place here
Kenosha Pass
5. Gang bragged they were rebel raiders
KENOSHA HOUSE
KENOSHA
GRANT
Deer Creek
Elk Creek
Some think treasure buried along here
10. Gang made escape through here - Fairplay posse followed short distance
7. Berry attempted to organize posse here
6. Gang spent night here
JUNCTION HOUSE
DENVER
OMAHA HOUSE
SHAFFER'S CROSSING
8. Gang spent night here
9. While Fairplay posse camped near here
15. After battle Sparks' posse spent night here
SLAGHTS
11. Gang had meal here - left just ahead of Denver posse
Reynolds among first prospectors at Tarryall
Singleterry's head went on display here
HAMILTON
TARRYALL
(Ghost towns)
JEFFERSON
MICHIGAN RANCH
4. Gang stole horses here
ALMA
COMO
DAN McLAUGHLIN'S STAGE STATION
3. Gang robbed stage station
FAIRPLAY
2. Gang robbed deMary along here
19. Grant posse left Fairplay led by Holliman
18. Robbed ranch along here on way to Fairplay
The Reynolds Saga - in 20 parts
GARO
24
17. Gang returned here, found it empty - left.
GUIRAUD'S RANCH
1. Gang made rendez-vous here
HARTSEL
24
COLORADO SPRINGS
BUENA VISTA
16. Holliman captured near here --- and fainted
20. Four members of gang captured near Canon City - while last three escaped through here

A well-known but fallacious drawing of the execution of the Reynolds Gang. This represents Cook's version which had six of the gang executed by soldiers. There were only five men executed and most authentic versions of the deed had two, and possibly three, soldiers do all the shooting. This drawing was made for D. J. Cook's book *Hands Up*. *Denver Public Library Western Collection.*

Tarryall (dubbed by those who didn't receive the welcome they wanted as "Grab-all"). History books say it was Jim himself who stood up on the soapbox and claimed this new town would show "fair play" to all those who came there, thus giving the town its name.

But Jim soon climbed down off his soapbox. Making speeches was not his forte, and prospecting was too slow. Jim organized a gang of highwaymen. They say he first got the taste for it by robbing a lonely traveler of $100. Reynolds knew the area as well as anybody and he was smarter than most run-of-the-mill highway men, so he got a pretty effective business going. There are no authoritative estimates of his take, but since history later made Reynolds an important character, just about everything in South Park that was lost, stolen or strayed was blamed on him. One serious student of the Reynolds Saga estimates the Reynolds take, those first few months, was about $3,000. It certainly would have been more had not other developments occurred.

First off, Reynolds got himself arrested, an occupational hazard in his line of work. He was taken to Denver and thrown into jail. His cellmates were Charley Harrison and a fellow named "Captain" McKee. Another thing that happened was the Civil War. One can't be sure if Jim got patriotic while in prison, but when he and the boys broke out of jail they headed south.

There are two lines of thought on what happened next. One side says Jim himself suggested and planned the big move to rob Colorado of all its gold. Another side says the South needed gold more than gunfodder and selected Jim because of his particular background.

At any rate, Jim the Bold was heading back to Colorado within a few short weeks with twenty-three hand-picked Confederates . . . to rob Colorado of all its gold. This was the summer of 1864.

In the flyleaf of Reynolds' diary was the oath that gang members presumably swore to:

"I do solemnly swear or affirm that I will bear true allegiance to the Confederate States of America and the President and all officers appointed over me, so help me God. I further swear that I will aid or assist all true southern men and their families wherever they may be at a reasonable risk of my life whether in the army or out of it. I furthermore swear that I will not reveal, divulge, or cause to be divulged, any of the grips, signs, passwords or proceedings of the order, except to those who have been regularly initiated or to whom it may by right belong, and if I should be so vile as to violate this my solemn oath or obligation I shall be taken and hung by the neck until I am dead, dead, dead, and my bones left on the plains to bleach as unworthy of burial."

The gang had an auspicious beginning. They robbed a wagon train in New Mexico of $63,000. The first trouble began right after that. The gang members argued over division of the loot. Some say Reynolds was quite righteous about the use of the money, while others were not so patriotic. Anyhow, some of the gang parted ways here. Reynolds claimed all the loot for the South. According to most histories, the gang buried the loot in the Spanish Peaks region (there's another buried treasure for you), before the gang headed north.

With Jim Reynolds, who had promoted himself to a full-fledged southern colonel by now, was his brother John, and also

Owen Singleterry, Jake Stowe, Tom Holliman, John Bobbitt, John Andrews, Jack Robinson and Tom Knight.

The group split up as they rode north so as not to attract suspicion. They made their way to South Park by way of Canon City. They rendezvoused at Adolph Guiraud's ranch between present-day Hartsel and Fairplay. The Guirauds were hospitable so the gang behaved itself.

Shortly after setting out the next day they robbed Major H. H. de Mary, manager of the famous Phillips Lode. De Mary was known for carrying large sums of gold dust on his person but at this time he had only about $100.

The next stop was Dan McLaughlin's Stage Station, about two miles south of the old ghost town of Hamilton and not far from the present site of Como. The stage station was used by the McClellen and Spotswood line.

The gang had a gay, talkative time as they waited for the stage. When it came, they grabbed the reins and surrounded it and its passengers.

Here's where legend and fact begin to run wild.

A popular early story of the holdup says a drunk and a Fairplay prostitute were on the stage along with the driver, Abe Williamson, and Billy McClellen, owner of the lines. According to one story or another, everybody who was anybody in South Park, including Father Dyer, the Snow-Shoe Itinerant, had money in the stage strongbox. The most play is given the amount of the take. Generations of story-tellers have rounded the figure off at $100,000 for convenience sake, and this is the figure most often heard. More reliable sources estimate the figure at $60,000. And a couple of latter-day historians who love to take the meat and bones off legend and leave it sick, say the "treasure" probably wasn't over $5,000.

McClellen was relieved of $400 in cash, a gold watch and a revolver. Williamson had no money. The latter-day historians say the treasure in the strong box was estimated at about $3,000 in gold dust, the first shipment of the Orphan Boy Mine. Down through the years, however, most other historians estimated the gold dust at between $40,000 and $60,000, and some of these were fairly reliable chroniclers of Colorado history.

Another amount for speculation was the money taken from the mails. These were pretty productive times in South Park and many people there, including the prostitutes, were sending their earnings home; in some cases so the people back home could head out west.

Nonetheless, the bone-pickers estimated the mail take at between $1,200 and $1,500. Others put it as high as $10,000. Another story says $40,000 in currency and three cans of gold dust and amalgan worth $8,000 from saddle bags. Of course, there's no way of telling because the bandits didn't keep tidy books for posterity.

The bandits were full of bravado but weren't bloodthirsty. There's no record of their ever killing a man. Mayhap that was their problem. After they left the scene of the crime, McClellen and Williamson, and two people that were in the stage station while all this was going on, scattered helter-skelter in all directions to warn the populace. One of the persons in the stage station was a young fellow named William H. Berry, who worked at the fledgling *Rocky Mountain News.* Berry scurried off to warn Hamilton. He traveled on, no doubt feeling a bit like Paul Revere, warning all the places along the way. He tried to round up a posse at the

Is the Reynolds Gang Treasure buried in this valley? Hall Valley, scene of much of the activity during the chase of the gang, wanders off in the distance. The old Hall Valley Smelter guards the entrance of the valley. *U.S. Geological Survey photo.*

Vernon Crow shows the old handmade knife he found and the tree in which he found it. The Reynolds Gang treasure is supposed to be nearby. *Photo courtesy Orin A. Sealy.*

Junction House, on the road to Denver, but the men there were too faint-hearted. Anyhow, Berry got back to Denver and the *News* in time to meet the deadline and give the paper a clear scoop.

Meanwhile, back with the Reynolds gang, everything was serene. They traveled in style. They stopped at the Kenosha House on Kenosha Pass and bragged to one and all that they were rebel soldiers here on business—to rob the state treasury in Denver of all its gold. They also said they were Quantrill Raiders.

They said a lot of things, but you couldn't believe highwaymen any more then than you can now.

They next stopped at the Omaha House and had a good night's sleep.

Meanwhile, a 30-man posse had started out from Fairplay. The gang might as well have put up signposts, but the Fairplay posse apparently didn't want to mess with them. The posse traveled in any direction just to stay out of the gang's way. At one time the posse had a nice outdoor breakfast just six miles from the Junction House, where the gang was having breakfast in comfort.

After Berry got to Denver, the big city was in a quandary as to whether to send out a posse or just to wait until the gang meandered into town. Finally, after thirty hours of discussion and sleeping on the problem, they sent out another 30-man posse under Captain Maynard. The Denver posse was fairly hot on the trail when Reynolds figured he'd better take to the hills.

Our hero, you remember, knew the mountains in this area just about as well as anyone alive. He and the gang holed up far up the north fork of the South Platte River, on Handcart Gulch. They probably never would have been caught if it hadn't been for the fact that just about everybody wanted to get into the act. The news had reached over the mountains and the busy mining camps up Breckenridge way. A posse from the Swan River, under Jack Sparks, set out in pursuit. It so happened that they headed south over the mountains at just about the point where the north fork of the South Platte headwaters begin and the gang was holed up.

It was shortly after nightfall when the posse rode over the mountains, and they could see a distant campfire. They parked their horses and crawled silently toward the fire. They thought it was probably another posse, but they didn't want to take any chances.

The gang had just finished dinner and were stashing away their loot when the posse closed in. According to just about all reports, the gang had wrapped up the loot in cloth or buckskin, put it in tin cans and hid it. The posse was quite excited and their reports differ, but that is the general presumption. Sparks gave each man in the posse a different gang member to shoot in a surprise attack, but one of them jumped the gun. With short warning, the gang scattered in all directions and out of the campfire light. In the sudden burst of gunfire, three men were seen to fall. Fearing ambush, the posse went after their horses, circled around the battle site and then checked in at the Kenosha House for the night.

The next day they returned to the scene. It was immediately apparent the gang had hurriedly left the site and they didn't return during the night. Here, too, was the body of Owen Singleterry, killed in the crossfire. Virtually all the supplies carried by the gang were scattered around the scene, including two coats, six blankets, two revolvers, a shot gun, four pairs of gloves, a lot of hairpins, three pairs of saddlebags, four muskets, one spy glass, sundry traps and other items. Near the fire were several letters taken from the stage. A few greenbacks were thrown about and there was one package of amalgam gold.

This part of the story has given historians a lot of food for thought. Some think that if any treasure were buried, it was buried near the campfire—a short distance from where the gulch runs into the main stream—either before the shots were fired or in a hurry afterward. Members of the posse later stated that the rest of the loot was apparently carried off on the persons of the surviving gang members. This line of reasoning doesn't hold up too well, however, since little or nothing was found on the men who were captured later and it is doubtful if they kept passing it on like standard-bearers. So, if they did carry it off, they must have buried it before they were captured.

If one is inclined to puncture a good legend, one might come in here with the best possibility of all—that the posse, either as a group or later as individuals, returned and found the treasure.

But, by and large, posses were wholesome groups. Dr. Cooper, a member of the Swan River posse, severed the head from Singleterry and took it to Alma where it went on display for all the wholesome-minded people.

After the close call in the mountains, the gang, now reduced to eight, dispersed in several directions.

Tom Holliman rode off alone and finally reached a house about thirty miles from Canon City. Here he holed up to get some much-needed rest.

Unfortunately for Holliman the posse also took off in all directions. One group arrived at the house a few hours later and took Holliman without any trouble. In fact, Holliman was far from the typical villain one sees on television nowadays . . . he fainted.

When he was revived, fearing for his life, he instantly agreed to tell all. He did, and was taken to Fairplay for safekeeping.

About this time four more members of the gang returned to the Guiraud Ranch, but they found the Guirauds gone and no food in the cupboard. Desperate, the four men headed for Fairplay, the only place they could think of nearby where there was plenty of food.

However, they soon came to a ranch and took it over, much to the terror of the occupants. Two highwaymen took naps while the other two ate, and then the procedure was reversed. Before the news of the four men could leak out, they had disappeared into the night.

Their audacity set Fairplay astir. The town set up a guard all around. One member of the guard got so excited he shot a member of the posse through the leg.

A day later the largest and best equipped posse of them all headed out from Fairplay. At least seventy-five heavily-armed men with eight wagons and several horses set out. And leading them was no less than Tom Holliman.

The huge posse, under the command of Captain Shoup, traced the gang, or at least four members of it, to the Canon City area. They finally converged on the four renegades a few miles east of Canon City.

Meanwhile, a Captain Kerber was chasing John Reynolds, Jake Stowe and John Andrews to the south where they escaped into the mountains of New Mexico.

Captain Shoup led the five captured members back to Denver in triumph. The arrival of the gang in Denver gave the town a bit of excitement. Even then they were greeted by some as rollicking Robin Hoods. The imprisonment of the gang seemed to solidify some of the haphazard Southern sentiment in Denver, or, at least, so officials thought. This possibly explains the army's strange conduct from here on out.

In the first place the five captives were given a secret military trial—a breach of some tradition or other. The records of the trial were never made public, another breach. The five men were sentenced to be hanged. But, fearing possible recriminations in Denver, the army decided to shuttle the men down to Fort Wise near Pueblo.

A company of the Third Colorado Cavalry under Captain Cree

left Denver to escort the captives to Fort Wise. The soldiers returned to Denver a short time later. Cree said all five of the men were shot while trying to escape about thirty miles southwest of Denver near the old gold rush town of Russelville.

Next to the Sand Creek Massacre, perhaps no other act by Colorado soldiers has been so condemned. Captain Cree later said he received verbal orders to shoot the men. The old western scout, Uncle Dick Wooten, happened by the scene a short time later and found skeletons of men lashed upright against trees with bullet holes in their heads. Early Colorado historian Frank Hall said the whole affair was "unworthy of civilized people."

The legend concerning the treasure seems to start from here . . . and there are many variations on the same theme.

A popular story is that Jake Stowe died of wounds he received in the original ambush shortly after he escaped into New Mexico. John Andrews was killed in a barroom brawl. John Reynolds bummed around gambling here and there until 1871, when he thought it was safe to return to Colorado for the treasure. Enroute, however, he was caught stealing horses, a capital offense at that time. But before he was hanged, Reynolds told his executioners of the treasure and drew a crude map of its location. The executioner gave the map to Albert Brown. Brown took J. N. Cochran of Denver in as partner.

The two men followed the directions carefully in traveling up Geneva Gulch, where the treasure was said to be buried. They found evidence of the Reynolds ambush, including the skeleton of Singleterry's headless body. Some of the landmarks on the map were trees, and the two men were disgusted to find that many of the trees in the area had burned down in a recent forest fire. They searched and searched whenever they had time the next few years but never found the treasure.

Another tale is based on a popular discrepancy of many of the stories. Although the most authentic say three members escaped into New Mexico, a few tales say that only John Reynolds and Stowe escaped. John Andrews was captured along with the rest, according to this version, but was only wounded when the others were shot down near Russelville. He made his way back to Denver, and after recovering he located Reynolds and Stowe in New Mexico. The three recovered the loot at Spanish Peaks, and when that was spent they began to plan a return to South Park for the other treasure. But in robbing ranches for fresh horses Stowe and Andrews were killed by posses. John Reynolds then took on another partner, an outlaw named Brown. In a robbery enroute to Fairplay Reynolds was shot and wounded. In his dying breath he told Brown about the treasure and drew a crude map of the area. Accord'ng to stories the directions by Reynolds were:

"You go up there a little ways (along Geneva Creek) and find where one of our horses mired in the swamp. On up at the head of the gulch we turned to the right and followed the mountain around a little farther, and just above the head of Deer Creek we found an old prospect hole at about timberline. There was $40,000 in greenbacks, wrapped in a silk oilcloth, and three cans of gold dust. We filled the mouth of the hole up with stones and ten steps below we stuck an old butcher knife in a tree about four feet from the ground, broke the handle off, and left it pointing to the mouth of the hole."

Brown claimed to have searched for the treasure for several years and finally made his way up to Wyoming to become a drunkard.

This is one version of the treasure story and is generally discredited as a hoax.

Another tale concerns the arrest of one of the escapees in Texas, who told of the treasure and drew a map for the sheriff who had treated him decently.

Another story says the treasure is buried in a cave not far from Shafer's Crossing. Another says it's just a few feet off the road from the old Webster Pass road where the road crosses Elk Creek.

A Denver newspaperman, Gene Lindbergh, a few years ago, ran across an oldtimer in the Handcart Creek region who seemed to have a fairly authoritative idea of where the treasure was buried. The oldtimer, Vernon L. Crow, came to the area as a boy, and while he was a boy, a hired hand came to his ranch. The fellow said he was a nephew of one of the members of the Reynolds gang and was looking for the treasure. The hired man told Crow all about the treasure and its location.

Perhaps nobody around at that time got to know the area better than Crow. And in his meanderings he said he ran across a crude dagger with its point missing. He believed it was the treasure knife. Another time, Crow found a small park which he believes was the Reynolds' gang campsite. Above the park were the ruins of an old makeshift corral, which he believes the gang used for their horses. And eventually Crow found a mark on a dead tree that he believed was where the knife was thrust into the bark. A short distance from the tree was a rock set in the ground, like a marker on a grave. Crow dug up the spot and found the skeleton of a man, buried with his boots on and a bullet hole in his skull.

Some stories say the gang buried a fatally wounded member near their campsite, although others claim the loot was buried in a hole about the size and shape of a grave.

Crow said he combed the area around the tree quite thoroughly but couldn't find another place where the treasure was likely to have been buried. Although, he admits, he wouldn't know where to begin his search and hasn't dug around much.

The location of the treasure area, according to Crow, is a good distance up Handcart Gulch. He said the trail up Handcart Gulch starts at the old ghost town of Hall Valley, some ten miles northwest of Grant. Just below the ruins of the old Hall Valley Smelter, Handcart Creek flows into the north fork of the South Platte River. Through aspens and spruce trees, you travel up a sharp glade from the townsite. It is almost impossible to see any trail now, but about a half mile upstream were stone breastworks, which are often mistaken for a natural rock ledge. Uptrail is a little hidden park in an aspen grove. Near its center is a line of stones where once a lean-to stood. Higher on the slope it levels into an area roughly square, about seventy-five feet on each side. To the right the bank drops down steeply into Handcart Gulch and Handcart Creek. Here a deep trench still runs around what was once a makeshift corral. In the trees at the edge of the clearing, farthest from the creek, stockade timbers lie where they fell, side by side in what was once a solid wall of logs, set upright in the trench. The ax marks are still visible. A mile or more upstream on the same side of the creek is the grave. And the tree with the dim scar is nearby. Near the grave a large iron springs bubbles on the right-hand bank. (One reason why electronic detectors are useless.)

To summarize, the most authoritative narratives have the treasure a short distance up Handcart Gulch, although enough people think the treasure is up either Geneva or Elk Creek to look for it there. And, then again, some studious people don't

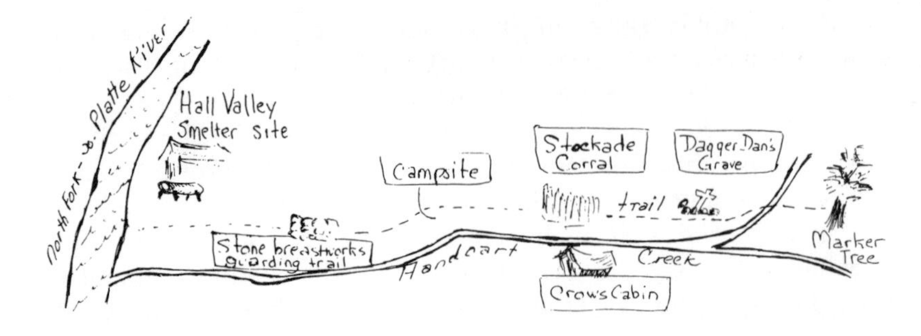

think there is a treasure at all, at least a big enough one to merit the name.

If you decide to look, don't tell the people up there who sent you. They are sick unto death of all this treasure talk. Fortune hunters have torn down fences and fence posts, trampled fields and dug holes all up and down three gulches.

They wish they had never heard of Jim "The Bold" Reynolds and his infernal treasure.

66. THE LOST MINE OF DEAD MAN'S GULCH

Dead Man's Gulch was named for the slaughter of one of the first prospecting parties in South Park. Eight prospectors and fourteen horses were caught in an ambush. Seven of the men and all fourteen horses were killed, and their bleached bones were found by some of the early prospectors over Kenosha Pass.

Dead Man's Gulch is on Kenosha Hill, not far from the site of Tarryall, the first town in South Park.

Tarryall was still growing and going strong in 1863 when two peculiar-acting Germans began to arouse the curiosity of the townspeople. Each morning, with regularity, they left the camp and headed over the mountain. A lot of prospectors did that, and not too many people paid much heed for the first few weeks.

However, each camp had its leeches. Down on their luck at the local diggings, the leeches would attempt to follow other prospectors out of town, hoping to latch onto something nearby. The Germans didn't cotton to being followed. Whenever anyone even looked as if he was going to follow, the Germans turned back and wouldn't work that day. As the weeks went by, the Germans would be gone more and more, and they acted more strangely.

In the fall of 1863, one of the Germans was seen working alone near Dead Man's Gulch. The visitor asked the German where his partner was and the German replied casually that their mine had caved in and his partner had been killed. The surviving partner didn't seem crestfallen at the death of his colleague. In fact, when the incident was recalled later, he seemed rather happy. He told the visitor they, he and his partner, had mined between $6,000 and $7,000 in gold dust off bed rock, and he was preparing to head back to Germany and enjoy himself, and then come back in the spring.

The German refused to divulge the location of his mine. (This, apparently, became more of a mystery than whatever became of his partner—it demonstrates how people thought in those days.)

The German departed and was never seen again in South Park. Prospectors searched the width and breadth of Dead Man's Gulch the next few years, but found no evidence of the lost mine, the legendary wealth of which grew through the years.

Eventually, in 1885, long after Tarryall and other workings in the area had died, rancher David Baker found traces of a mine in Dead Man's Gulch. He found an abandoned shaft, the opening of which had been obscured. Wood chips were found in the shaft and Baker said that the trees showed that the chips had been taken from them about twenty years previously.

Baker and some of his friends sunk a shaft of about fifteen feet and found traces of gold as well as a peculiarly-shaped tin can with the word "patented" pressed into the tin.

Baker and others believed the mine was the German's lost mine but they had no real evidence to support their assumption. And they didn't find any trace of the partner.

67. THE WHITTLER'S LOST MINE

An oft-told story of lost gold down around Breckenridge way is the tale of the Whittler's Lost Mine.

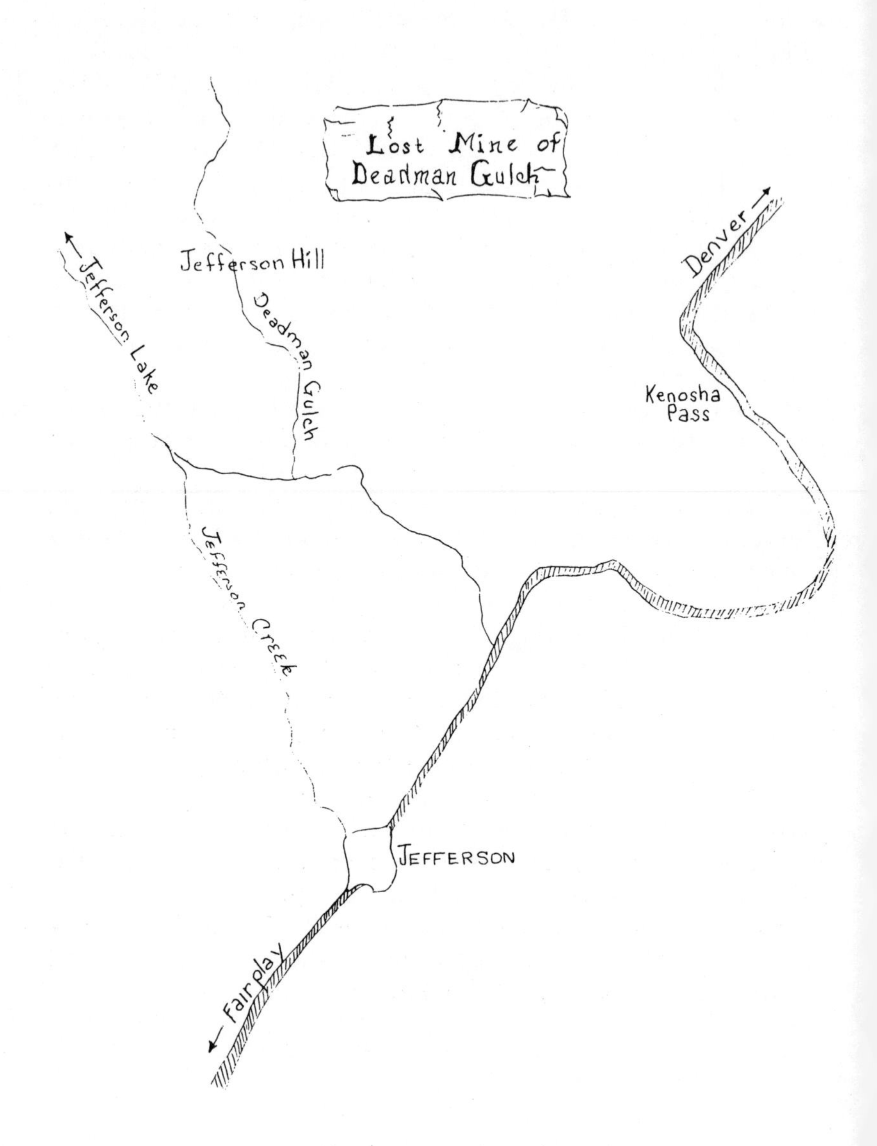
Lost Mine of Deadman Gulch
Jefferson Hill
Jefferson Lake
Deadman Gulch
Denver
Kenosha Pass
Jefferson Creek
JEFFERSON
Fairplay

It seems a certain hunter in the early 1860's would ride into Denver in the fall with his pack full of skins and "pleasant quantities" of gold. He told everyone he shot the bears near Breckenridge. He kept mum about the source of the gold.

The distinguishing trait of the hunter was the small wooden shovels he whittled all the time. He said he whittled the shovels to help clear the snow away from his cabin in the mountains, and it had become a habit.

After a few years the hunter got lost in the crowd coming west. But the story of his mine, the location of which he had never told, lived on. Many searched for it although they had only a vague idea of where it might be.

In the 1890s, some thirty years later, a Breckenridge prospector happened onto a rundown cabin, a mine tunnel and a mine dump in strange land high above the mining town.

The mine could well have been just another abandoned location, were it not for its unique feature. Small wooden spades, worn down almost to the handles, were found on the mine dump. Another spade was found in the tunnel.

The prospector was sure he had found the Whittler's Lost Mine, known in legend to be rich in gold. The ore was black, tacky stuff. The prospector had nothing in which to put ore samples but a tobacco pouch. This he loaded with the best-looking ore, put one of the wooden spades in his pack, and headed for town.

He lost the trail on the way back, however, and by the time he had recovered his bearings he had no idea of directions. He also lost his tobacco pouch full of ore. He was in one hell of a mess.

He was still excited when he got back to town, however, feeling fairly certain he could find the site again. He took a friend into his confidence and showed him the wooden spade.

The two men made several prospecting trips into the mountains but never found the old cabin and the mine.

68. THE LOST TENDERFOOT MINE

The Lost Tenderfoot is the favorite quest of treasure searchers in the Breckenridge area. An item in the 1900 *Denver Republi-*

can told of several prospectors having their "annual try" at the Lost Tenderfoot Mine. Directions for finding the mine are so simple, or seem so simple, that many were sure they would find it. Nobody has found it yet . . . and they're still looking.

The story begins in the fall of 1880 when a novice prospector, or tenderfoot, stopped for lunch in the mountains high above Breckenridge. He could see the Warrior's Mark Mine to the east and Breckenridge far below to the northwest.

At the spot, the tenderfoot saw a rock jutting out edgewise from the ledge nearby. He idly banged his prospector's pick against the rock.

It didn't fall, although it was cracked clear through. On closer inspection he saw the reason why.

The rock was held to the ledge by a pale metal filament—wire gold!

The excited young man gouged out about twenty pounds of it, the wire gold, and started back for town just as the snow—the first snow of the season—began to fall.

He sent the gold to Denver and got back $400 for it—a pretty fair country price for twenty pounds of ore. Tenderfeet don't have poker faces, and the news got out. Breckenridge stirred with excitement that winter.

The tenderfoot, and several others, headed back toward the spot as early as they could the following spring. They failed to find the ledge after a full summer of searching.

Experienced prospectors and tenderfoots have been searching ever since. The ledge has either disappeared or has eluded them all.

Oldtimers believed the ledge was located on Bare Mountain, although it could be on Red Mountain.

A few years ago, the *Denver Post* cautioned:

"The top of Bare Mountain is largely covered with broken and disintegrated red sandstone. Anyone searching for the lost mine, say experts, should dig holes at intervals to the bed rock or a flow-streak, using the gold pan to pan each different stratum until he finds one that pans gold. Then he should follow the flow streak until it shows the vein or ledge from which it was eroded by the actions of the elements."

So, your work is cut out for you.

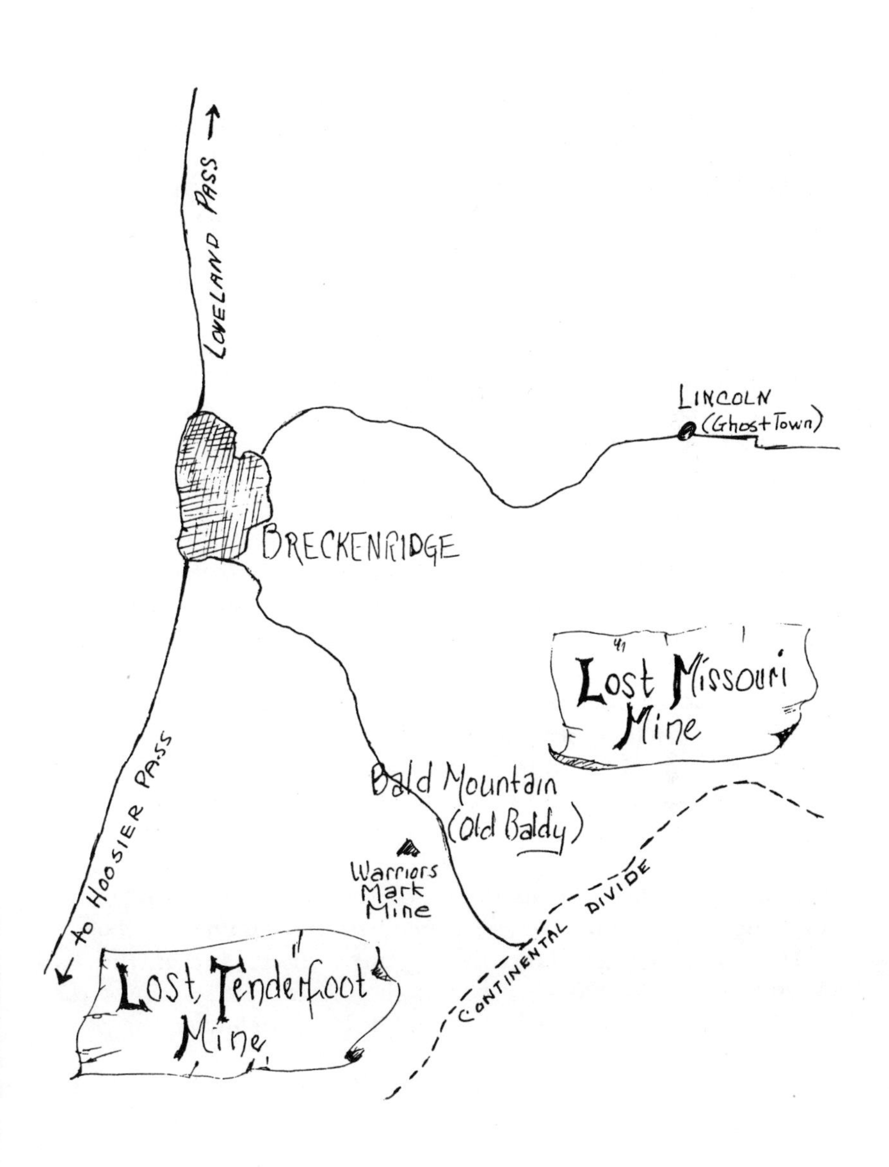
LOVELAND PASS
LINCOLN
(Ghost Town)
BRECKENRIDGE
Lost Missouri Mine
Bald Mountain
(Old Baldy)
Warriors Mark Mine
to HOOSIER PASS
CONTINENTAL DIVIDE
Lost Tenderfoot Mine

69. THE LOST MISSOURI MINE

In the 1860s Breckenridge and its neighbor, Lincoln, now a ghost town, were bustling with gold miners and gold prospectors. Came dawn, the prospectors fanned out in every direction. Nobody paid much attention where anybody else went unless one's actions differed from the norm.

Two of the Lincoln prospectors were from the "show-me" state, Missouri. Nobody paid them much heed until the town noticed they set off for the hills at night and returned at dawn to sleep during the day. When word of this got around, all Lincoln began paying closer attention to the men from Missouri. It soon became evident that the men had large quantities of gold about them. Apparently, however, no one took the trouble to trail the men. They were seen returning to camp from around Big Baldy.

The two men continued to mystify the camp until the winter of 1861 when they returned to Breckenridge. When the Civil War broke out, they returned to Missouri. They were never seen again, and they left no clue as to the location of their apparently rich mine.

The mine left behind by the Missourians became the subject of several search parties the next few years, but there has been no evidence it was found—if there was a mine in the first place.

The location of the mine has never been verified, but the story of the rich Missourians has. Lafayette Seaman, the first coroner of Summit County and later manager of the Tabor Investment Company, verified the existence of the two men. Seaman was working a placer mine out of Lincoln in the summer of 1860.

Historian George Bancroft suggested in 1914 that the two Missourians may have worked nights, because the mines they worked—possibly on rich Farncomb Hill—belonged to others during the day.

XIV. *THE NORTHERN MOUNTAINS*

70. THE LOST MINE OWNER

There's a fairly rich mine, the Entre-Mile, located near the once rip-roaring town of Teller in Larimer County, which never gained its rightful place in the sun for want of tender, loving development.

The mine was, and is, located at the head of Michigan Creek on the western slope of Mt. Richtofen. It was discovered in 1879 by John Moore and brothers John and Alexander Lefevre. The mine developed very rapidly and was soon shown to be of more than ordinary value. The ore ran very high in silver, from the surface down.

But before any great amount of work was done, the three owners were offered a good price for the mine from a company formed in Vandalia, Illinois.

The new owners equipped the property with a steam plant, including a pump, and sunk a shaft to a depth of 200 feet. Along the way they opened up some rich ore deposits, much of it a very high grade ruby silver.

The Entre-Mile faced the same problem all the mines in that area did then. Many good mines were found in this section of northern Colorado, but it was so remote that much of the profits

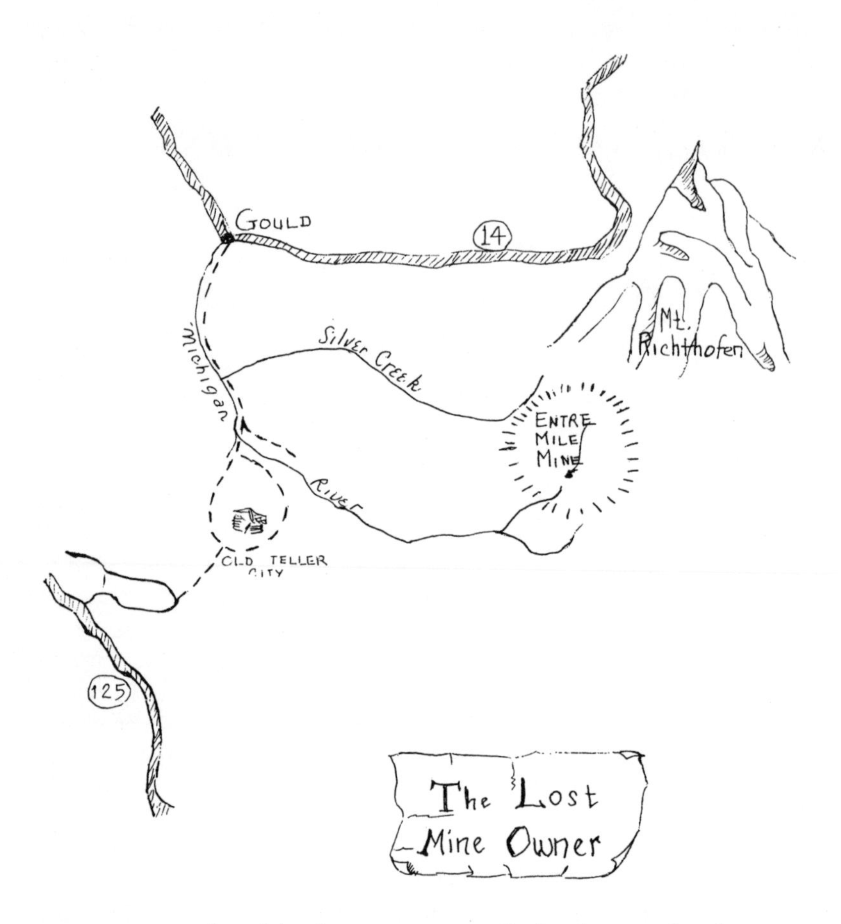

were eaten up by shipping expenses. Only the good mines survived until better transportation came to Larimer County.

The Entre-Mile was considered one of the better properties in the neighborhood and its development continued. But it was mismanaged, the owners disagreed, the company got into debt before realizing any profit, work was suspended, and the mine was abandoned.

In 1885 the property was sold at auction in Vandalia to cover debts. The selling price was $60,000.

But to the surprise of the miners in the area, the mine was never worked again. Not that many didn't want to work it. Several times during the next fifteen or twenty years, prospectors and mine owners have verified the worth of the mine and have attempted to purchase the property, but the owner was never located. Officials in Vandalia combed the records, verified the sale and all the particulars, but the name and whereabouts of the purchaser were never found.

Around 1900 a mining engineer made an extensive examination of the mine and took samples of ore that ran 600 ounces of silver to the ton. But he also found that water had seeped into the shaft and the frigid temperatures at that high altitude had caused the water to freeze until the pump and the hoist were encased in one huge cake of ice.

Within the next few years the entire area was abandoned. Now, even the trails leading to Teller country have been covered over by time. It is about the most lonely and desolate area in all of Colorado.

But it had its day—except for one very good mine.

71. GRAND LAKE GOLD

Several men who had made their pile in the early California gold rush were returning to the east when they were attacked by Utes near the present site of Steamboat Springs. Only four of the men survived. Temporarily winded and needing a rest from the grueling trip, the survivors stopped alongside the shores of Grand Lake for a few days of hunting and fishing.

They buried their gold in a Dutch oven near a huge boulder on the eastern shores of the lake. To further mark the spot they drove a knife deep into a nearby tree.

Then they went about their hunting and fishing.

But the Indians wouldn't leave them alone. Resenting the poachers in their happy hunting ground, a band of Indians attacked them. Three of the four men were killed. The fourth escaped and returned to his home in the east, feeling fortunate he was alive.

The survivor told his story and then died a short time later.

One story says the Frenchmen were not attacked by Indians, but simply decided to leave the gold here and come back and get

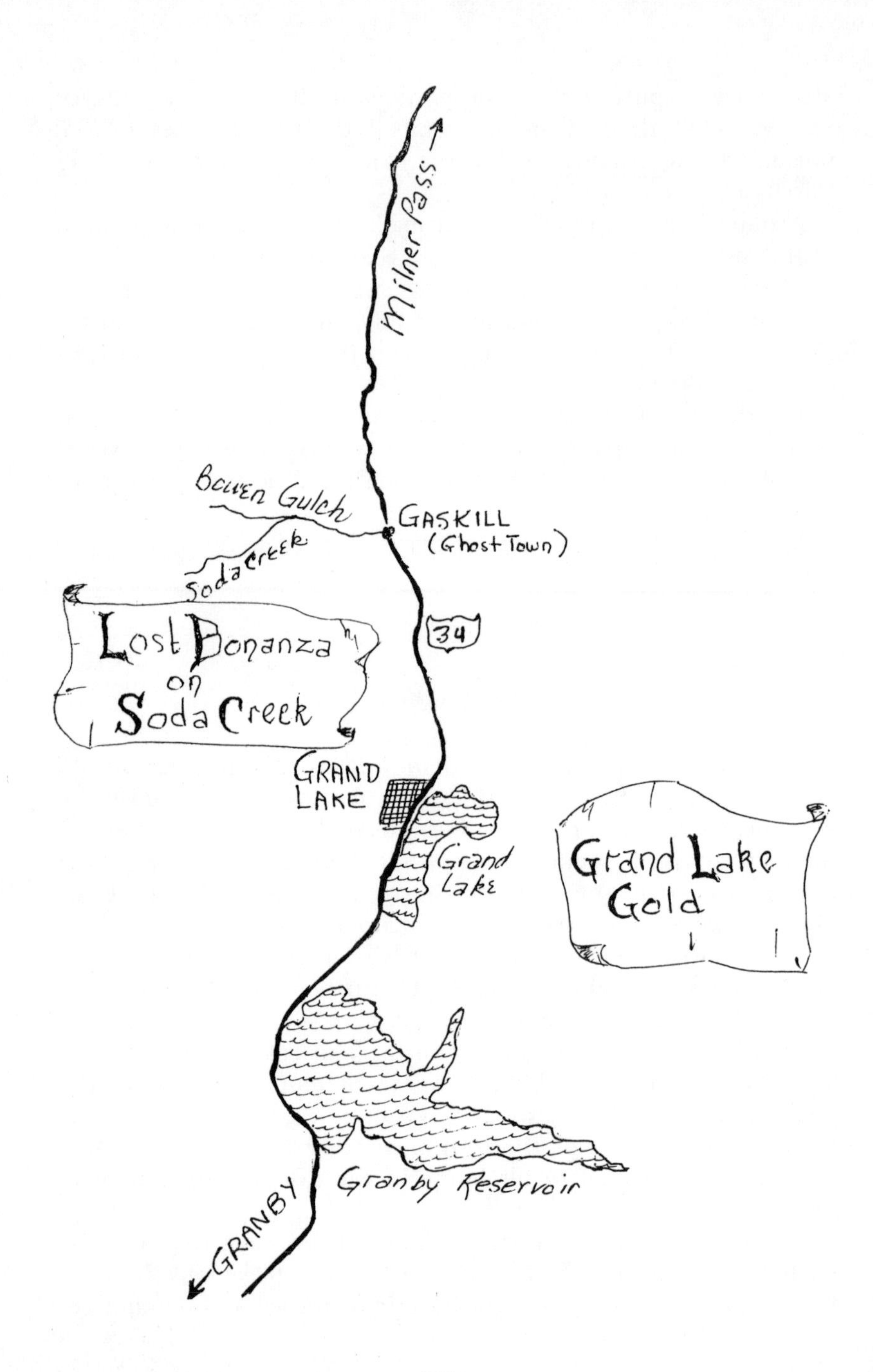
Milner Pass
Bowen Gulch
Soda Creek
GASKILL
(Ghost Town)
34
Lost Bonanza
on
Soda Creek
GRAND
LAKE
Grand
Lake
Grand Lake
Gold
Granby Reservoir
GRANBY

Grand Lake years and years ago when only an old trapper's cabin was seen along its shores and a rich California gold cache lay buried along the bank.

it the following year—they were tired of carrying it. This doesn't seem logical, however.

The land has changed greatly in the intervening 110 years. Tractors and bull-dozers working on the immense Big Thompson project, scraped the ground, pushed over the trees; dynamite uprooted the boulders.

In recent years a cottage was built on or near the spot where the treasure was said to be buried. Before that, the Indians burned down many of the trees here.

Perhaps the tree with the knife stuck in it was destroyed by fire, and the knife fell to the ground, eventually buried beneath the sands of time.

Or, mayhap, a lonely stranger, not knowing the legend, passed by and spotting the knife in the tree, salvaged it for himself. A knife might have been enough treasure for him.

72. LOST BONANZA ON SODA CREEK

Isaac Alden, who claimed to be a direct descendant of John Alden, came to the Grand Lake area in the 1880s, when he was in his twenties. Alden knew there was plenty of gold in Colorado and like most young fellows he wanted to get some of it.

He prospected all over the area. He didn't have much luck until one day when he was up on Soda Creek in the once lively mining area around Gaskill. Weary, Alden rested on a boulder and idly picked up a rock and broke it with his prospector's pick. The rock showed signs of copper. He picked up several samples and went on his way.

When he got home he tested the metals himself and it seemed like some rusty gold. He still wasn't sure so he took them to Grand Lake and sent them to an assayer in Denver by stagecoach.

At the end of a month he got the report back from Denver—the samples showed $1,600 gold to the ton.

Alden scurried back up to Soda Creek. He had been enough of a prospector to have made a careful study of the area before he left. The main landmarks were the huge boulder on which he had sat and an overturned tree nearby with its roots upended. He was sure of his directions because he had discovered the samples in the early spring. There was snow on his side of the creek and the other side was green and clear.

However, in the intervening months, the landscape had changed considerably. The snow had melted and several large boulders now lined the creek. And a fire, apparently set by lightning, had burned several trees—including, apparently, the overturned tree with roots upended—to ashes.

Alden searched up and down the creek the rest of the summer . . . and the following summer. In fact, he searched Soda Creek off and on for the rest of his life . . . and he died at the age of ninety.

He always said he wanted to take $100,000 from "his mine" and then sell the property.

But Isaac Alden didn't take it with him.

73. ESTES PARK GOLD

Estes Park, northern Colorado's mountain wonderland, is not known as a mining area. There was some mining nearby, but, for the most part, its mountains are unblemished by prospect holes and mine shafts.

No mountain area is untouched by legends, however. Estes Park has had its share. Here are some of them.

Hunter's Gold

In 1875. a party from Boulder journeyed over the mountains for a hunting expedition into Estes Park. In the party was a man named Barber who was above all else a prospector and had his eyes on the ground for signs of gold as well as deer tracks.

During the expedition he gathered up several rock samples and stuffed them in his hunting jacket. On his return home, the press of other business filled his thoughts and the jacket was put away.

Months later Barber was visited by an assayer friend and the rocks were suddenly called to mind. Barber showed them to his friend. The assayer looked them over with a magnifying glass and declared there were a few worth testing. He took them with him and, later, making the usual tests at his shop he found one sample that showed high gold content, worth thousands of dollars per ton.

He rushed back and told Barber. The two of them decided to take the most practical course. They would keep their find a secret and return to Estes Park the following spring, presumably on another hunting expedition. Barber took what seemed the same trail the party had taken nearly two years before. But they didn't find any gold.

The two of them searched much of the rest of the year, and the years that followed, but found no gold.

Years later, Barber told others the story and said he thought it was in the Wind River and Glacier Basin drainage area. The region has been well searched, however, without success.

The Lost Artist Lode

One of Colorado's most famous artists was Albert Bierstadt, and perhaps his most famous painting was of Loch Vale. He did the painting in the Estes Park area. He maintained that the mountain park was one of his favorite spots. He painted there often.

On one of his trips he picked up what looked like a gold nugget. When he returned to civilization, and when he had the opportunity, he had it tested. It showed good gold content.

The artist showed friends the nugget, and told them where they could find some more just as pretty. Later, he even conducted a party up to the park, to the spot where he thought he found it. But they couldn't find another one.

Bierstadt and his friends returned to Estes Park frequently after that, Bierstadt to paint, his friends to prospect.

Dying Prospector Mine

A dying prospector, who finally gave in to the fact he couldn't take it with him, told bedside friends of the gold strike he had made on Specimen Mountain in the Estes Park area.

With shaking hands he drew a map of the mountain. Although crude, the map seemed complete enough to take anyone to the spot.

Beautiful but rugged Loch Vale country near Estes Park where the famous Colorado artist found a gold nugget while enroute to his favorite art subject. *Picture courtesy Erika Schramm.*

But, on future explorations, it was found the map neglected too many landmarks to be useful. Many searched, however, with and without the map.

One of the many parties that attempted to locate the lost lode became lost itself. They wandered around the mountain wonderland for nearly three days before they made their way into a ranger station, cold and hungry, and sick to death of lost mines.

XV. *EAST OF THE FRONT RANGE*

74. SPIRITS JOIN THE SEARCH

A. M. Pryor, a Denver realty agent in 1914, was sure he could find the spot where train robbers had hidden their loot some twenty years before. But he needed help.

Pryor, who was also an amateur hypnotist, enlisted the aid of Mrs. Elizabeth McNeeton, who had called upon Pryor's powers to end her ailments, and Arthur Betterman, a bootblack at the St. James Hotel, where Pryor was staying.

According to Pryor, old records stated the train robbers were seen crossing a bridge across the Platte River at 47th and Downing Street with their loot in hand. When the posse finally caught up with them and killed them a short distance beyond the bridge, the loot was gone.

Pryor, Mrs. McNeeton, Betterman, and a John Siler, who was hired to do the digging, set off for the bridge. But their venture met unexpected complications at the scene when they found three bridges, any one of which could have been the bridge used in the flight of the train robbers.

However, the problem was soon remedied. Pryor put Mrs. McNeeton and Betterman into a hypnotic trance along the banks of the Platte. After short flights into the spirit world, Mrs. McNeeton and Betterman agreed upon the bridge. They said the spirits also agreed upon which pillar of the bridge the loot was buried under. Siler began digging.

But here the spirits parted ways. Siler found no loot near the surface. The spirits were questioned further. Mrs. McNeeton said her spirit told her the treasure was another foot and a half deeper. Betterman's spirit claimed it was only a foot deeper.

While Mrs. NcNeeton and Betterman were negotiating with the spirits, twelve-year-old Dewey Miyorks chanced by. He saw the digging and he saw the two bodies lying on the bank. Dewey put two and two together and went home and called the cops.

Patrolman Gavin answered the call. Patrolman Gavin was an unimaginative police officer who didn't believe in spirits in the first place. Pryor attempted to explain that it was all a legitimate business venture, but Patrolman Gavin didn't like the looks of it at all, and ran them all into the station house. Pryor, Mrs. McNeeton, Betterman and Siler were booked at City Hall and kept in jail overnight.

While the four were in the cooler, small neighborhood boys widened the hole at the bridge and found no treasure.

If small boys can't find a treasure—no one can.

75. THE LOST SPANISH BULLION CASE

Late in 1905, gaudy advertisements appeared in several eastern newspapers, particularly in New York City and Boston, telling of the rediscovery of a long lost Spanish mine near Silver City in New Mexico.

The discovery was made by George DuBois and his son, Lee, who lived in Silver City and were shown the ancient mine by an Indian guide.

After the discovery, the DuBoises moved to Denver to organize a company and develop what they said would be "one of the richest mines in the entire west."

One of the first men they met in Denver was Dr. R. C. Hunt, a dentist, who happened to be casting around for a place to invest his money. The DuBoises told Dr. Hunt of the Spanish Bullion Mine. They showed him rich ore samples they said came from the mine. He invested $10,000 in the enterprise. In return, Dr. Hunt was made first president of the newly-organized Spanish Bullion Mining Company. Another prominent Denverite, Danton Pinkus, invested in the company and was made a vice president.

Seven more names were added to the company roster: William E. Wilson and W. B. Cameron of Boulder; A. E. Keables, C. L. Blackman, Arthur Leven, David Lawrence, and E. W. Sebben of Denver.

The names of all these men appeared in the advertisements, but the name of Dr. Hunt was most prominent. For such a potentially great mine, stock was cheap, and it sold rapidly although sales were limited to the east.

It so happened, however, that an alert and ambitious Federal investigator, Charles Riddiford, chanced to notice the ads in a Boston newspaper and he sent for information.

Information, glowing information, was sent forthwith, and to young Riddiford it was too good to be true. Riddiford displayed the information before his superior and was granted permission to investigate. He went to Silver City.

Riddiford found what seemed to him to be nothing more than a limestone cave, with plenty of loose dirt and debris on the floor. The mining engineers he hired concurred and, after thorough investigation, could find no mineral of any value.

Riddiford returned to Denver and confronted Dubois and his son with the evidence. The two men denied any and all allegations, producing their own samples and assay charts that showed high gold content. But after persistent and grueling questioning, the two men admitted their fraud.

Within days, the DuBoises and all other members of the company were indicted on three counts of using the U.S. mail to defraud. Although no accurate records were kept, it was estimated that $80,000 in stock had already been sold.

Shortly thereafter, the DuBoises repudiated their confession, saying it was made under duress.

The trial was held in the late summer of 1907 and received great notoriety throughout the country. United States District

Attorney Harry J. Berne of Kansas City journeyed to Denver to try the case which he called "one of the rankest frauds ever perpetrated in this or any other state."

The *Denver Republican* called it "one of the most novel although palpable frauds in mining history."

Wildcat speculation was rampant in those days and, although many petty swindles and frauds were tried all the time, this trial marked one of the first major trials involving a large, legally-drawn corporation and involving national interests, in the history of mining and the west.

The consequences could be far-reaching in stamping out wildcat mining speculation and get-rich-quick schemes.

Another aspect of the case drew and kept the interest of the public, nationally as well as locally. After DuBois and his son repudiated their confessions there was constant speculation about who was right and who was wrong. Some believe to this day that the Lost Spanish Bullion Mine could have been one of the biggest mining enterprises in the west, had not its owners been unfairly persecuted. Testimony brought out in the trial only tended to confuse the issue more.

The trial was one of the most exciting of the times. It was marked with numerous angry outbursts, charges and countercharges. The prosecuting and defense attorneys were dramatic in their presentation and cross examination. But the most colorful ingredients of the trial were the people put on the stand.

The prosecution had a solid case, parading expert after expert to the stand who told of the worthlessness of what the prosecution insisted was no more than a cave. One of the most telling and colorful witnesses was long-time Silver City miner Jack Flemming who said:

"When the good Lord built Bear Mountain he left a big hole in there and then got busy somewhere else and forgot to put in any minerals to make the poor prospector happy."

Another damning witness was Theodore Stegner of New York City, who was hired by Blackman to sell stocks. Stegner said under oath that Blackman told him, "We have got a good thing and are going to catch a lot of suckers." Blackman also said, according to Stegner, that the company figured on making at least a million dollars out of the scheme.

Much of the case for the defense was based upon the testimony of a mining engineer named Lindeman. Lindeman was one of the top engineers in the west, and was said to have built the first house in Denver. His father put forth many mining advances and Lindeman's Lake in Alaska was named for him.

The highly respected man estimated the Spanish Bullion property was worth about twenty million dollars, and that from $600,000 to $800,000 of loose ore was in sight. He said:

"The cross cutting from one vein to the other showed every sign of being done by human hands. Also I saw that the passages had been filled in with broken rock and masses of ore. The regularity of the passages was another fact that convinced me that it was an old Spanish mine."

Lindeman, who spent more time at the site than any other expert, also said he found some evidence that the Aztecs had worked the mine before the Spanish.

His testimony cast doubt on the charges from that time forward. The prosecution found rebuttal against such a learned man difficult, but they heaped it on.

Time and time again the defense attempted to introduce ore samples as evidence, but the attempts were defeated as the prosecution claimed it would be impossible to prove that such samples came from the Spanish Bullion property. Angry clashes took place between the defense and prosecution over the samples, the defense stating they should be able to present samples if the prosecution did.

DuBois, for awhile, seemed an effective witness. He told in great detail how the old Indian guide showed him the mine, how he had the ore sampled and tested time after time, and how the Spanish company was formed legally. He denied all allegations against him and said his earlier confession was made under duress.

But his testimony broke down somewhat under cross examination. In a shouting contest his position of hurt innocence was greatly weakened.

Another hope of the defense was the audience, filled with the families and friends of the defendants. The defendants had nineteen children in all, and they were all there, every day. Frequently the wives would raise handkerchiefs to their eyes.

Berne attempted to counteract the sympathy aroused for the defendants in his summation by citing the thousands of dollars the accused took from widows and mothers throughout the country. He said many put their last cent of life savings into the nefarious scheme. He claimed the rape of the innocent would continue if these men were not brought to justice.

The jury was out several hours. They returned with a verdict of guilty, asking leniency for Dr. Hunt and Pinkus.

Before sentence was pronounced, Judge Lewis gave the defense attorney opportunity to file for a new trial.

In the meantime, the defendants brought a carload of ore which assayed at $26 dollars a ton. They also stressed claims, only touched upon in the trial, that the cave was only the beginning of Spanish Bullion property, and that the best part of the property was far up in the gulch, off any wagon trail.

In filing for a new trial, the defense attorney claimed the defendants showed their good faith by building dwellings for miners and starting construction of a road up the gulch.

The defense attorney also charged 109 errors in the trial, not the least of which was the fact that the prosecutor prejudiced the jury by his continuous use of the word "slag" instead of "ore," and "cave" instead of "mine." The defense also objected strenuously to the use of ore samples submitted by the prosecution, while the defense was not able to use its own.

Judge Lewis, in denying the petition for a new trial, discounted the errors and discounted the recent shipment of ore. He said there still was no proof that the ore came from Spanish Bullion property, and that the defendants had had two years to show their good faith and they had failed to do so.

On the day after Christmas in 1907, Judge Lewis passed sentence. He said the defendants deserved no mercy. He said, however, that the wives and children of the defendants must be considered. They had suffered enough.

George and Lee DuBois and C. L. Blackman, who first concocted the scheme, received the stiffest sentences: thirty days in jail and $1,000 fines each. Wilson, Cameron, Keables and Lawrence, willing confederates in the plan, were sentenced to fifteen days in jail and $500 fines. Leven and Sebben, $100 fines and costs. Dr. Hunt and Pinkus, innocent dupes in the scheme, were fined $50 each, and were given a stern talk on how to invest their money wisely in the future.

Of more lasting consequence were the steps taken in most of the states to prevent such schemes from succeeding in the future.

Even during the trial, officials in Colorado and other states held meetings on how to safeguard against wildcat speculation and fraudulent schemes. The result was that the laws were strengthened and the effectiveness of such get-rich-quick schemes were greatly hampered.

It wasn't until some forty years later when a metal called uranium skyrocketed into prominence that widows and mothers throughout the country were again robbed of their pennies and dollars in an effort to get rich quick.

76. GEORGETOWN'S HIDDEN VAULT

The first bank in Clear Creek County used to stand at the corner of Rose and Fourth Streets in Georgetown. It was established by George T. Clark and Company, with backing from the First National Bank in Denver. The bank was the center of some tremendous business transactions in the early days.

One of the exciting events in the bank's colorful history was the run on the bank that occurred in the '70s. When the panic began, just a few persons rushed to the bank to withdraw their money; this brought others, until by mid-morning a long line was waiting outside on the rumor the bank was running out of gold.

The bank officials were frantic. They feared they would not have enough money on hand to cover the deposits. Then one official got a bright idea.

The bank dispatched a wagon to Central City and it returned with a load of gold bullion. They unloaded the bags, plainly marked gold bullion, at the front door of the bank—right through the people waiting in line to get their money.

Of course, the shipment put an end to the panic, and by the end of the afternoon, much of the money withdrawn from the bank had been deposited again.

The circulating medium at the time was gold dust and $20 gold pieces coined by Gruber, Clark and Company in Denver. In the late '60s and '70s, it was necessary to keep large sums of money at the bank. And since there were so many unsavory characters in town, it was often necessary for banks to have hidden vaults.

The bank was torn down after it outlived its usefulness. After a few years the property was purchased by Edward Riley.

In 1912, a hole began to sink immediately behind where the bank used to be. It developed that the hole was an old hidden vault of the bank. It had been reinforced with heavy timbers which had finally rotted out under the weight of the earth.

That's all Georgetown got to know about the vault.

Riley fenced it off and did all the investigating himself and wouldn't tell anyone about it.

His reticence gave birth to the legends about the hidden vault.

It seems that no one, not even those intimate with the bank, knew of the vault. The story got around that perhaps only one man knew of the vault and that he died suddenly, taking the secret with him. It only followed that there were perhaps many valuables and much gold still buried there.

Riley didn't give anyone any peace of mind. He never did tell anyone about the vault and said, many times, if he ever found anything, it was nobody's damn business but his own.

Oldtime Georgetown residents say he said this in such a way that made them believe he had found something.

77. BOX ELDER LEAD

In the fall of 1862 a bunch of pioneers gathered in Denver and decided to join together in their search for meat to lay in for the winter ahead of them. The group decided to break into small groups and fan out in search of venison.

One group headed for the Box Elder region about thirty miles northwest of Denver. They erected a makeshift shelter for their headquarters and began their hunt. As most of the pioneers did, they caulked the holes in their shelter with mud.

They were quite successful in their quest for game. Too successful, in fact, because they soon discovered they were running low on bullets. One night, while discussing the problem, one of the party happened to notice the mud caulking. Small particles that looked like lead were seen in the mud. On closer inspection it did turn out to be lead.

The next day they went to the spot where they had found the mud and found large quantities of leaden particles. They used the lead chunks for bullets, finished their hunt, and returned to Denver with plenty of meat for the cold winter ahead. The use of the lead particles for bullets became a well-known story at the time, but only because of the ingenuity displayed by the hunters. At that time placer mining was the craze in Colorado. Nobody bothered much with ore deposits, let alone lead deposits.

A few years later, however, when the value of the find was realized, the story was recalled and many attempted to find the spot, but could not.

78. LOST MINE ON HICKS MOUNTAIN

Douglas McClain was an electrician and the founder of the Firemen's Fund Life Insurance Company. He was also a consumptive. His doctor back east said he didn't have much time left to live unless he gave up working and went to a better climate.

So, Douglas McClain headed for Colorado, naturally. This was in 1893.

The Colorado climate and his doctor, F. J. Bancroft, did wonders for the man. After two years in bed, Dr. Bancroft said that McClain was well enough to travel to the doctor's ranch near Evergreen. After a short time, McClain was able to putter around the ranch, then take longer and longer walks in the woods. The '90s was a time of great gold excitement in Colorado. McClain's TB was arrested, but he got the gold fever along with everyone else.

His walks turned into prospecting jaunts, although the area around Evergreen is notorious for being deficient in gold.

However, one fall he was out rabbit hunting when he became lost in the heavy timber on Mount Bergen. He was lost from ten o'clock in the morning until 9 o'clock at night.

About dark it began to snow and he hurried on his way, although he wasn't too sure where his way was.

While searching for a route, he noticed a ledge of peculiar-looking rock. It looked like a vein of gold, about eighteen inches

wide. He later said the outcropping was at the bottom of a gulch under a high earthen bank. McClain chipped off a few samples and went on. At 9 o'clock that night, at the height of the blizzard, he stumbled into the Witter ranch on the opposite side of Hicks Mountain from the Bancroft ranch.

The next day, McClain had the samples assayed and found that the ore ran to about $1,000 a ton. He immediately purchased a stagecoach ticket to Denver and told his doctor the news. Dr. Bancroft provided McClain with the necessary equipment needed for a mining venture, including a pony and blank location notices. McClain hurried back to the ranch, but to his disappointment, the snow stayed in the mountains, and he had to postpone his prospecting trip until the following spring.

That spring of 1896, McClain took what he thought was the same route he took the year before, but he didn't locate his golden ledge. He made a careful study of the region, charting his trip from the Bancroft ranch to the Witter ranch, and was positive the find was made on Hicks Mountain. It had to be if one considered his winding up at the Witter ranch.

McClain looked for the gold all that summer, spent the following winter studying the region again and preparing for more prospecting trips the following spring and summer. He never did find the golden ledge.

Dr. Bancroft said McClain was not an experienced prospector and made little note of the surroundings. He, McClain, had become lost before and absent-mindedness was one of his characteristics. It is possible he became lost on Mount Strain instead of Mount Bergen. Nonetheless, the gold must have been on Hicks Mountain, although it could be anywhere on the mountain. McClain maintains that the gulch was either Witter Gulch or the next big gulch from it, running into Bear Creek.

It is possible the high earthen bank above the gulch gave way during the winter and obscured the golden ledge.

Anyhow, the find has been verified . . . but never found.

McClain returned to the east in 1910, hale and hearty, but not as rich as he should have been.

79. UNDERWATER GOLD AT STANDLEY LAKE

Standley Lake, just outside Denver, covers a bed of gold and coal . . . if anybody wants to spend the money to dig it out.

The Standley Reservoir site in Jefferson County was filed for and financed in 1902. Owners of right-of-way land at the eastern end of the proposed lake bed sold quickly. But residents at the western end refused.

They said they had done some drilling on their land and discovered that the ground was underlain with a bed of gold ore about eight feet thick at a depth of 800 feet. The ore was valued at about $30 per ton. On top of this, they said, were some coal beds.

The west-enders hired a lawyer and fought the land acquisition.

There was a long-drawn-out legal battle, including a trial. At the trial several mining engineers, hired by the state, said one of the samples did show some gold and that the ground was underlaid with coal. But, engineers said, they could tell little from the surface. They said mineralization often occurred, or usually occurred, before coal beds.

Condemnation proceedings were drawn up, but the west-enders threatened to fight all the way.

Finally, as a compromise, the dam people asked only for the

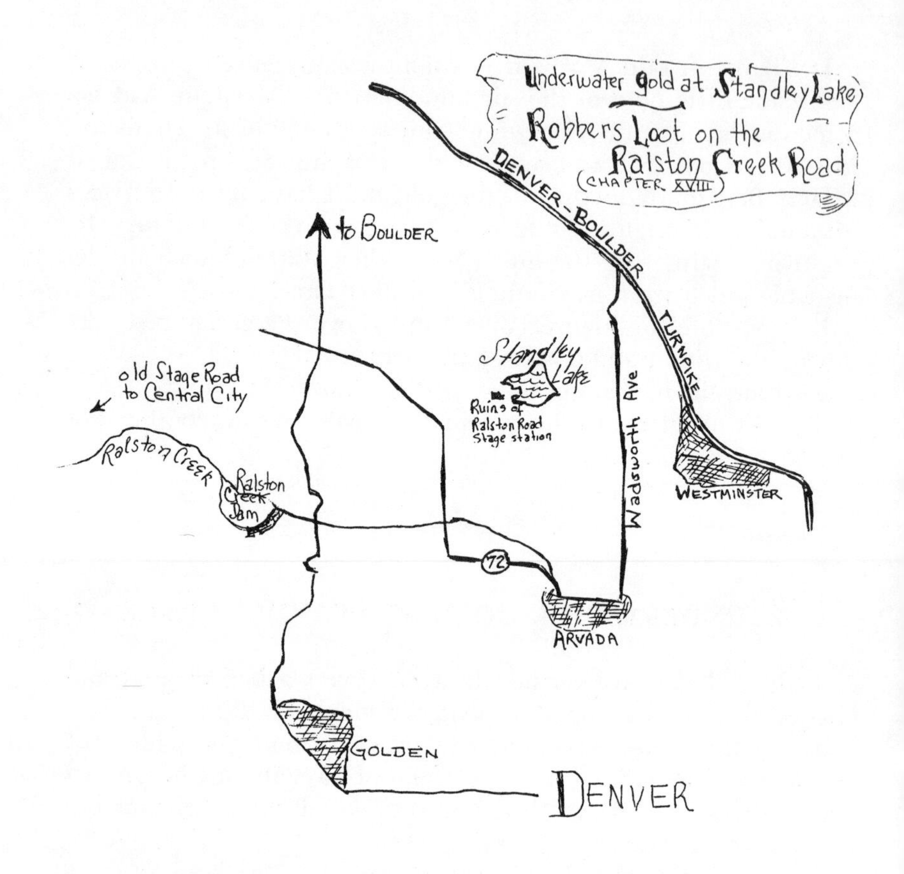

surface rights and since much of the west-enders' land was still above the water line and since they could still drill if they wanted to, the west-enders agreed.

A few years after the dam was completed, a mining engineer had opportunity to go over the drill samples (which he hadn't done before).

He said all of the seven drillings showed gold, averaging between $12 to $45 per ton. Experts at the trial claimed only one of the samples contained gold.

The engineer, who happened to be George J. Bancroft, also estimated the ore zone between fifty and 100 feet thick.

There is gold and coal under Standley Lake. It will cost a little to take it out . . . but it's there.

80. THE DEVIL'S HEAD TREASURE

In the foothills between Denver and Colorado Springs is a great mound of rocks known as Devil's Head, named, oddly enough, because of its slight resemblance to a devil's head. It is in a wild area off the beaten track and is seldom visited. But Devil's Head was well known to the Indians. They spun many a legend about it.

Rock hounds know the steep slopes, too. Ever since 1883 when W. B. Smith uncovered a rich deposit of topaz, people have been searching for the mother lode of this precious gem. They say the rare stones found were some the finest yet discovered in the United States.

It was also known to the highwaymen. The region made an ideal hideout, and the Devil's Head was an ideal lookout.

One gang held up a government train in the early '70s near Big Springs and made off with an estimated $60,000 in gold eagles. The men hid in the wooded area near Devil's Head. But, alas, the posse knew the country well by then and headed directly for the hideout.

Realizing the posse was closing in and that it would be foolish to stick around and fight it out, the train robbers made plans to leave the area until things cooled off. They buried their loot and marked the spot by jabbing a knife into a nearby tree—a popular method of marking treasures in those days.

Some stories say the men were killed shortly thereafter. True or not, they did not come back in the next few years.

The story was long forgotten until one day in 1923, when an old man ventured into the region and set up a tent near Devil's Head. He spent many days there and was busy each day, combing the area very closely. Eventually, he was spotted by Forest Ranger Roy Dupre. The man's actions aroused Dupre's curiosity and he kept an eye on him.

One day, a cloudburst drove the stranger into the ranger station. The old man was untalkative, but the forest ranger was determined to discover what he was up to. Finally, the stranger told the story of the robbery so many years ago, in which he had been a participant.

Views from Devil's Head and the ranger station where Ranger Dupre viewed an old man looking for the long lost treasure. *Photos by Erika Schramm.*

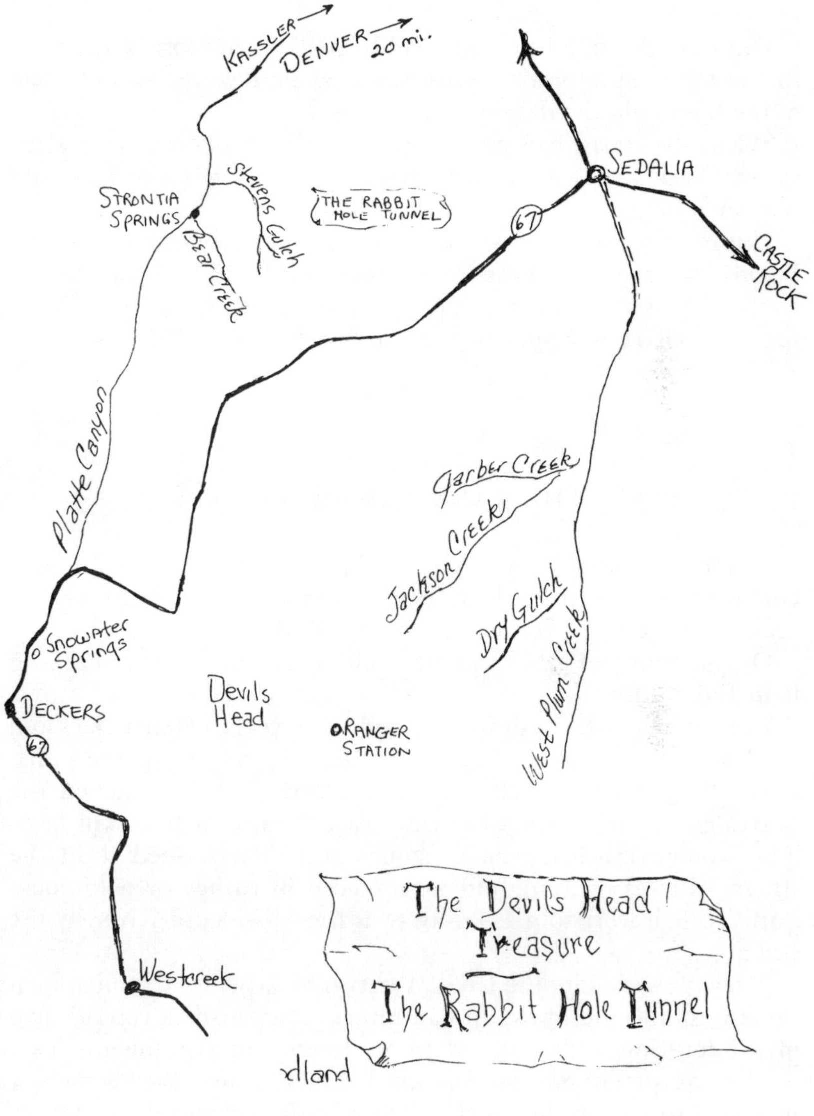

The Devil's Head Treasure
The Rabbit Hole Tunnel

KASSLER
DENVER 20 mi.
SEDALIA
STRONTIA SPRINGS
Stevens Gulch
THE RABBIT HOLE TUNNEL
Bear Creek
67
CASTLE ROCK
Platte Canyon
Garber Creek
Jackson Creek
Dry Gulch
West Plum Creek
Snowater Springs
DECKERS
67
Devils Head
RANGER STATION
Westcreek

Dupre said he doubted that the man would have told the story if he were not just about at the end of his rope as far as finding the tree with the dagger.

Dupre told him a forest fire had burned down most of the trees in the intervening years. This was a whole new forest and none of the trees held the dagger.

When the storm had passed over, the disconsolate man trudged wearily back to his camp, gathered up his soaked possessions, and wandered off.

Dupre said the old man had concentrated his search near the Windy Pass area. And the forest ranger made no bones about the fact that he scuffed his way through the region many times, looking for a charred dagger in the leaves.

81. THE RABBIT HOLE TUNNEL

There is a well-known but well-lost gold mine in Steven's Gulch near Strontia Springs, an old station on the Platte Canon branch of the Colorado and Southern Railway.

Only a family of rabbits knows its location and they are keeping it in the family.

Indians had been mining the gold for years. Henry Jackson, part Negro and part Indian, lived near the mouth of the gulch most all of his life. When he was a little boy he watched the braves go up the gulch and bring back the ore in buckskin bags. The women crushed it with stones and then washed it in the stream. Pieces of solid gold were placed in turkey or wild goose quills, which were sold as far away as the Mississippi River by the Indians.

A few years before the Civil War two St. Joseph, Missouri, men came west and found the Indian mine. They made a careful map of the location and returned to St. Joseph for equipment. Part of the equipment was an ox-drawn wagon which they somehow managed to get up the gulch, filled it with ore, and then they returned to St. Joseph and sold it.

They gave a copy of the map to a relative in St. Joseph and then they headed back to the mine. They never made it. Near

Devil's Head they were murdered, presumably by Indians. When they didn't return, a party organized by the St. Joseph relatives came to Colorado. They found the bodies of the two men and they found where the tools were hidden, but they didn't find the gold.

Before they left they gave the map to Jackson so he could continue the search. If he found it, he agreed to let them know. But Jackson never found the mine.

In 1911, a Denver man named Carl Johnson was hunting around Steven's Gulch when he ran across what seemed to be several veins of rusty quartz. Johnson, who worked in a Denver testing plant, picked up a few samples. In testing, one of the samples showed a good color.

Johnson wasn't able to return to Steven's Gulch until 1913. At that time he didn't even find the veins he had found before. One of the landmarks he searched for was a clump of underbrush. He remembered seeing a rabbit run into a hole hidden by the brush when he found a good sample.

He didn't think anything about it at the time, but the more he mulled it over afterward, the more he believed the rabbit hole was the secret of it all. Miners, especially those who had not registered their claims, obscured the opening of their claim with underbrush so that no one else would find it. Johnson was sure that was the case here.

But in all of his subsequent trips up the gulch he never found the rabbit hole, nor did he find any more rusty quartz.

XVI. *CACHE LA POUDRE AND THE PLAINS*

82. THE LOST DUTCHMAN MINE

Perhaps the most told story of lost treasure in northern Colorado is the old, old one of the lost mine near Fort Collins, dubbed by story tellers through the years as Colorado's "Lost Dutchman Mine."

The saga began long before Fort Collins was a grown-up city, when it really was a fort.

One year, an Irishman and a Dutchman came into the fort, bought supplies with gold dust and went on a nine-day binge before heading back into the mountains. They drank too much and the soldiers tried everything to loosen their tongues, but the pair did not divulge the source of their gold.

The next trip into the fort, the Irishman and the Dutchman bought a donkey with which to carry the ore. During their ensuing binge, the soldiers hired a noted scout to track the two back to their gold mine. But three days after the two had left the fort, the scout, who was not rigged for a long and cold trip, returned, saying he had lost them in the heavy snow.

The third time into the fort, the Irishman and the Dutchman traded the donkey in on an ox, saying the donkey was not strong enough to carry the ore.

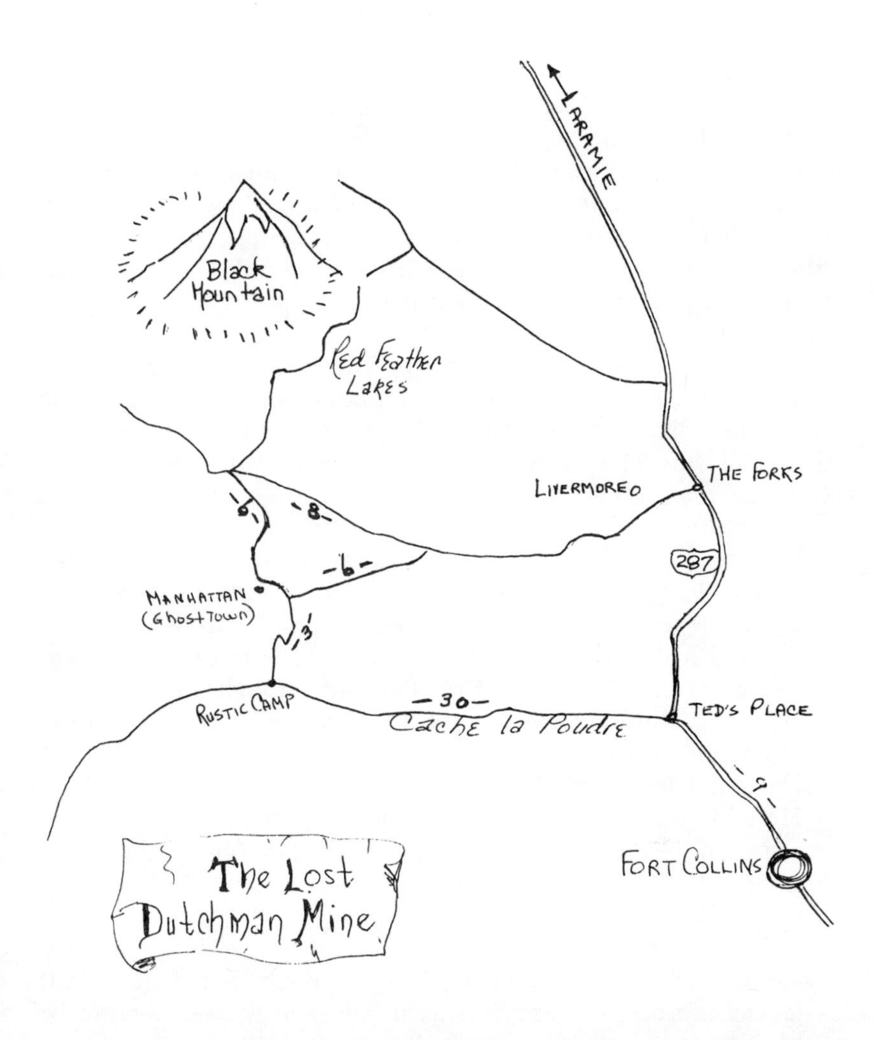

On the fourth trip in, the ox staggered under the weight of the gold. The two men couldn't begin to drink away all the gold they had.

On the next trip, the men came in without the ox, explaining that the animal was killed by a bear. They still had enough gold to go on an extended binge. After about three weeks of drinking and brawling, the Irishman killed the Dutchman.

The head of the garrison was away at the time so the soldiers decided it was a wonderful opportunity to find out the location of the gold mine. They threatened to hang the Irishman if he did not tell them. The Irishman stubbornly refused. Finally, to show the Irishman they meant business, the soldiers produced a rope. They tied it around his neck. The Irishman still held out. Finally, in desperation, the soldiers decided to show the Irishman how it felt to be hanged. They strung him up, meaning to cut him down immediately. But the Irishman didn't cooperate. Because of his many and extended drinking sprees, his heart gave out and he died.

The story became famous during the next few years and its dimensions grew rapidly. One of the best-known stories evolving from the original took place around the turn of the century. Teller is Billy Melins, prominent lumberman who came to Fort Collins from Nebraska in 1899. He got a job hauling lumber to a mill on the Cache La Poudre.

On one of his many trips to the old mining town of Manhattan he found the town was frantic over a visitor who had become lost. It seems the son of some tourists wandered too far from town on a burro and hadn't returned. Search parties scoured the neighboring wild region all the rest of the day and through the night, but to no avail. However, the boy returned to Manhattan himself the next day under his own steam.

He told a weird story.

He said he had become lost but the burro finally came upon a near-invisible trail and began to follow it. The boy gave the animal free rein since he apparently knew more about the area than the boy did.

Eventually, the winding trail led to a deserted cabin. The boy inspected the site and found the decaying bones of a large animal —legend says an ox—near the cabin door and what seemed to be gold dust on a shelf inside the cabin.

Melins, who knew the story of the Lost Dutchman mine, and was continually looking for it in his wanderings through the area, immediately looked around for an experienced prospector to guide him to the cabin.

The only one on hand, however, was a half-crazy old soul whose mind was known to wander, evidently because he was suffering from too many excursions alone. Melins was warned not to take him, but the lumberman was most anxious to find the mine and did not accept the advice. He obtained careful directions from the returned youth and took off . . . with the balmy old prospector.

The two eventually found the faint trail and followed it until they came to a small clearing. And there was the deserted cabin, ox bones and all. At the sight, however, the prospector lost all his composure and dashed up the path, past the cabin, and into a mine opening behind the cabin, Melins trying to keep up with him.

The old prospector had no sooner rushed into the mine tunnel than he rushed out again, followed by a huge bear. Melins said the crazy old fellow jumped at Melins, trying to wrestle the gun away from him. Melins said they were lucky both of them weren't killed. The bear, apparently as frightened as the prospector, scampered off into the woods. The prospector had lost all reason, saying he was going to kill Melins to feed the bear and allow him —the prospector—to escape.

Melins returned to Manhattan, feeling lucky to be alive and thoroughly disgusted with prospecting.

He did try to find the cabin a few months later, however, but was unsuccessful. He said as near as he could tell the mine was on the north slope of Black Mountain, well toward the top. He said it was in heavy timber and could well be overlooked unless one followed the nearly invisible trail.

Through the years many, many people have searched for the mine. There have even been some stories of the trail, the cabin and the mine being found, then lost again.

Scoffers believe there never was a mine, that the Irishman and the Dutchman were in reality highwaymen who ambushed and robbed miners returning from California gold fields. A much traveled road back from California was just over the hills north of Fort Collins.

People who don't believe there ever was such a mine claim Billy Melins was a tall-tale teller and just wanted to add something to the legend.

People like that don't believe in Santa Claus.

83. GUNSHOP LEAD

Clay Peterson was one of the early residents in old Fort Collins. He ran a gun shop on what would now be Jefferson Street.

One day a stranger came into his shop to have his gun repaired. While Clay worked, as was his habit he chatted with the customer. Eventually, Clay had occasion to mention the shortage of lead which placed a hardship on his profession.

At that, the stranger dug down into his bag and produced a rock, heavy with lead, asking Peterson if it would do him any good. The stranger said he had found it along the trail from Fort Laramie in the hills north of Fort Collins. He said Peterson could have it.

Peterson wasn't sure if he could use it but he thanked the stranger graciously and went on to other topics. A few days later Peterson had the rock tested and it did show plenty of lead . . . but also about one-third silver.

During all his spare moments the next few years, Peterson searched along the trail to Fort Laramie, but found no rocks such as the one the long-gone stranger had.

Finally Peterson gave up his gunshop and his search for silver, and began raising cattle in the White River area.

84. FRENCH TREASURE CACHE ON THE POUDRE

There is another story of buried treasure on the Cache La Poudre near Fort Collins. It was unknown until 1911 when a French Canadian named Jacques LaBorgeans happened into Fort Collins on purpose to look for it.

In attempting to organize a search party, LaBorgeans told this story. He said his uncle, who bore the same name, was an early western fur trader and trapper who followed the rush to the California gold fields in the early 1850s. LaBorgeans said his uncle was lucky and amassed a fortune after five years of finding and storing his gold. With eight friends he headed back home in 1857.

They stopped at the military camp of La Porte, above Fort Collins, where many early mountain men used to stop. After a rest the nine continued on their way back east. But a short distance out of La Porte, about where Windsor is now located, they were pursued by a band of Sioux on the warpath.

The nine managed to hide their gold at the foot of a conspicious bluff, but were caught shortly thereafter by the Indians, scalped, and left for dead.

Freighters passed by the fight scene a few hours later. Upon investigation, they saw signs of life in LaBorgeans. They nursed him the best they could and carted him to Fort Leavenworth. He had received a severe blow on the head and lay hovering between life and death at a government hospital at Fort Leavenworth for five months before he finally recovered his health and his memory.

Then he returned to his family in Montreal, fully intending to come back to Colorado some day and recover his treasure. But the years passed and finally, when he realized death was near, he told the story to his nephew, giving him as explicit directions as his memory would permit. Surprisingly enough, the nephew said, he remembered the area in great detail.

If LaBorgeans ever located the treasure the fact was never known. The land has changed greatly since his uncle traveled through it. If LaBorgeans, the nephew, did find the cache, no doubt it would have been recorded.

It may still be buried at the base of a conspicuous bluff not far from Windsor.

35. THE TREASURE OF ROBBERS ROOST

About a mile north of the once very-active stage station of Virginia Dale is a table mountain. The mountain is a mile long and about a quarter of a mile wide. It has a grass top, ideal for grazing horses, but the rim is of shale rocks and there are only a few difficult trails through the perpendicular cliffs on all sides of the mountain. They say only the bad men, for the most part, knew the trails at all.

Indians found Table Mountain ideal for a lookout. From the mountain they watched the white men come and they sent smoke signals, often to organize an attack on a wagon train or pioneer group.

Later, bandits and highwaymen took over Table Mountain. They even improved upon what nature had made almost ideal

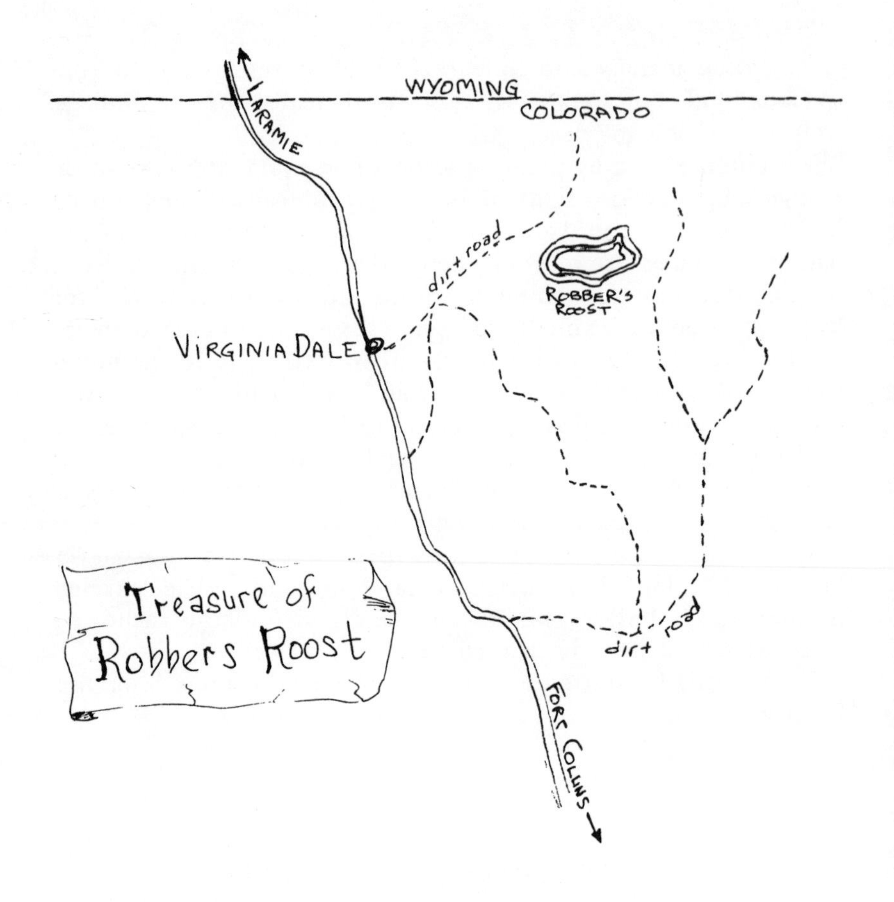

for them. They built a shelter atop the mountain and installed reinforced lookouts and battle stations. A handful of robbers could hold off an army. It was only after the army threatened to train heavy artillery on the spot that the renegades sought greener table mountains.

But for years before that happened, many a highwayman called this home. And the mountain was known far and wide as Robbers Roost. From their lookout they could see a stagecoach approaching for miles. And after they robbed it they found safety atop the mountain.

There are many stories of buried treasure here. With so many highwaymen and so many robberies, there are bound to be. One above all the others seems the most authentic—at least there was

$60,000 in U.S. money missing in this area and no one seems to know where it went to.

The $60,000 gold shipment was bound for Fort Laramie, and represented several months' back pay for the soldiers stationed there. When the stagecoach carrying the strong box arrived at Virgina Dale stage station, it was supposed to meet a body of troops who were to convoy the stage the rest of the way.

But the soldiers were late to the rendezvous, and after waiting awhile, the impatient stage driver decided to go on alone and meet them along the road, thus saving some time.

The stage was only a few minutes out of Virginia Dale when the bandits struck. However, the soldiers arrived just after the robbery and took off in hot pursuit. The bandits scattered in their flight. During a lively chase it was believed all the bandits were killed.

After a short search the strong box was found in the creek, but

Robbers Roost in 1883. It was here that Jack Slade's gang of highwaymen preyed upon stages and wagons passing through Virginia Dale below. *U.S. Geological Survey photo.*

despite the fact the robbery and the chase had only lasted a few minutes, the box had already been blown open—both the top and the bottom had been blown off—and the money was gone. None of the money was found although the entire area was searched thoroughly.

Of course, the prime suspect was Jack Slade (see Italian Caves) who happened to be superintendant of the stage station at the time. Many believed he was ringleader of the bandit gang and tipped them off when a particularly rich shipment came through.

He solidified his role as a top suspect a short time later when he left the area, taking with him, they say, a great deal of money.

86. TREASURE OF ITALIAN CAVES

The Italian Caves, a short distance from Julesburg, is a favorite picnic spot now. It also is a favorite spot for treasure hunters. Full many a fortune seeker has probed the mysterious caves for legendary treasure, but none has been found. It's a fun place to look anyhow.

There are several stories of treasure being hidden here. Jules Beni and Black Jack Slade are the most prominent figures in many of these legends.

Jules Beni once ran a trading post near here. Legend says that he also had as a hobby, highway robbery. His trusty little band of highwaymen was partly made up of Indians, so when Jules directed them to rob a rich stage or wagon that had stopped at his trading post, the stage driver or wagon master could always say they were attacked by Indians.

Tradition says Beni hid much of his loot in the Italian Caves.

Later, the Leavenworth and Pikes Peak stage made a stop at Beni's trading post. Jack Slade, for some reason or other, was made division chief of the stage line.

There are several stories on how the feud between Beni and Slade got started. Some say it was over a girl, the Rose of Julesburg, some say Slade believed Beni was robbing the stage company for which Slade was responsible. But perhaps the most authentic

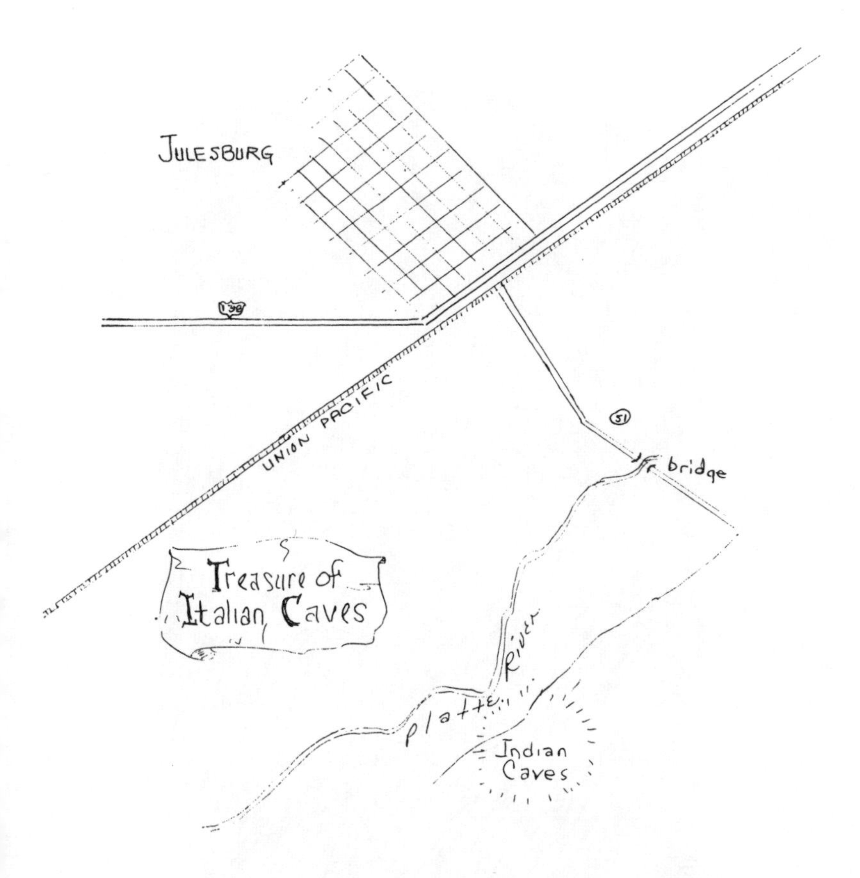

reason for the feud was that Jules Beni's highwaymen were too much competition for Jack Slade's robber band.

Anyhow the feud got red hot. Slade had terrorized that part of the country with his whip. Legend says he could snap a cigarette out of a man's mouth at twenty yards. For fun he used to cut through a cowboy's belt straps so the cowboy would drop his chaps.

Slade showed Beni he meant business when he, Slade, whipped off Beni's ears. This pretty much embarrassed Beni who swore he would kill Slade. A few days later Beni's bullet-riddled body was found.

Beni was the third man known to have died at the hands of Jack Slade, whom Mark Twain called "the cruelest-looking man" he ever met.

Early drawing of Jack Slade. Mark Twain said he had the cruelest eyes of any man he had ever met. *Colorado Historical Society photo.*

Slade was born in southern Illinois. He killed a man at the age of thirteen in a quarrel. Slade beat the man to death with a stone. Slade's father promptly sent the boy to Texas as a train boss. From there he wandered all over the frontier, spreading fear wherever he went with his whip and his gun.

His next killing occurred in Wyoming where he shot Andy Farrer in a saloon. Slade never turned down a dare in his life.

Andy dared Slade to shoot. Slade shot, Andy died. After he had shot him, Slade tried desperately to save Farrer's life.

They say the only person Slade was afraid of was his wife, who was said to have had the worst temper in northeastern Colorado.

Slade was only thirty when he took over as division chief of the Leavenworth and Pikes Peak line. It was shortly after this that the feud with Beni began. Beni was said to have been the third man Slade killed, although many another killing has been attributed to him.

Anyhow, the Beni killing was Slade's last. It was the beginning of the end for him. He cleared out of Colorado with a posse in hot pursuit. He escaped the posse but the *wanted* posters sent out on him resulted in his being hanged by a vigilante committee in Virginia City, Montana.

With the homelife he must have had, perhaps he was better off.

87. THE CLIFFORD BURIED LOOT

In 1847 or 1849, bandits stole "hundreds of thousands of dollars" in Sacramento, California, and headed east with U.S. troops in hot pursuit. Most of the gang was killed in the chase, but two survived and made their escape through Colorado.

They finally came over the mountains about where Denver was to be and followed an easterly trail along, or near, the Smoky Hill Trail. A short distance out on the plains they decided to lighten their load by burying their loot in a dutch oven in a gulch a few miles east of latter-day Clifford.

They marked the location with three stone markers with the date "1847" chiseled on each of them. This has led some historians and treasure-hunters to believe the year they traveled through was 1847. Some believe, however, that they marked the stones thusly to throw everyone off the trail, and they actually came through Colorado in 1849. The latter case is the more plausible to the author.

After burying their loot, the two continued on their way to Chicago.

About thirty years later a stranger came into the area of Clifford

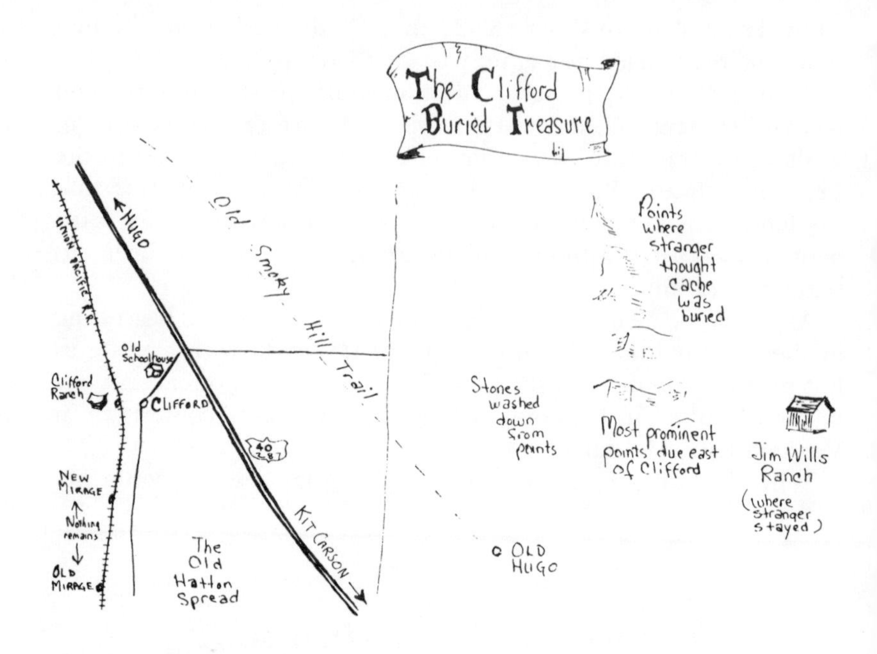

and was offered hospitality near Hugo at a sheep camp run by James Will. The stranger spent his time off by himself, searching for something. After a few days of apparently futile effort, he prepared to return to Chicago. Before he left, however, he told his story to James Will.

The story was no more than local legend until the late 1920s when a man named Elkins found a marker with the date 1847 on it. Elkins brought the stone into the *Eastern Plainsman* newspaper office in Hugo. The stone recalled the legend and the rush was on. The area all around where the marker was found was dug up, but no ancient treasure was located.

It was again forgotten for a short while. Then in 1934, Tom Hatton of Clifford found a stone near town inscribed "D. Grover and Joseph Fox-Lowe—Aug. 8, 1847." This too, was taken into the *Plainsman* office. Another rush started with the same result as the first time.

The buried treasure is more than just local legend now. Residents of the area are continually on the alert for the third stone marker and a possible cache of the treasure.

There are many possibilities here. When more and more men

came west they found many lonely grave markers along the trail. Most were destroyed as the west became populated.

James "Bud" Will, nephew of the original, said the stranger who stayed at his uncle's place spent all of his time investigating a series of prominent points running north and south east of the old railroad stops of Clifford and Mirage. Will, the nephew, said the stones were found below these points and could have been washed down in the rain. Will believes the treasure area is on the three most prominent points, due east of Clifford.

Will brought up another curious event that took place several years ago that may or may not have anything to do with the buried treasure, but many Hugoites think it does have something to do with our story.

It seems an army officer got off the train at Clifford one time and

Jim "Bud" Will stands on the point near Clifford where he believes the treasure is buried. One of the original bandits returned years after the California robbery and stayed at the ranch operated by Will's uncle.

headed off toward the points to the east. The fact that he got off the train at Clifford was curious enough. Clifford was never more than a loading stop for the Clifford ranch and other ranches in the near vicinity. Once in a while, ranchers living here or visitors would get off at the stop, but this strange officer, according to everyone around, had no business being there.

The body of the army officer was found a few days later a short distance below the points east of Clifford. He had been murdered. His murderer had never been found. Why the officer was murdered and why he was here in the first place had never been determined.

Old man Hatton, the original Jim Will, and others are dead now. Trains no longer stop at Clifford and at Mirage, a short distance down the line from Clifford. The treasure area is wide-open country, ranched by Jim Will, the nephew, his son, also named Jim Will, and others.

Until the third stone is found, or the treasure itself, the mystery is hidden by sage and sand.

Of course, some of the neighbors have a very plausible belief that could mean the end of the mystery. The skeptics say the stranger who returned in 1880 to look for the treasure actually did find the loot and told the story just to play a trick on the local residents.

Then, there is also the chance the other survivor of the holdup returned before 1880 and picked up the loot without anybody's knowing about it.

There's no honor among thieves.

XVII. *GOLD DUST*

88. Chest of Gold on the Ralston Creek Road
89. Murdie's Lost Gold Mine
90. Lost Mine on Embargo Creek
91. Lost Mine on Mogate Peak
92. The Fishing Hole Treasure
93. Two Barrels of Coins

POCKET CHANGE

94. The Lost Saxon Mine
95. Bent's Gold on Crow Creek
96. Buried Treasure of Bent's Fort
97. Treasure of Spanish Caves
98. Sunken Treasure of Silver Lake
99. Buried Loot of the Bloody Espinozas
100. The Baby Doe Buried Treasure
101. Spanish Treasure on Blanca Peak
102. Gothic's Lost Mine
103. Lost Phantom Mine
    and, Pierre's Lost Mine, The Lost Pin Gold Mine, Bandit Treasure of Grand Valley, Buried Treasure of Natural Fort

FORTUNES FOUND

104. Hunt's Successful Search
105. A Jar of Gold Dust
106. Found Fortune near Querida
107. The Chamber of Wealth

GOLD DUST

The story doesn't end. There is always another lost treasure farther up the creek, just over the mountain. As long as there are people and gold still glitters, there will be lost mines and people looking for them. Perhaps many lost mine stories are lost now, the treasures are still there, but the stories are lost.

All the old timers have a story of their own. Temple H. Cornelius, a veteran in the ever-mysterious San Juans, recalls many he has heard or experienced in a recent book which he did with John B. Marshall, *Golden Treasures of the San Juan.*

Many stories haven't been told.

Here are some other stories of lost mines and buried treasures I ran across in my research. They didn't seem as important as the others. The money may have been more, but money isn't everything. The search is the thing.

88. CHEST OF GOLD ON THE RALSTON CREEK ROAD

The Ralston Creek Road was a shortcut between Central City and Denver. During the early days of the gold rush, the stages and ore wagons rumbled over the road at breakneck speed.

Only the stage and wagon drivers, a peculiar breed at best, maintained their sanity on the run. To make matters worse was the fact that highwaymen infested the road. The old stone house just at the water line of the Ralston Creek Dam was a well-known rendezvous for the bandits.

Our legend says that highwaymen lifted a chest of gold from one of the stages and buried it nearby. Many bandits, they say, buried their loot on or near the site which later became the Ralston Creek Dam. Many dug for it before the deluge came.

Some people still go up and poke around once in a while . . . on their way to other places.

Ruins of the old stage station on the Ralston Creek Road from Central City to Denver. The stage stop was a favorite hangout for highwaymen. Standley Lake is in the background.

89. MURDIE'S LOST GOLD MINE

The Murdies were, and are, prominent in Gunnison country. They were pioneer residents and civic leaders. Adam Murdie was a leader in early Tin Cup. W. D. Murdie and John Murdie were important names in Gunnison.

W. D. Murdie's father was a locomotive machinist in Topeka, Kansas. Each summer, on his vacation, he would come to Gunnison to visit his son and do a little prospecting.

One year, just before returning to Kansas, Murdie's father was crossing a stream in the Taylor Park area that was low and clear. He saw a sparkle in the bed of the stream and stooped to investigate. He found a vein of ore about fifteen inches in diameter.

He dug out a good-sized sample. An assay showed the ore contained 2400 ounces of silver and 95 ounces of gold to the ton, worth about $5,000 a ton.

Murdie thought he had made a pretty clear map of the area, but when he returned to Taylor Park the following year, he could not find his vein of ore. In fact, members of the family searched the region thoroughly in the next few years. They rounded up some good fish but no fortune.

90. LOST MINE ON EMBARGO CREEK

Many, many years ago, two men made a good strike on Embargo Creek, not far from Creede. During the summer they worked their claim. Came winter, they took only what gold they would need to carry them through the winter in Santa Fe. They stored the remainder of the gold at their mine, hoping to accumulate a fortune after a few years, and retire.

One winter, however, they were murdered by bandits. The bandits were never able to find the mother lode. Neither has anybody else.

91. LOST MINE ON MOGATE PEAK

The tale of the Lost Mine on Mogate Peak is much the same as that of Embargo Creek.

The primary differences were the two men spent their winters in Taos and that they were much more indiscreet.

They wintered with sufficient funds and spent quite a lot on booze. They drank too much and in doing so they talked too much.

Outside the tavern they were accosted by ruffians. When their lives were threatened, they divulged the location of their mine. They were murdered anyway.

The murderers didn't find the mine, however. Murderers are too impatient.

92. THE FISHING HOLE TREASURE

There's another story down along the border about the big payroll robbery that didn't quite come off. It seems the paymaster of Fort Garland would drive down to Fort Union twice a year to pick up the pay for the men and officers at Fort Garland. He drove an old horse-drawn ambulance and usually had a convoy of four mounted soldiers to guard the treasure, which was several thousand dollars in gold dust.

On one trip—his last one—the paymaster and the soldiers were ambushed a short distance south of Fort Garland by a gang of highwaymen. Three of the soldiers were killed immediately, the other died a short while later.

However, the sudden ring of bullets frightened the horses pulling the pay wagon. They burst forward, taking the wounded paymaster with them.

The paymaster was found a little later up Trinchera Creek. He was dying and the wagon was empty. The paymaster's last words told of hiding the chest of gold in his favorite fishing hole to prevent the bandits from getting it.

Many a soldier had seen the paymaster head up the creek to fish. A few had even gone with him. They all had their ideas about where the fishing hole was. They found many a good fishing hole, but nary a chest of gold.

93. TWO BARRELS OF COINS

For three generations the Gomez family has been digging in the shade of the Sangre de Cristo Mountains for two barrels of coins.

The coins were presumably buried by Henry Sefton, the man who built the first toll road crossing the Sangre de Cristos. Sefton, who apparently did a land-office business and didn't have many needs, put the toll coins in the barrels and then buried them.

Sefton knew the Gomez family and on his deathbed told of the treasure. After Sefton's death, the Gomezes bought the ranch and started digging.

One might jump to the obvious conclusion: that such a tale is a good way to sell a ranch at a good price. The Gomez family, however, doesn't think so.

POCKET CHANGE

There is no end to the story.

Many a lost mine is so lost, much of its story is lost along with it. Some are the same stories all over again. Once in a while an oldtimer would take a story and change its location. No doubt, some story tellers and writers heard vague stories, gave them names and locations to make up for the substances they lacked.

These stories I haven't told. In many cases I couldn't find out enough about them to tell. Perhaps you know the story and can tell me.

94. For example, there were a few references to a LOST SAXON MINE, lost very early near Empire on Berthoud Pass. It seemed to be a popular story in its day, but, apparently, all the story tellers are dead.

95. There are a couple of stories of lost gold attached to Bent's famous fort on the Arkansas River. Judge Wilbur F. Stone's historical sketch of Pueblo County says William Bent's children found some gold nuggets on Crow Creek while returning to the fort from Fort Bridger in 1848.

Nobody knows if they went back for more and if they found the spot again if they did.

96. Another oft-told tale with little basis in history is the gold buried in the walls of the fort. No doubt, the person, or persons, who created the legend had a good reason for the gold's being there. The history books, however, don't provide that reason. Nor is it recorded if the gold, or evidence of it, was found when the walls came tumbling down.

97. There are stories that have made their way through South Park about hidden gold in SPANISH CAVES, near the ghost

town of Buckskin Joe. Some say it is bandit's loot, some say it is Spanish treasure. Ancient Spanish arrastras were found nearby.

Wherever there is a cave, there is a story of lost treasure that goes with it. A cave just can't hold up its head without it. Highwaymen were known to make wide use of caves for hideouts. No doubt they hid their loot there, and no doubt many didn't return from a foray. Prospectors often took refuge from Indians in a cave. They may also have left their gold dust behind in an attempt to lighten their load to escape. Such stories inhabit so many of the caves throughout the state. The more mysterious and remote the cave, the better the story. On the other hand, the closer the cave to a well-traveled road wherever highwaymen might have practiced their evil trade, the more logical the story. I hope I haven't offended the many caves by leaving out their stories.

98. Down around Silverton there is a joke that has been going around for decades about draining SILVER LAKE to salvage all the high-grade gold left there.

High graders are miners who wanted to get ahead in a hurry. They smuggled from the mines some of the bosses' best real estate in their pockets, lunch buckets, hat brims, hollow pick handles and anything else they could make use of. Much of the time they sold the high-grade ore directly to a crooked buyer. Sometimes, they stashed their loot until they had collected a sufficient amount to make it worth while or until they could leave the area in luxury.

From these cases come the legends.

There are such stories in most of the state's richest mining areas, Leadville and Cripple Creek in particular.

The Silverton story goes that many a high-grader hid his take near the shore of the lake, and before he was able to return for it, it had floated gently out to sea.

Before we leave the subject, we would be remiss if we didn't mention the graves involved in highgrading. Dishonest miners often found cemeteries a handy place to hide their stolen ore. There were many reason for this. In the old west graves were being opened up and being closed every day for burial. Nobody would suspect anybody found digging in a graveyard. Also, the turf was loose in the graveyard and therefore an easy and unsuspicious place to bury a cache. Caskets were also handy hiding places. There are cases of caskets coming out of a mine, presumably containing a miner, or miners, who were killed in cave-ins or explosions, that also contained some good ore.

So much for that.

99. There are stories of the BLOODY ESPINOZAS leaving a buried treasure here and there. One is mentioned on UTE PASS. It's possible, but the Espinozas seemed more interested in killing people and spreading terror in the 1860s than in storing treasure.

100. Another oft-told but doubtful, story concerns the BABY DOE BURIED TREASURE at the Matchless Mine near Leadville. The story goes that Baby Doe, during those long years that she lived as a hermit at her husband's mine, actually did mine some silver and hoarded it nearby. Anything is possible, but it would seem that she wasn't so far gone that she wouldn't tap her hoard to buy some coal rather than freezing to death, as she did in 1935.

101. A fellow down in Walsenburg said he knew a spiritualist once who saw the location of a SPANISH TREASURE ON BLANCA PEAK one night in a dream. The spiritualist followed it up and claims he did find some ancient Spanish relics on the peak, but no gold. Maybe he's still looking . . . even after death.

As the fellow down in Walsenburg said, "You can't tell about them spiritualists."

102. Another oldtimer says "there's one of them lost mine stories down around Gothic." But he didn't remember the particulars, and, apparently, no one else can.

There are a few stories mentioned in one published collection or another and no particulars are included. Sources were vague and I have found no substance in my research (this is not to say there isn't any). These include:

103. A map on lost mines in the west tells of a LOST PHANTOM MINE near Steamboat Springs, found and lost in 1881. This may be one of the stories told in this book, although I wasn't able to track down the reason for the name.

And there were:

PIERRE'S LOST MINE in Las Animas County.

THE LOST PIN GOLD MINE near Grand Junction.

BANDIT TREASURE OF GRAND VALLEY.

THE BURIED TREASURE OF NATURAL FORT (no location).

FORTUNES FOUND

If one can link lost treasure stories to treasures found, there are also many of them. Some I have already presented. Here are some others.

If they do nothing else, they at least prove that finding a lost treasure is possible.

104. The following story of HUNT'S SUCCESSFUL SEARCH appeared in the *Daily Central City Register* in 1871.

"The News (Rocky Mountain) furnishes a singular story of buried treasure.

"There lived in Denver in 1863 a man by the name of B. C. Hunt. He bought a lot, built a house, and then went into the far country of Idaho where he has since lived and prospered.

"He left a man by the name of Dunn to rent the House, make returns, etc.

"Finally, Mr. Dunn ceased to answer the letters of his principal and Mr. Hunt lately came to Denver to hunt Mr. Dunn and see what he had done with the property and the rent.

"He found that Mr. Dunn had been dead several years and his property demolished.

"Then he (Mr. Hunt) remembered that before he left he had buried a bag of gold dust at one corner of the house worth over $1,200.

"He got a man to help him and after considerable work they found the buckskin bag in an excellent state of preservation.

"Taking the gold to the mint he found it to be worth over $1,200 and weigh 67.97 ounces."

105. In 1888, two ranchers sought shelter in an abandoned cabin near Harrisburg, a ghost town between Leadville and Denver.

After eating, the ranchers sat in the doorway of the cabin for their before-bed smoke. One of them, whose name was Holsom, as was his wont, sat digging in the dirt just outside the door with his knife.

Eventually, he hit something solid. He dug deeper and discovered that a glass jar was buried only a few inches below the surface of the ground.

The rancher struck a match and found the jar was half full of gold dust. The next day the ranchers, half believing they were mistaken about the contents of the jar, took it to town and had it analyzed.

They received $6,000 for their efforts.

The ranchers said the cabin was often used by travelers going to and from the boom town of Leadville. But why the jar of gold dust was buried by the cabin door and then abandoned, no one will ever know.

106. One day in 1882, twenty-five sacks of most healthy tellurium were found hidden near Querida. It appeared as if the sacks had been hidden for several years. It was surmised that they had been stolen and the thieves didn't get a chance to return for them. Since the find was worth a fortune, it was believed that the bandits were killed before they could return, since death would have been the only deterrent from claiming such a rich reward.

107. A fellow named Olaf Berg found a long-lost lode in the vicinity of Naylor's Lake up around Payne's Peak in 1906.

The lost mine had been referred to in legend as the "Chamber of Wealth," and had been lost for twenty-five years . . . no record, by any means.

CATCHING UP: ADDENDUM TO SECOND EDITION

The first edition of this book lured many a novice and further encouraged the army of amateur and professional treasure hunters already in the field. A good many of them have written to me or telephoned me asking for additional details I might have, asking my opinion on the more authentic stories, and if I had heard any other tales.

To all I replied that I had included what I considered all the pertinent details in the stories, at least all the details I knew. As to the more authentic stories, I told them I thought that, for one reason or another, about a half dozen stories seemed the most likely: The Treasure of Timber Hill, Buried Treasure in Bull Canyon, Lost Treasure on Slate Mountain, The Devil's Head Treasure, and the Clifford Buried Loot.

It seems that more treasure hunters have concentrated on the Treasure of Treasure Mountain, The Devil's Head Treasure, the Clifford Buried Loot, and that old standby, the Reynolds Gang Gold. Some meticulous treasure hunters who had all the necessary paraphernalia spent many an hour searching for the above. One man even bought property on or near Treasure Mountain to enable his systematic search. Another spent several consecutive week ends in a detailed search for the Clifford Buried Loot. And there have been enough inconsiderate treasure hunters digging up, trampling on or over private property, and tearing down fences, etc., in search for the Reynolds treasure, that there was a rumor at one time that the local people, in a posse, were on their way to get me and string me up.

Many of the treasure hunters would report to me regularly, usually before or after a trip. After a while, however, I would hear no more from them. This indicates to me that they either got discouraged in the hunt or found their fortune and are now taking life easy in some Latin wonderland.

But, except for the story of the treasure found below, I have heard of no other Colorado treasure found. That doesn't mean they won't be found. Millions of dollars in lost treasures are found each year. Many are uncovered by a freak of nature, as was the one below, many are found by a bit of luck or coincidence, but most are tracked down by long and careful work.

Except for the Treasure Mountain story, there are no new facts to add to those contained in the first edition, at least no facts that I believe pertinent to the search. As to the Treasure Mountain story, volumes could be written about it. In fact, it would be a good book in itself. Much of the additional material not contained in my original story concerns the many stories of searches still underway or that have taken place in the past. To incorporate this information into our study would, it seems to me, only tend further to confuse the search. If there is a treasure there, I believe it will be found one day. It may take luck, but more than likely, it will be found through hard work.

As to any additional stories I have heard, there are many. Some of my treasure-hunting friends put me on to other stories that I did not have in the original volume. Following are a few of the new stories that I thought most interesting.

ANOTHER TREASURE FOUND

The "Treasure of the Platte River Bridge" was one of the more obscure lost treasures bundled into the first edition of this book. Due to its obscurity, the unique attempt to find the treasure seemed more noteworthy than the losing of the treasure itself.

But this is one treasure that has been definitely found. Spirits didn't find it. The probing of countless numbers of treasure hunters during the intervening 70 years didn't find it. It took a cloudburst and a minor flood.

The cloudburst of June 15, 1963, washed down the Platte and apparently shook the treasure from its sandy grave. The event prompted professional treasure hunter Ray Andis of Denver to check along the banks of the river. Andis knows his way around, treasure-hunting-wise. He doesn't discount any story. He knows what to look for and when to do it.

When the cloudburst set the usually-peaceful waters of the Platte a-swirling, Andis had a hunch that it might shake up something long buried. Sure enough, he found a few coins along the shore near the Washington Street bridge. One coin was an 1856 two-cent piece. The find excited Andis and he lost little time calling on his treasure-hunting partner, Bill DeBaca. DeBaca has a lot of treasure-hunting savvy himself. He also has an electronic metal detector.

The two men and their electronic friend found what had been hidden about 70 years. Altogether they swept out 192 coins, many dating before the Civil War, several rings, three guns, some pewter jewelry, and some other odds and ends, including the rotted remains of the chest that hid the treasure lo these many years. The two men sold much of the find to collectors, netting about $500 for their efforts.

News of the find attracted other treasure hunters. They weren't as lucky as Andis and DeBaca, but some of the others did find some coins that had washed between the rocks near the treasure site. Jess Bollinger and Robert Redding, also treasure-hunting partners, swept out some coins a few days later.

The treasure didn't bring anybody a fortune, but it did rekindle much faith in lost treasure stories, and encourage them to keep looking for treasures still lost.

ROYAL GORGE GOLD

One of the treasures Bill DeBaca plans to search for, aided by his share of the Platte River find, is said to be located near the Royal Gorge. Details of the treasure were told to him a few years ago by Mrs. Maude Proctor, who was then seventy.

Mrs. Proctor's family homesteaded near Copper Gulch, near the Gorge, when she was a girl. She heard the many tales of outlaws who headquartered in the gulch. One of the better known stories concerned the robbery of a $75,000 gold shipment. The outlaws soon afterward vacated the area. It wasn't known whether they had been killed during another outing or whether they had taken the gold with them.

Maude roamed the area freely as a child. One day, near the Elsie Mine, she discovered a hidden cave that contained evidence of earlier habitation. Odd marks were blazed on trees close by that led to a circular pattern of rocks.

She thought little of this at the time, but pieced it together years later. She became certain that the treasure, or a treasure, was buried under these rocks.

But when she finally decided to investigate, she discovered a forest fire had burned down the trees and the rocks had been scattered in the intervening years.

She not only took DeBaca into her confidence, she took him to the area, showed him the cave and outlined the general area in which she believed the rock pattern had been. DeBaca purchased a metal detector and prepared for a detailed search. But before he could undertake his quest, he was drafted into the army. Shortly after his discharge and before they could make another trip, Mrs. Proctor died.

DeBaca and his partner, Ray Andis, have continued their search whenever possible. In fact, further encouraged by their recent find along the Platte River, DeBaca is making plans to take leave of absence from his job with the city of Denver, and devote full time to his search for the Royal Gorge treasure, and any others in the neighborhood.

A GREATER, MORE MYSTERIOUS LA CAVERNA DEL ORO

We were forced to leave our story of "La Caverna Del Oro," or perhaps more properly, "The Spanish Caves," shortly after our heroes had found a new entrance above the known entrance. It was a poor time to leave but it had to be. Now, we can report the progress up to this time—three years later.

The new opening has enlarged our story considerably. Even so, enlarging it has tended to add to the mystery of the fabulous cave.

The three or four organized expeditions into the new opening have uncovered many things but the spelunkers involved claim the study has just begun. They have connected the new opening with the cave mapped previously. They still have not mapped and charted all the chambers and portals in the new section and would not even guess how large the cave will turn out to be. What has been explored in the new section has already doubled the size of the cave known just three years ago, and made it one of the five or six deepest caves in the United States.

Many bones of elk, deer, bighorn sheep, and other animals have been found in the cave, even in sections where one would not believe such bones would be found. However, no additional finds have been uncovered that would tell more of the human history of the cave.

Even as this second edition goes to press, a scientific and technical expedition is being formed to begin to chart this new area. Perhaps, book sales and spelunkers willing, there will be yet another chapter in our story. Worthy spelunker John Streich, who will help lead the expedition, said a thorough study of the cave may take years and perhaps only a small part of the entire cave is now known.

Streich also warned amateurs against attempting exploration on their own. He said the new, uncharted areas of the cave had made it many times more hazardous than it was before. The cave is a real challenge to even an experienced caveman. Footing is treacherous. Many vertical shafts fall several feet and most of the openings are sudden and unexpected.

Those interested in spelunking are urged to contact Streich or other official spelunkers. They can provide additional information on this cave and others, and can provide details on how you, too, can become a spelunker and do exciting things safely.

PAT KELLY'S LOST MINE

Walter "Pat" Kelly was a well known figure around Lake City. He was a manager of the famous Golden Fleece Mine and was also a sheriff in Lake City for several years. He was said to have buried some bones of the men eaten by Alfred Packer—the only man ever tried for cannibalism in the United States.

Kelly spent all his spare time prospecting, always sure he would one day find "that big one." Finally, after years and years of looking, he believed he had found it. However, he made his find just before the heavy snows set in. Kelly left a marker at the site and headed back to Lake City, not worrying about mapping the area since he figured he knew the way well enough.

But before the spring thaws set it, Kelly fell and broke his neck. They laid him out on a slab in the Lake City morgue thinking he was dead. The next morning they found him turned around on the slab. The only one who could have done it was Pat Kelly himself—who wouldn't die until he got comfortable. What made his death even more colorful was the fact that the whereabouts of his mine died with him. It's still near Lake City somewhere, waiting.

Anyone wanting further details about Pat Kelly and his mine can ask his daughter Nancy Burk, the county clerk of Lake County.

THE CHERRY CREEK TREASURE

Two versions are told of a story that puts about $400,000 in gold bars in the shape of four-leaf clovers somewhere midway between Denver and Colorado Springs. Many of the details in both stories are similar. They vary, however, in how the gold happened to be hidden in the first place.

It seems that a man named Thomas R. Gavin was contracted to bring in the raw gold by the Clark and Gruber mint of Denver. (One oft-told version is that he was hired by the Denver mint. This would be difficult at best since there was no such thing in the 1860's when the story was said to take place.)

Gavin hired Peter Larkin and James Bullock. They picked up the gold at the "Pikes Peak gold fields," melted it down into ingots the shape of four-leaf clovers, and set out for Denver.

One version says the three men got into an argument after a card game the first night. The story goes that Gavin killed the other two and was mortally wounded himself. Unable to lead the gold-carrying burros the remainder of the way to Denver, he buried the gold in the holes of a groundhog colony. By the time he reached Denver, gangrene had set in. He lived just long enough to tell the story to relatives. But he was unable to be specific as to the distances. Search as they did, no one has dug up the right groundhog town.

Another version says the three men were ambushed along the headwaters of Cherry Creek. They put up a good fight, but eventually the two were killed and Gavin was mortally wounded. He lived long enough, however, to get together a posse of miners and prospectors working along Cherry Creek. The outlaws, unable to move rapidly with their heavy loot, had disposed of it before the posse caught up with them and killed them.

A careful search was carried out by many between the site of the crime and where the bandits were killed, but no gold four-leaf clovers were ever found.

One trouble with the story is that it is most doubtful that the "Pikes Peak gold fields" produced that much raw gold, or much raw gold at all in the 1860's. Since Pikes Peak was the goal of many in the first months of the Pikes Peak Gold Rush, there was some prospecting that actually took place around the towering peak. But the results were so poor that it began talk of the "Pikes Peak Hoax." There was also much panning for gold along the headwaters of Cherry Creek, but if anyone— or even a whole army of prospectors together—should pan $400,000 in gold, there certainly wouldn't be any talk about a hoax.

However, it's possible that that much gold had been found in other diggings at the time, and the men merely picked it up around Colorado Springs. There are enough details that jive to give some credence to the story—and to encourage plenty of people over the years to dig up a vast number of groundhog towns and other probable treasure locations in the vicinity about midway between Denver and Colorado Springs, around the headwaters of Cherry Creek.

THE GOLDEN CAVE

A story from the Creede area concerns a young nitro freighter named Curt Garner, put out of work by the coming of the railroad shortly after the turn of the century. He set out to look for a job but chose a poor time to do so. He hadn't been on the road long, heading north, before it began to snow. The snow became heavier and the trail more difficult to follow. Twice he became lost. The second night out he was fortunate to find a cave for refuge. The cave contained enough wood for a fire. He warmed himself, cooked the rabbit and grouse he shot during the day.

The light of the fire also did much to light up the corners of the cave. He noticed a vein of rock that stood out from the rest. He broke off a piece of it and stuffed it in his mackinaw.

The next day he wandered into a home in Biedell Camp about thirty miles north of Creede. The ore was found a couple of days later. It was taken to one of the nearby mines which boasted an assay office and found to be worth $2,342 a ton. The mine officials promised Garner a fair sum for his claim on the mine.

That—of course—is where the trouble began.

The snow continued for days. The entire region was covered with a deep blanket of snow, particularly in the high mountains over which Garner had traveled. It was several days before Garner could ride over the area, and it wasn't until the following spring that he could make a detailed search of the area. Many others from Creede and Biedell who had heard of the story searched the area carefully. Nary a "cave of gold" did they find.

Garner searched for his cave every day he could during the next three years. The third year, in his desperation to find what was rightly his, he stayed out too long and was caught in another snow storm. He wasn't as fortunate, or as strong, as he had been the first time. He was nearly dead from pneumonia when he finally wandered into Biedell. He died a few days later despite the efforts of the best people in camp.

With him died the only living contact with the golden cave.

ET CETERA, ET CETERA

And the stories continue. There are a number of stories that need additional checking.

- There is one about $55,000 in loot that Butch Cassidy and his Wild Bunch might have hid near Powder Springs just north of Brown's Hole. They "might" have hidden it here and they "might" have left it here, but it's doubtful.
- There is a story of a fellow named Gabe Espinoza who was believed to have buried a treasure on or around Mount Evans and then went off and got himself killed in a duel—about fifty years ago.
- Another duel near Saguache years ago didn't kill the owner of the secret treasure, but sent him to the penitentiary for life. He is still there and his treasure is said to be in the shaft of the old mine where he left it.
- Another fellow who went to the pen for life was said to have been an ingenious thief near Bonanza who stole a fortune in gold bars and hid them well—about forty years ago. The bars are still where he hid them.
- There is a vague story about a drunken prospector who frequently ventured into Fairplay with a load of "fabulously" rich nuggets. On one trip he got involved with a blacksmith and his sixteen-year-old daughter. She got raped and killed. A few months later the drunken prospector got shot along the trail by a mysterious assailant. The blacksmith, the girl's father, returned to Germany with his sudden wealth. And the mine was never found. It's all very complicated. The unusual part of the story is that it took place in Fairplay two of three years before Fairplay was born.

A WORD OF THANKS

Through an oversight in the last edition I failed to acknowledge the fine book *Golden Treasures of San Juan* by John B. Marshall and Temple H. Cornelius (Sage Books, 1961) . The book is heartedly recommended for a closer and colorful look at the lost treasure stories in and around southwestern Colorado.

Temple H. Cornelius recently published another volume, *Sheepherder's Gold,* which contains a dozen more exciting tales of treasure (Sage Books, 1964, $4.50).

Other persons I wish to thank for new information are Jess Bollinger, Robert A. Redding, Nancy Bank, Bill DeBaca, A. E. Raehrs, Richard Cone, and two men whose last names are Crane and Bilotte. I hope you all find your life's treasure.

BIBLIOGRAPHY

Baggs, Mae Lacy, *Colorado, the Queen Jewel of the Rockies,* Boston, The Page Company, 1918.

Baker, James H., editor, and Hafen, LeRoy, associate editor, *History of Colorado,* prepared by the State Historical and Natural History Society of Colorado, Denver, Linderman Co., Inc., 1927.

Bancroft, George Jarvis, Lost Mine Legends and Western Stories and Material, an unpublished collections written in 1914 when Bancroft was Mining Page Editor of the *Rocky Mountain News.* Collection donated to Denver Public Library Western History section by Caroline Bancroft.

Baskin, O. L., *History of the Arkansas Valley, Colorado,* Chicago, O. L. Baskin & Co., Historical Publishers, 1881.

Botkin, B. A., *Treasury of Western Folklore,* edited by Botkin, New York, Crown Publishers, Inc., 1951.

Brigham, Lillian Rice, *Historical Guide to Colorado,* Denver, W. H. Kistler Co., 1931.

Brigham, Lillian Rice, *Colorado Travelore,* Denver, Peerless Printing, 1938.

Cairns, Mary Lyon, *Grand Lake: The Pioneers,* Denver, World Press, 1946.

Cairns, Mary Lyon, *The Old Days,* Denver, World Press, Inc., 1954.

Carhart, Arthur H., *Colorado,* New York, Coward-McCann, Inc., 1932.

Cook, John W., *Hands Up,* Denver, W. F. Robinson Printing Co., 1897.

Crofutt, George A., *Grip-Sack Guide to Colorado,* Denver, Alvord Co., 1881.

Davidson, Levette J., and Blake, Forrester, editors, *Rocky Mountain Tales,* Norman, U. of Oklahoma Press, 1947.

Dawson, T. F. Dawson Scrapbook, several unpublished volumes of newspaper clippings given the Colorado Historical Society.

Denver Posse of Westerners, *Westerners Brand Book,* Denver, Artcraft Press, 1946-48; Golden Press, 1949; U. of Denver Press, 1950; Denver, Artcraft, 1951; Denver, Arthur Zeuch, 1952; Boulder, Johnson Publishing Co., 1953, 1954, 1955, 1956, 1957, 1958, 1959.

Denver Post Empire Magazine, *Rocky Mountain Empire,* Edited by Elvon L. Howe, Garden City, N. Y., Doubleday & Co., Inc., 1950.

Dobie, J. Frank, *Coronado's Children; tales of Lost Mines and Buried Treasures of the Southwest,* Dallas, Southwest Press, 1930.

Dunning, Harold Marion, *Over Hill and Vale,* Boulder, Johnson Publishing Co., 1956.

Eberhart, Perry, *Guide to Colorado Ghost Towns and Mining Camps,* Denver, Sage Books, 1959.

Ellis, Amanda, *Legends and Tales of the Rockies,* Colorado Springs, The Denton Printing Co., 1954.

Ellis, Amanda M., *The Strange Uncertain Years,* Hamden, Conn., The Shoe String Press, Inc., 1950.

Ferguson, Robert G., *Lost Treasure: The Search for Hidden Gold,* New York, Vantage Press, 1957.

Fergusson, Harvey, *Rio Grande,* New York, Tudor Publishing Co., 1945.

Fossett, Frank, *Colorado, Its Gold and Silver Mines,* New York, C. G. Crawford, 1880.

Garrard, Lewis, *Wah-To-Yah and the Taos Trail,* Glendale, Calif., The Arthur H. Clark Co., 1938.

Griswold, Don and Jean, *A Carbonate Camp Called Leadville,* Denver, U. of Denver Press, 1951.

Hafen, LeRoy and Ann, *The Colorado Story,* Old West Publishing Co., 1956.

Hafen, LeRoy, *Pikes Peak Gold Rush Guidebooks of 1859,* edited by Hafen, Glendale, Calif., Arthur H. Clark Co., 1941.

Hallenbeck, Clive, *Legends of the Spanish Southwest,* Glendale, Calif., The Arthur H. Clark Co., 1938.

Hall, Frank, *History of the State of Colorado* (4 vols.), Chicago, Blakely Printing Co., 1889-95.

Hedges, William Hawkins, *Pikes Peak . . . or Busted,* Evanston, Ill., Branding Iron Press, 1954.

Hollon, Eugene, *Beyond the Crossed Timbers,* Travels of Randolph B. Marcy 1812-1887, Norman, U. of Oklahoma Press, 1949.

Horgan, Paul, *Great River, the Rio Grande* (2 vols.), New York, Rinehart & Co., Inc., 1954.

Inman, Co. Henry, *The Old Santa Fe Trail, the Story of a Great Highway,* Topeka, Kan., Crane & Co., 1916.

Johnston, William Cameron, *American Treasure Hunters Guide,* published by author, 1952.
Kelly, Charles, *The Outlaw Trail,* New York, the Devin-Adair Co., 1959.
Lavender, David, *The Big Divide,* Garden City, N. Y., Doubleday and Co., Inc., 1948.
Lavender, David, *One Man's West,* Garden City, N. Y., Doubleday and Co., 1956.
Long, Margaret, *Smoky Hill Trail,* Denver, W. H. Kistler Co., 1943.
Lovelace, Leland, *Lost Mines and Hidden Treasure,* San Antonio, Naylor Co., 1956.
Nasatir, A. P., *Before Lewis and Clark,* edited by Nasatir, St. Louis, Published by the St. Louis Historical Documents Foundation, 1952.
Ormes, Robert M., *Guide to the Colorado Mountains,* Denver, Sage Books, 1955.
Pearl, Richard M., *Colorado Gem Trails,* Denver, Sage Books, 1951.
Penfield, Thomas, *Lost Treasure Trails,* New York, Grosset and Dunlop Inc., 1954.
Perkin, Robert L., *First Hundred Years,* Garden City, N. Y., Doubleday & Co., 1959.
Pike, Zebulon, *Zebulon Pike's Arkansaw Journal,* edited by Stephen Harding Hart and Archer Butler Hulbert, 1932, published by the Stewart Commission of Colorado College and the Denver Public Library.
Porter, Clyde and Mae Reed, *Ruxton of the Rockies,* collected by the Porters, edited by LeRoy Hafen, Norman, U. of Oklahoma Press, 1950.
Quiett, Glenn Chesney, *Pay Dirt,* New York, D. Appleton-Century Co., 1936.
Rockwell, Wilson, *Sunset Slope,* Denver, Big Mountain Press, 1956.
Ruxton, George F., *Life in the Far West,* edited by LeRoy Hafen, Norman, U. of Oklahoma Press, 1951.
Sage, Rufus, *Letters and Scenes in the Rocky Mountains* (2 vols.), edited by LeRoy Hafen, Glendale, Calif., The Arthur H. Clark Co., 1956.
Sporleder, Louis B., *Huajatolla, Colorado's Mystic Mountain,* Pueblo, 1916.
Sporleder, Louis B., *Romance of Spanish Peaks,* Pueblo Co., O'Brien Press, 1960.

Sprague, Marshall, *Money Mountain,* Boston, Little Brown and Co., 1953.

Stone, William Fiske, *History of Colorado* (4 vols.), Chicago, S. J. Clark Publishing Co., 1918.

Thomas, Alfred Barnaby, *After Coronado, Spanish Exploration Northeast of New Mexico, 1696-1727,* translated and edited by Thomas, Norman, U. of Oklahoma Press, 1935.

Wellman, Paul Iselin, *Glory, God and Gold, a Narrative History,* Garden City, N. Y., Doubleday & Co., Inc., 1954.

Willison, George, *Here They Dug the Gold,* New York, A. L. Burt Co., 1931.

Wolle, Muriel Sibell, *Stampede to Timberline,* published by author, Boulder, 1957.

Works Progress Administration, *Colorado, A Guide to the Highest State,* New York, Hastings House, 1941.

Works Progress Administration, *New Mexico, A Guide to the Colorful State,* new and revised edition by Joseph Miller and Henry G. Alsberg, Hastings House, New York, 1953.

Works Progress Administration, *Arizona, the Grand Canyon State,* New York, Hastings House, 1940.

NEWSPAPERS: The Denver Post; Rocky Mountains News; Denver Republican; Steamboat (Springs) Pilot; Dolores Star; Great Divide, Denver; Denver Times; Daily and Weekly Central City Register; Walsenburg World-Independent; Gunnison Courier; Illustrated Rocky Mountain Globe; Grand Junction Daily Sentinel; Eastern Colorado Plainsman (Hugo); Flagler News; Aspen Times; Montrose Press; Denver Liberty Press; Leadville Herald; Trinidad Chronicle-Times; Leadville Herald-Democrat; Silver Cliff Prospect; Fairplay Flume; Breckenridge Summit Mountain Journal; Central City Weekly Register-Call; Pagosa Springs Sun; Colorado Sun; Silverton Standard; Castle Rock Record Journal; Pueblo Chieftain; Crested Butte Republican; Washington Post; Aspen Democrat-Times; Rocky Mountain Herald; Cheyenne County News (Cheyenne Wells)

MAGAZINES AND PAMPHLETS:

Desert Magazine

True West

Colorado Magazine, Published by the Colorado State Historical Society
Mining Journal
The Trail
Municipal Facts
Estes Park Trail
Colorado Topics, Hyde, Colo., Washington County

ACKNOWLEDGMENTS

A book such as this is a compilation of what has been said or written before. There is nothing new in it, except, perhaps, some personal observations. By and large, however, I had thousands of collaborators. Some, of course, were of greater help than others.

It is of these I would like to take special note and give my special thanks.

First I would like to thank my wife, Sandy. She was a great help to me, typing, drawing, proofing, and suggestions. My mother, Eve Bennett Haberl, too, was of great aid with her proofing, suggestions, and encouragement.

A lot of people helped me gather the material.

There was kindly old Judge Don Vigil of Trinidad, and Andrew Merritt of Walsenburg, both of whom have endless stories of the past. Robert Dunne of Querida knows a lot of mining and mining legend. H. M. McMillan of Silverton is an interested student of the San Juans and the many stories these mountains have to tell. Mrs. John Burgener and the Reynolds of Salida were of special help, too.

Of course, much of the material came from the Western History Section of the Denver Public Library and the State Historical Museum. I would like to extend my heartfelt appreciation to the staffs of these two institutions Mrs. Alys Freeze, Mrs. Opal Harbor, Mrs. Christine Larsen, Jim Davis, Mrs. Kathryn Hawkens, and Mrs. Mary Hanley, at the library; and Mrs. Agnes Spring and Mrs. Laura Ekstrom, at the museum.

Others who offered special help were Pinky Warell, Francis B. Rizzari, Fred Swenson, Stan Weston, Carl Haberl, Jim Ward, Don Bloch, Tom Hutton, Howard Roepnack, Gene Lindbergh, Jim "Bud" Will, Fred Smith, Erika Schramm.

And I can't forget John Streich and his most interesting club—the Colorado Grotto of the National Speological Society.

Most of the stories came from newspapers. There were special collections of clippings that were of great help, such as T. F. Dawson's scrapbook. Any student of legend and mining cannot afford to overlook these many volumes in the library of the Historical Museum.

Also, there was a newspaper series than ran a few years back entitled "Golden Phantoms" by Editha L. Watson.

The mining legends collected by George J. Bancroft and written for the *Rocky Mountain News* back in 1914, have been compiled into an interesting little booklet and donated to the Library by Caroline Bancroft.

There were also some good stories in the old *Mining Journal.*

I could go on and on. I got a lot or a little from each of the books in the bibliography. Space prohibits me from singling out special volumes.

Let's just say it was good to have so much help. Thanks to each and all of my collaborators.

PE

INDEX

WYOMING

Steamboat Springs
Grand Lake
Glenwood Springs
Grand Junction
Leadville
Breckenrid
Fairplay
Buena Vista
Gunnison
Salida
Montrose
Ouray
Lake City
Silverton
Creede
Wolf Creek Pass
Alamosa
Durango
Pagosa Springs

NEW MEXICO

1. Spanish Peaks
2. Arapaho Princess Treasure
3. The Golden Mummy
4. Alex Cobsky's Secret Mine
5. Lost Mine on Veta Creek
6. The Old Spanish Fort
7. Gold of Greenhorn Range
8. Treasure of Apache Gulch
9. Sunken Treasu
10. Gold Nuggets
11. Lost Tungsten
12. Spanish Treasu